BETWEEN BABEL AND BEAST

THEOPOLITICAL VISIONS

SERIES EDITORS:

Thomas Heilke
D. Stephen Long
and C. C. Pecknold

Theopolitical Visions seeks to open up new vistas on public life, hosting fresh conversations between theology and political theory. This series assembles writers who wish to revive theopolitical imagination for the sake of our common good.

Theopolitical Visions hopes to re-source modern imaginations with those ancient traditions in which political theorists were often also theologians. Whether it was Jeremiah's prophetic vision of exiles "seeking the peace of the city," Plato's illuminations on piety and the civic virtues in the Republic, St. Paul's call to "a common life worthy of the Gospel," St. Augustine's beatific vision of the City of God, or the gothic heights of medieval political theology, much of Western thought has found it necessary to think theologically about politics, and to think politically about theology. This series is founded in the hope that the renewal of such mutual illumination might make a genuine contribution to the peace of our cities.

FORTHCOMING VOLUMES:

Christopher D. Marshall
Compassionate Justice: An Interdisciplinary Dialogue with Gospel Parables on Law, Crime, and Restorative Justice

Artur Mrówczynski-Van Allen
Between the Icon and the Idol: Man and State in Russian Thought and Literature: Chaadayev, Soloviev, Grossman

Between BABEL and BEAST

America

and Empires

in Biblical Perspective

PETER J. LEITHART

CASCADE *Books* • Eugene, Oregon

BETWEEN BABEL AND BEAST
America and Empires in Biblical Perspective

Theopolitical Visions 14

Copyright © 2012 Peter J. Leithart. All rights reserved. Except for brief quotations in critical publications or reviews, no part of this book may be reproduced in any manner without prior written permission from the publisher. Write: Permissions, Wipf and Stock Publishers, 199 W. 8th Ave., Suite 3, Eugene, OR 97401.

Cascade Books
An Imprint of Wipf and Stock Publishers
199 W. 8th Ave., Suite 3
Eugene, OR 97401

www.wipfandstock.com

ISBN 13: 978-1-60899-817-3

Cataloging-in-Publication data:

Leithart, Peter J.

    Between Babel and beast : America and empires in biblical perspective / Peter J. Leithart.

    xiv + 200 p. ; 23 cm. —

    Theopolitical Visions 14

    ISBN 13: 978-1-60899-817-3

    1. Bible — Criticism, interpretation, etc. 2. Christianity and culture. 3. Church and state — United States. I. Series. II. Title.

BR516 .L39 2012

Manufactured in the U.S.A.

To my unborn grandchild.

Contents

Introduction ix

PART I *Empires in Scripture*

1 A Tale of Two Imperialisms 3
2 Rod, Refuge, Messiah, Beast 15
3 The Good News of Empire 34
Conclusion to Part I 52

PART II *Americanism*

4 Heretic Nation 57
5 Chanting the New Empire 84
Conclusion to Part II 110

PART III *Between Babel and Beast*

6 American Babel 115
7 Among Beasts 136

Conclusion 151
Endnotes 153

Introduction

Time was when you could hardly toss an egg without hitting a freshly published critique (and critic) of American empire. Since the Soviet bloc dissolved and left the United States the remaining "hyperpower," and even more since Bush II's aggressive pursuit of Islamism, publications on "American empire" have exploded. Critiques come almost equally from the left and right. Gore Vidal opposes American empire; so does Pat Buchanan. Michael Moore is anti-war; so is Andrew Bacevich. Leftists denounce American empire because it exploits the rest of the world; critics from the right usually focus on the dangers that America's global power poses to free institutions at home, on the theory that America, having regressed from Republic to Empire, will follow Rome's path to the end and finally collapse altogether. Some critiques are informed, others less so. Among the best are painful accounts of the appalling stupidity and shameful abuses of America's covert and overt meddling and bullying. A few, a very few, defend American empire. Niall Ferguson writes wistfully about the need for a more assertive America, while Thomas F. Madden has characterized both the Roman and the American empires as "empires of trust." Empire studies have become a cottage industry among theologians as well. Fresh studies of Bible-and-empire, Jesus-and-empire, Paul-and-empire, Revelation-and-empire flow freely from the presses, and everyone who writes in the resurgent subdiscipline of political theology touches on the theme. Publishers seem to have discovered that adding "empire" to a title will pique interest in an otherwise unrelated book. But I wax cynical.

Anti-imperial frenzy peaked during the second Bush term. The stream of publications has become a trickle. It seems as if under Obama's internationalist leadership, the United States has rolled up its empire and packed it away in a forgotten closet at the State Department. Though I missed the crest of the publishing wave, I take confidence in the hope that another wave is coming, especially if we have a Republican President beginning in 2013. Whatever has happened since Obama took office, America is still everywhere with its fingers in nearly everything, and that gigantic fact about our world is not going to change anytime soon.

I have three main reasons to add another book to the pile. First, I found myself bumping into questions about imperialism at every turn during my research for *Defending Constantine* (IVP Academic, 2010), but I did not have the opportunity to work through the issue as thoroughly as I wanted. *Between Babel and Beast* is a book-length footnote to that earlier book, a footnote full of epicyclical footnotes of its own—a detachable, errant appendix. If you are not the kind of person who likes reading footnotes, you ought, as Lemony Snicket would say, set this book down immediately and look for something less wonkish for your beach reading.

Second, though I agree with today's consensus that the Bible is an inherently political book, I have been dissatisfied with much of what has been written about the Bible's treatment of empires. Most scholars recognize that the biblical portrait of imperial power is complex, but scholars rarely accept that complexity as a norm for political theology. Typically, the anti-imperial threads of Scripture are taken as a political canon-within-a-canon, while the places in Scripture that seem to give aid and comfort to empires are marginalized as unfortunate or treacherous lapses. Thus even scholars who recognize that the Bible is not consistently anti-imperial will talk of the New Testament's "anti-imperial gospel." It is an ironic reversal of nineteenth-century readings, which highlighted apparently pro-imperial portions of the Bible to justify the White Man's Burden. In *Between Babel and Beast*, I have done my best to understand the complexities of the biblical account of empires and, more importantly, to accept these complexities as a framework within which to reason about contemporary international politics.

My reading of Scripture will offend scholars whose political sympathies incline toward the left, but the reading of American history that occupies the latter half of this book will offend Christians whose political sympathies incline toward the right. My third, pastoral concern of *Between Babel and Beast* is to challenge popular understandings of American history and the political stances that result from them. For a generation, conservative Christians have accepted and taught a one-sidedly rosy view of America's Christian past, and in practice Christians have confused "restoring America" with promotion of God's kingdom and His justice. Against this American mythology, I contend that the "American faith," though unthinkable without the heritage of Christendom, represents a heretical departure from the political heritage of the church. American Christians need to assess our past accurately if we are going to act faithfully in the present. Until American churches actually function as outposts of Jesus' heavenly empire rather than as cheerleaders for America—until the churches produce martyrs rather than patriots—the political witness of Christians will continue to be diluted and co-opted.

I expect to offend many, perhaps everyone. Stumbling blocks must come, Jesus said, but setting up stumbling blocks is not an end in itself. *Between Babel and Beast* will achieve my aims only if readers who stumble here or there are provoked to reassess the trail they follow and to contemplate a change of course.

The book is divided into three parts. Part I is a survey of the biblical presentation of empires, beginning with the pre-flood cities of Cain and Lamech and ending with the fall of the harlot city Babylon in Revelation. Politically, the Bible is a tale of two imperialisms. In response to the rebellious imperialism of Babel, Yahweh calls Abraham to be the father of a nation that will eventually become a nation of nations and the founder of a mountain city that will attract all the nations to worship the one God, learn His Torah, and beat their swords into ploughs. Israel is the first form of that Abrahamic empire, and in Christ the church is Israel's fulfillment. Part I traces this history of clashing imperialisms to develop a biblically based typology that discriminates three types of world empires competing with the Abrahamic: Empires may be Babels that impose a uniform political and cultural pattern on the world; Beasts that devour the saints and drink their blood; or, in some few cases, Guardians of the people of God. The Bible is not for or against "empire" because it does not concede that empire in the singular is a useful category of political analysis. The key question for Scripture is, how does this political entity treat the people of God?

Parts II and III are historical. Part II first examines the fundamental theology of the American order, a quasi-Christian, biblically laced heresy that I have labeled "Americanism." I love America. I love being American. I love much of what America has achieved, and I am grateful for what God has done through Americans and American institutions. But Americanism is different. Americanism has three founding moments: Its sense of vocation was established by the Puritan settlers of New England; its political eschatology emerged in the era of the Founding; its version of patriotic sacrifice was one of the chief legacies of the Civil War. Americanism often sounds like Christianity, but it is not. For Americanism, the American nation takes the place of the church as the sacred community. Americanists read the Bible looking for types and shadows of America, and view the constitutional order as the *novus ordo saeclorum*, an eschatological form of social and political order. In Americanism, America is the world's future visible already in the present. Because Americanism has no church, it acknowledges no public Eucharist (perhaps the causation should be reversed). Instead, like many modern nationalisms, Americanism makes devotion to the polity the central form of sacrifice. Americanism rarely occurs in a pure form; the heresy I describe is a kind of "ideal type," but its power in American history and in the American present is real.

Americanism is an inherently expansionist faith. Americanists cannot leave the rest of the world in the darkness of monarchy and aristocracy and theocracy. America doesn't *have*, but *is* a mission. In chapter 5, I show how this missionary nationalism has affected American foreign policy *throughout* its history. As many scholars have pointed out in recent years, the notion that America lived in splendid isolation until it was dragged kicking and screaming into the world in the early twentieth century is an ahistorical myth, and a dangerous one. Americans have conceived their mission in different ways: Sometimes the force of the American example is enough to transform the world; sometimes America functions as a sanctuary for the oppressed; for a century and a half, America, inspired by Americanism, has been all too ready to resort to force to remake first a continent and then the world into America's image.

Using the biblical typology of empires developed in Part I, Part III examines America's recent appearances on the world stage. To be sure, America promotes democracy, free trade, and religious freedom in various ways. But Americanist slogans are more misleading than not. We claim to be promoting global democracy, but we are often quite happy to suppress democracy and give aid to thugs when it serves national interests. We claim to be leading the world in free trade and the establishment of a global market, but we use tariffs and international institutions in which we have majority share to tilt the world economy in our favor. Religious freedom is enshrined in our Constitution, but we cozy up to regimes that brutally suppress religious minorities—Christians, in particular—so long as these regimes serve our purposes. When they stop serving us, we dump them. Inspired by Christian values and by the quasi-Christian ideology of Americanism, America is more benevolent than many great powers. But in the end, we are another great power, another nation of "the world," acting in our interests while telling ourselves that we have the best interests of the world at heart. Insofar as we want to make the world into our image, we are a Babel. We are not a beast, but we freely consort with beasts if it will serve our political ends. I wonder how long we can stay in the cage without taking on bestial habits ourselves. For now, though, America stands "between Babel and beast."

Between Babel and Beast is written for Christians, and my main practical message is a simple one: Remember who you are, and to whom you belong. Remember that you belong to Jesus first and last; remember that the church, not America, is the body of Christ and the political hope of the future; remember that no matter how much it may have served the city of God, America is in itself part of the city of man; remember that the Eucharist is our sacrificial feast. It is good for Christians to be salted throughout our polity—in the White House and bureaucracies, in the military, in international institutions. But Christians in those positions are called to *be* salt. American churches have too long discipled Christians in Americanism, and that makes Christian involvement in the American polity far smoother than it ought to be. Churches must repent of our Americanism and begin to cultivate martyrs—believers who are martyrs in the original sense of "witness" *and* in the later sense of men and women ready to follow the Lamb all the way to an imperial cross.

∼

I received help at various stages of this project from James Jordan, Rich Bledsoe, Doug Jones, Toby Sumpter, Joshua Appel, Chris Schlect,

Brendan O'Donnell, Eric Enlow, Jim Rogers, Stanley Hauerwas, John Milbank, Tom Farr, Paul Marshall, Michael Cromartie, Eric Patterson, Gen. Ron Burgess, Richard Garnett, Davey Henreckson, Steven Wedgeworth, Brad Littlejohn, Doug Bandow, William Cavanaugh, and Woelke Leithart. I was blessed to have students from South Africa, Indonesia, Kenya, and Canada in my master's seminar on empire during the fall term of 2011, and I learned much even from the American students. Many thanks also to Charlie Collier and the rest of the team at Wipf & Stock for their hard work in making this book a reality.

After I finished the manuscript for *Between Babel and Beast*, I learned that Lindsey Tollefson, my oldest daughter, was pregnant with her second child. The book will be born before he or she is, and I hope that my little effort will have made the world a marginally better place for him or her to enter and inhabit. I dedicate it to my unborn grandchild in the hope that his or her love for the Lord Jesus will put every other love in its proper place.

PART I

Empires in Scripture

CHAPTER 1

A Tale of Two Imperialisms

Old Testament history is bracketed by empires.[1] Just after Babel collapsed, Yahweh called Abram from Ur of the Chaldeans, but two millennia later Israel was under the hegemony of neo-Chaldea's successor, Persia. One can simplify this history by cherry-picking favored texts, characters, or events and presenting them as the sum total of the biblical portrait of "empire."[2] On the face of things, though, Israel's history with empires is too long and complex to be summarized in a single stance or an easy slogan.[3] The Bible refuses to smooth the historical phenomenon of "empires" into a singular "empire." For Scripture, it is not case that empire is empire is empire, which is the oddly ahistorical assumption implicitly adopted by some of the most historically sophisticated biblical scholars of our day. Empire differs from empire; Babel and Persia cannot be collapsed into one another.[4] As living political orders, no empire is static over time. Rome is sometimes the church's protector, sometimes a bestial devourer of holy flesh, sometimes the monstrous steed of a harlot-city drunk with saintly blood.[5]

The line between Israel and empire is not, furthermore, a clean one. Assyrians conquered and exiled Israel, but long before then, Israel conquered and subjected Canaan. Romans killed Jesus and His followers, yet centuries before Constantine, imperial categories, titles, and terminologies were being "reinscribed" in Christian thought and practice.[6] These "reinscriptions" are more fundamental than usually acknowledged. They are not accidental but essential, not a late aberration but inherent in the original biblical outlook and integral to the gospel.

Babel (Genesis 10–11)

The Bible hints that imperial political structures existed before the flood. Cain built the first city as a bridal city for his son Enoch, for whom the city was named,[7] and one of the descendants of Cain, Lamech, boasted of his bigamy and his vengefulness (Gen 4:22–24). Cain's murder of Abel was followed by a great flourishing of culture, civic and rural. Cain's descendants developed techniques of husbandry, invented musical instruments, and experimented with metallurgy. Though not explicitly designated as an imperial system, the history of Cain's descendants points to the sacrificial origins of cultural and political order.[8] The first overtly imperial program in the Bible was the post-flood establishment of two great cities, Nineveh and Babel.[9] Nimrod first established Babel, Erech, Akkad, and Calneh in the land of Shinar (Gen 10:10), and later founded Nineveh. Nineveh consisted of four cities—Nineveh, Rehoboth-Ir, Calah, and Resen—which together constituted a four-cornered civic "world" that built on but expanded Cain's urban program (Gen 10:11–12).[10] We learn little more about Nimrod's Nineveh, but the text tantalizingly suggests that imperial power—rule of a people or city by another—is inherent in political order. Any political structure larger than a household involves imperial supremacy in this general sense.[11] In ruling Israel, David governed preexisting tribal and clan political units. David the king was a ruler of "princes" (1 Chron 21:2; 27:22; 28:1), an imperial "king of kings."

Genesis is divided into sections by ten *toledoth* statements, typically translated as "these are the generations of." Chapter 10 begins with a *toledoth* statement, and the next occurs in 11:10, so the Babel episode in Gen 11:1–9 is enfolded in the account of the "generations of Shem, Ham, and Japheth." Babel is among the things that the sons of Noah "birthed." Genesis 11 begins with an unspecified group of migrants ("they" in 11:2), and the antecedent must be the "sons of Noah" (10:32) or some subgroup of the sons of Noah. Genesis 10:30 specifies the antecedent: the descendants of Joktan, brother to Peleg and son of Eber, a descendant of Shem (10:25), and these Joktanites settled "from

Mesha as you go toward Sephar, the hill country of the east" (v. 30). The eastward-migrating bands in 11:2 are Joktanites, descendants of Shem, cousins to the "Eberites" that made up the family of Abram.[12] Abram and the Babelites had the same ancestry. Genesis specifies two groups among the builders of Babel. "Nimrod the mighty hunter" is the obvious one (10:9–10), but was assisted by the Joktanite clan of the Shemites. Prior to the flood, the faithful Sethite "sons of God" had married Cainite "daughters of evil," an erotic and cultural mingling that eventually compromised and corrupted nearly every member of the faithful line of Seth and filled the earth with violence (Gen 6:1–4). After the flood, it happened all over again as the Joktanite descendants of Seth offered their support for the Hamite/Nimrod Babel project. With sons of God "intermarrying" with the daughters of men at Babel, it was only a matter of time before there was another catastrophic "flood."

Prior to Babel, the earth "was one lip and one set of words."[13] The two terms are not identical in Scripture. Typically, "lip" (שָׂפָה) is used for religious confession and worship (Pss 12:2–4; 16:1; 40:9; 45:2; 51:15; Isa 6:5, 7; 29:13),[14] while "words" (דְּבָרִים) has a more strictly linguistic significance. What unified the men at Babel was not merely language but a single liturgical confession. The distinction between "lip" and "words" illuminates what might seem to be another poetic repetition: "Let us build for ourselves a city and a tower" (v. 4). Babel was a double project, including both a city, which corresponds to the "words" of common speech, and a "tower" (ziggurat) for the liturgy of international community. That the head of the tower would, they hoped, "reach heaven" is another indication of the religious character of the project. Like every temple in the ancient world, the Babel tower was conceived as a connection point between heaven and earth, gods and men. Babel aimed to create a "gate of God" in Shinar—"gate of God" being the original meaning of the name "Babylon." The fourfold repetition of "one" (אֶחָד; vv. 1, 6) emphasizes that their aim was uniformity. Babel, a prototype of all the antitypical "Babels" that appear later in the Bible, was intolerant of linguistic, cultural, and especially religious difference. Not all imperial orders demand homogeneity, but those that do so perpetuate the Babel project.[15] The distinction between tower-lip and city-words also corresponds to the racial distinction among the sons of Noah. Hamites built Babel, but they were assisted in the project by Shemites from the line of Joktan. At least part of the proto-priestly line of Shem, in other words, consecrated the Babel project.[16] For the moment, Shemites shared a single "lip" with the rest of humanity. Since Yahweh Himself admitted that, unified, Babel would be able to achieve almost everything (v. 6), we need to be careful not to underestimate the nearly omnipotent power of Babelic empire.

They also, of course, aimed for Name. This too was a religious goal, a bid for immortality. Like Homeric heroes, they hoped to overcome the threat of death by achievements that would earn them everlasting reputation. If not eternal life, at least they could achieve eternal name. Exalting the name, like building a tower to heaven, was an implicit assault on Yahweh's Lordship. They succumbed to the serpent's temptation to become like gods. Like the later king of neo-Babylon, the men of the first Babel wanted to set a throne among the stars, ascend above the clouds, make themselves "like the Most High" (Isa 14:13–14). Augustine recognized similar motivations behind the Roman drive for imperial mastery. Lust for glory first inspired Romans to throw off the rule of kings, but, having toppled the Tarquins, their lust was unsatisfied, and they pursued mastery over others, their desire for glory transformed into a *libido dominandi*.

At the same time, Roman desire for glory was crossed by anxiety and fear, which paradoxically increased in proportion to Roman conquest and power. Fear of death drove the Roman imperial project—fear of enemies in the first instance. Fear was the source of *virtus*, the manly virtues of the Roman warrior. As Augustine pointed out, Scipio worried that Roman virtue would grow flaccid if the threat of Carthage were removed.[17] In a later period, Romans masked their anxiety about individual and political death with a drive for luxury, consumption, and the Pascalian distractions of entertainment.[18] Babel already displayed this same complex of motivations. The twin aims were to achieve "name" and to prevent "scattering" (Gen 11:4). Their fear of dissolution and lust for glory were two sides of the same motive: Glory-seeking was the solution to insecurity in a world of change and death, and glory-seeking fear, or anxious glory-seeking, took political form in the construction of homogenous empire.

The men of Babel were also inspired by an eschatology. Humans were created to spread throughout the earth, multiplying until the earth was full (Gen 1:26–28). Babel attempted to arrest scattering, and thus to stop time and history. In their passion to avoid death, they established a necropolis, a city of death because it was a city without change. Babel claimed to be the end of history, the achieved goal of human development, beyond which there is nowhere to go and nothing to do.[19] Babel was the political embodiment of an overrealized eschatology, which is always also an eschatology of fear. Babel's eternal walls were built to ward off the ravages of time. Long before Virgil, Babel announced the formation of an *imperium sine fine*; long before the American Founders, Babel claimed to have founded the *novus ordo saeclorum*. Babelic empires, though, inevitably misconstrue the cunning weave of time. It is not the case that the first remain first forever. We have it on the highest authority that the last become first, while the first are relegated to the back of the line.

As in the city of Cain, blood was Babel's mortar. Genesis 11 details the construction of the city and tower, echoing the earlier description of the construction of Noah's ark (Genesis 6). The echoes are not accidental: "the Babel project is a new Ark designed to protect humanity from the 'death' of scattering abroad just as the Ark of Noah saved humanity from the death of drowning. The Babel project is a counterfeit Ark"— that is to say, a counterfeit church.[20] The image of "tar" covering the bricks and stones of the city also evokes the biblical concept of covering (Heb. כָּפַר), which is basic to the biblical sacrificial system. Atonement occurs by covering, and in "covering" the city and tower the men of Babel made not only a counterfeit church but also a counterfeit altar: "The Babel Project is built on human sacrifice. . . . The bricks of the city and tower are human beings, whose spilled blood holds them in place, and who are put into sacrificial fire in order to make them firm and usable."[21] The Shemite descendants of Joktan assisted the construction of a false church, a tower of sacrifice built, like the city of Cain, on the blood of the innocent. Sacrifice founds and continuous sacrifice perpetuates the last, Babelic order of the ages.

Until Yahweh appears, the account is neutral, and the reader cannot be entirely sure if Babel fulfills or subverts God's purposes for humans. At the structural center of the passage, Yahweh takes a stand against the project and begins to dismantle Babel brick by brick. He ensures that all they fear happens to them. He confuses their lip and speech (v. 7) and scatters them (vv. 4, 9). They wanted to build a city reaching to heaven (v. 4), but Yahweh had to "come down to see" the tower (v. 7). They wanted a name, and they got one—not the name of fame they desired

Part I: Empires in Scripture

but the mocking name "Confusion" (v. 9). Whatever success Babel or its imitators boast, in the end Yahweh opposes all such projects.[22] In the long run, no Babel will succeed.

The Babel narrative provides a virtual definition of illicit empire. It was a religious project, the political form of an aspiration to divinity. It was a cooperative venture of ambitious politicians egged on by their cheerleader priests. It attempted to arrest time in a static political-eschatological *now*. Like Cain's city, it was built on the blood of sacrificial victims. It attempted to preserve a single "lip" and "set of words," and centralized both religious and political authority in a single city-with-tower.[23] Even Yahweh acknowledged that, acting as one, the men of Babel were virtually omnipotent (v. 6), but their vast and terrifying power was ironically subverted by the psychopolitics of the effort: their lust for glory was undercut by the fear and anxiety that enflamed their lust in the first place.[24] Most importantly, the Babel episode shows that, whatever success empires of this sort achieve, they are doomed, not because of imperial overreach, or because manly military values that keep an imperial project going grow weak, or because the pure blood of the founders is diluted by invaders and immigrants; Babel is doomed because it stands in direct opposition to the true World Ruler.

In a laconic nine verses, the narrative exposes the illusion of imperial schemes throughout history. "Babel" means confusion and points to the inversion of imperial projects enacted against Yahweh. The men who build Babel think of their project as a guarantee of international peace, unity, and order. Men who build empires (the builders are mostly *men*) always do. Blinded by the ideology and eschatology of Babelic empire, they think world order depends on their success in gathering scattered nations to one city and one tower, and exacting a uniform confession from them. World order depends on founding a political and religious center, an *umbilicus mundi* around which everything else will circle. Yet the result is the opposite. The guarantors of world order sow confusion. Empires that claim to stabilize are typically agents of international destabilization.

God's Imperium

Yahweh opposed the imperial project in its Babelic form, but the story in Genesis continues with an intriguing twist. Genesis 10 lists the descendants of Joktan before the descendants of his brother, Peleg. Joktan has thirteen sons (vv. 26-28), and these sons join in the doomed project at Babel. Peleg, meanwhile, drops from the text, and when he reappears his name is in the middle of a ten-generation list linking Shem with Abram (Gen 11:10-26). Noah lurks in the background. Ten generations link Adam to Noah, and another ten generations connect Noah to Abram. Noah's ark preserved creation through the flood—a rescue that the Babelites wanted to imitate—but the new Noah was not Nimrod or his Joktanite assistants. The new Noah was Abram, Yahweh's chosen agent for leading the world through the Babelic flood into a new creation. As new Noah, Abram was yet another new Adam, the Creator's agent for establishing new creation. Abram and his descendants were not merely one nation-among-nations. Israel represented nothing less than a rebirth of the race after the de-creation of Babel. Yahweh disrupted Babel, and He immediately began constructing a new human world.[25]

Given Yahweh's vigorous and thoroughgoing opposition to Babel, it is surprising to discover that His counter-imperial program shared many of the features of Babelic imperialism.[26] He promised Abram a "great name" (12:2). He assured him that he would produce "a great and mighty nation" (18:18), but not just one: "I have made you a father of a multitude of nations" (Gen 17:4-6, 16). Many nations would be incorporated into the single family of Abram, giving Abram's family an imperial cast. Abraham would thus become the father of kings (Gen 17:6, 16), a patriarchal "king of kings." The two great promises—land and seed—echoed the dual aim of Babel to build a city and a tower.[27] Eventually, Abraham's children conquer the land in which he is a pilgrim and build in it an actual city and a tower—Jerusalem and its temple, the true "gate of God," the true Babylon.[28] Crucially for the future, Abraham was promised that all other peoples would be judged by their treatment of Abraham's children (12:3). Nations and kings who bless Abraham will be blessed, whereas those who curse will be cursed. This establishes one of the Bible's key standards for evaluation of empires and political orders in general: How do they treat Abraham's seed? Do they serve as cherubic guardians, honoring them and showing favor, or do they become beasts who eat Abrahamic flesh and get drunk on holy blood?[29] Whatever their similarities of personality or policy, this was the abyss between Diocletian and Constantine.

Part I: Empires in Scripture

The interplay between עַם ("people") and גּוֹי ("nation") in Genesis 11–12 not only shows the connection between Babel and Abraham but also points to Israel's calling in the midst of the nations. In most of the Old Testament, Israel is a "people" and all other nations are *goyim*, but here the terminology is inverted. The men who built Babel formed a single עַם (11:6), and Yahweh promised to make a great גּוֹי from Abram (12:2): "it is precisely as the one chosen 'people' (*'am*) that Israel represents the oneness of the human race, and it is the *goyim* who are to experience the blessing and to be gathered into the 'great *goy*.'" Israel's particularism does not contradict her universal purpose since "it is in her 'particular' function and calling . . . that Israel is truly 'universal.'"[30] This Abrahamic vocation forms the background and foundation for the prophets' later vision of Zion as a place of international pilgrimage and peace, the capital of an Abrahamic empire:

> May he also rule from sea to sea and from the River to the ends of the earth. Let the nomads of the desert bow before him, and his enemies lick the dust. Let the kings of Tarshish and of the islands bring presents; the kings of Sheba and Seba offer gifts. And let all kings bow down before him, all nations serve him. (Ps 72:8–11)

> Now it will come about that in the last days the mountain of the house of the Lord will be established as the chief of the mountains, and will be raised above the hills; and all the nations will stream to it. And many peoples will come and say, "Come, let us go up to the mountain of the Lord, to the house of the God of Jacob; that He may teach us concerning His ways and that we may walk in His paths." For the law will go forth from Zion and the word of the Lord from Jerusalem. And He will judge between the nations, and will render decisions for many peoples; and they will hammer their swords into plowshares and their spears into pruning hooks. Nation will not lift up sword against nation, and never again will they learn war. (Isa 2:2–4)

> Foreigners will build up your walls, and their kings will minister to you; for in My wrath I struck you, and in My favor I have had compassion on you. Your gates will be open continually; they will not be closed day or night, so that men may bring to you the wealth of the nations, with their kings led in procession. For

the nation and the kingdom which will not serve you will perish, and the nations will be utterly ruined. (Isa 60:10–11)

In these visions, Zion and its future king are systematically set over against the confusions of Babel:

> Over against the unnerving fear of mankind "lest we be scattered abroad" is set the free and joyful resolution of the nations to go up to Zion. On the one hand there is the panic, the confusion, the scattering, and on the other the festive gathering. On the one hand the cry is: "Come, let us build ourselves a city and a tower with its top in the heavens," and on the other: "Come, let us go up to the mountain of the Lord, to the house of the God of Jacob." On the one hand there is the striving, "Let us make a name for ourselves," and on the other the longing to learn the torah that goes forth out of Zion, the city where the Lord has chosen to set his name. On the one hand is confusion and enmity, on the other an eternal peace.[31]

God's reign in Zion, not the city-and-tower of Babel, is the center of international order and the hope for global peace. Given Israel's centrality, even before the nations streamed to Zion, Yahweh governed the nations by governing the representative nation Israel. In Israel, in the chosen עַם, Yahweh carried out His "tenacious struggle" with "the primeval forces that dominate the life of Gentiles."[32]

Because of the call of Abram, the nations were organized around Israel.[33] Israel formed "the land" at the center of the world, like the land that emerged from the watery chaos during the creation week (Gen 1:2). All other nations were part of the turbulent sea that threatened to overwhelm the land and turn the world back to confusion. The new creation that took place in Abram divided sea and land, but simultaneously established a necessary connection between the two. Israel alone was the land, but the nations became "the ends of the land" (Deut 33:17; 1 Sam 2:10; Pss 2:10; 22:27; 59:13; 67:7; Isa 45:22; 52:10; Jer 16:19; Mic 5:4; Zech 9:10) and "the islands" (Isa 40:15; 41:5; 42:4). Gentiles formed the boundary of Israel's land, and as such they were incorporated as the frontier of Yahweh's empire that had Zion as its capital. The Gentile sea thus belonged to the land of the children of Abraham, and this implied that the Gentile would eventually share in their redemption as light and life spread from Zion to the frontier, from Jew to Greek.

The call of Abram did not leave the scattered nations to their own devices, to their own "lip," or to their own gods, which are nothings. Because Israel was the גוי and the nations a scattered עם, the Gentiles were incorporated into the purposes of God. Yahweh's choice of Abram and His establishment of Zion aimed from the beginning at the "ends of the land."[34] This Zion-centric topology and cosmology is essential for understanding the New Testament and the interactions of the apostles with the Greco-Roman world. For Jesus and His Jewish disciples, Gentiles were never understood "in themselves," but only as the borderlands of Zion's realm. This took on an added specificity when Yahweh Himself united the nations into a series of new Babels in the last half millennium before Christ.

The two sons of Eber thus set out contrasting paths of political salvation. The corporate salvation of humanity—unity among peoples, a link to heaven, a great name; life, instruction, and glory—can be pursued by following errant Joktanites to Babel or by following the wandering Pelegite Abram out of Ur to a land unknown. Israel too was an empire, though at first a shadow empire—not a nation imposing its will on other nations but the center of "a unified world community under God's rule." This was inherent in Israel's hopes, since they envisioned not "peace in isolation" but "a peaceful international community" gathered around Zion.[35]

Yahweh's imperial program ran at a tangent to the history of Babel. Yahweh confronted Babel, but instead of sending a chosen army of holy warriors to plunder the great city, He founded His empire by calling Abram *away from* empire. Abram began with an exodus from a "Babylon," Ur of the Chaldees (Gen 11:27–32).[36] Abram's initial attachment to Babylon was more than geographic. He worshiped the gods of the Chaldeans (Josh 24:14), which meant that he was integrated into the political order of Chaldea as well. Leaving his home meant leaving behind the gods of his own people to follow the God who called him away.[37] The fact that Yahweh could appear in glory (Acts 7:2) in Ur, and call an idolater from the Chaldean empire (Josh 24:14) to be the bearer of his own plan, reassured Israel exiled in Egypt. If Yahweh could reach to Ur to tear Abraham from his place, His arm is not too short to reach into Egypt. Later in Babylon or under Rome, the people of Abraham were never beyond the reach of His deliverance and protection. No matter how powerful Gentile empires were, Yahweh was always fully capable of reinitiating His imperial project.

Israel in Egypt

The promises to Abraham began to be fulfilled within a few generations. Joseph was sold into Egypt, and there he rose to become the first great "king" from the seed of Abraham. He became a paradigm of proper Israelite conduct within Gentile empires. He was faithful in his father's house, faithful in Potipher's house, faithful finally in interpreting Pharaoh's dream and in offering counsel about famine relief. As a result of his service to Gentiles, Joseph was elevated from every low place into which he was tossed—pulled from the pit, raised from the position of slave to become Potipher's chief steward, exalted finally from prison to sit at the right hand of Pharaoh. Joseph was the firstfruits of the promise to Abraham—a son of Abraham who taught Pharaoh's counselors wisdom, became lord of Pharaoh's house, was given power over Egypt and power to battle Pharaoh's enemies (Ps 105:16–24). In Joseph, God's *imperium* invaded Egypt, and a son of Abraham was exalted at the right hand of the Gentile king.

Joseph inverted the Joktanites of Babel and the sons of God of Genesis 6. He was a descendant of Shem and, like the Joktanites, he cooperated with a Hamite political project (Mizraim/Egypt is Hamite, Gen 10:6). He looked like a son of God marrying a daughter of men, and in fact he married the daughter of an Egyptian priest (Gen 41:45). Yet Joseph consistently witnessed to the God of his fathers, the God of heaven who reveals mysteries (Gen 41:16, 25, 28, 32), the God that even Pharaoh acknowledged (Gen 41:39). Joseph never faced a test that forced him to choose between service to Pharaoh and service to Yahweh, as Daniel later would. But his service to Pharaoh accomplished God's purposes, not only the purpose of feeding a world suffering from famine but also the more particular purpose of preparing the way for Israel to come under the wing of Egypt.

Conclusion

Israel's history is bracketed by empires, and Genesis–Exodus, which presents Israel's history in small prophetic compass, also begins and

Part I: Empires in Scripture

ends with empires. Abram's exodus from Ur anticipated Israel's from Egypt; Israel's entry into Egypt anticipated her later exile in Babylon; and Israel's exodus became a model for new exodus. At another level, Israel's history became a model for the history of the Gentiles nations. In the chiasm of biblical history, Yahweh scattered the nations at Babel, then gathered Israel from Egypt to the land; eventually, He scattered Israel among the Gentiles again. But all this was preparation for reversing Babel and gathering the nations to Zion, the mountainous tower that reached heaven. All this was preparation for uniting the nations to confess, with one lip, one great Name.

CHAPTER 2

Rod, Refuge, Messiah, Beast

Egypt initially provided an imperial refuge for Israel. Pharaoh gave Jacob and his sons the fruitful land of Goshen. Under Joseph's leadership, Egypt enabled Israel, with many other nations, to survive a great famine. The Egyptian empire honored Israel, and Pharaoh paid respect to the God of Israel. Over time, however, Israel turned to worship Egypt's idols (Josh 24:14).[1] Given the symbiotic connections of religious and political life in Egypt, worshiping Egyptian gods involved accepting the Egyptian imperial polity.[2] Israel in Egypt imitated the sons of God and the Joktanites who cooperated with Babel. They were not entirely unwilling participants in the program. Yahweh disciplined Israel by erasing the memory of Joseph from the minds of Pharaohs (Exodus 1–2), and Pharaoh's Babel project turned bloody. The hints of human sacrifice in Genesis 11 become overt in Egypt. Cainite Pharaoh filled the Nile with the blood of baby Abels, until the Nile became so much a river of blood that it turned to blood and called up Yahweh's Avenging Angel. Egypt was the original harlot-city, drinking the blood of the saints until it became drunk, stumbled around, tripped, and fell.

Eventually, Yahweh yanked Israel from Egypt in another Abrahamic "call" from "Babel."[3] Like Abram leaving Ur, the sons of Abram left Egypt behind and went to Sinai, a mountain that reached to heaven. There Yahweh Himself showed Moses the pattern for a tabernacle that connected heaven and earth, the tower of which Israel was to be caretaker.⁴ As Israel left Egypt, they plundered the Egyptians, taking the riches of Egypt as their own—imperial riches to be used to build Yahweh's house in the wilderness (Exod 12:35–36; 25:1–8).

Delivered from the burdens of Egypt, Yahweh sent Israel to the land, where Israel established a small empire of her own. Israel took the land in a war of utter destruction commanded by Yahweh. When the dust settled, the twelve tribes dominated a land that included non-Israelite sojourners, whom Israel was exhorted to treat with un-Egyptian kindness and justice (Exod 22:21; 23:9; Lev 19:1, 33–34; Deut 16:11, 14). Under the early kings, Israel annexed Moab, Ammon, portions of Philistia and Edom. These territories were forced into the Israelite *imperium* but the Psalms and prophets envisioned a time when the conquered peoples, along with enemies like Egypt, Babylon, Ethiopia, and Assyria, would be regarded as brothers, all children of mother Zion (e.g., Pss 60; 87; 108; Isa 19:19–24; 27:12–13). Israel's imperial conquests matured into a vision of a future order of international peace and brotherhood, the fulfillment of God's imperial promises to Abraham.

The path to God's empire never did run smooth, and before Israel's regional empire was transformed into a global church they were tested by Gentile empires, new Babels. As Israel's monarchy wound down, a new form of imperialism appeared—aggressive, expansive, and brutal. First the Assyrians, then Babylon invaded and conquered Israel, until Babylon was herself overtaken by Persia. Old Babel was tame by comparison, built on the peaceable appeal, "Come, let us build." Assyrians did not wait for the nations to gather to Nineveh; they rushed out to conquer and subject peoples. Assyrian city walls were decorated with scenes of flayed enemies; blood almost literally served for mortar.⁵ Empires began to take on a bestial face. Its appeal was no longer eschatological hope but naked fear. Yet this was Yahweh's design for Israel, the way toward the political redemption of Israel and the nations: Before they were ready for a fulfilled *imperium* of their own, Israel must pass through a fiery furnace.

Rod (Isaiah 10)

In the days of King Ahaz, Judah was in the middle of a political crisis. The Assyrians were on the rise, and the Northern Kingdom had allied with the kingdom of Aram to form an anti-Assyrian alliance. The allies moved against Judah to force Judah into the alliance, because three cords are stronger than two (Isaiah 7–8). Ahaz responded by sending Yahweh's temple treasure to Tiglath-Pileser to encourage the Assyrian king to attack Aram and so relieve the pressure on Judah (2 Kings 16). Isaiah repeatedly warned Ahaz that his politicking would not work. Nor, later, would the effort to ward off Assyria and Babylon by an alliance with Egypt (cf. Isaiah 31).[6] The Assyrians were a relentless plague of flies from the river Euphrates (7:18–29), and they would settle everywhere in the land—on the ledges, on the bushes, in all the watering places. The Assyrians were a razor to remove the glory-crown from every head in Judah, shave them bald like slaves (Isa 7:20). The Assyrians were a flood, as if the Euphrates had overflowed and filled Judah up to the neck (Isa 8:7–8). In chapter 10, Isaiah renewed and expanded the threats. The Assyrians would capture booty and seize plunder and trample down Judah as if they were clay on the ground, mud in the streets. From Ai, they would march through Migron, terrifying the city of Ramah and chasing away the city of Saul, Gibeah. All through the land there would be mourning and lamentation. Laish and Anathoth, just northeast of Jerusalem, were threatened, and the king of Assyria would come as far as Nob, just to the east of the mount of Olives, which is just to the east of Jerusalem (vv. 28–32).

Though Judah's world seemed to be falling apart, Yahweh assured Ahaz that He was in control. None of Assyria's actions were accidental. Yahweh orchestrated Assyria's rise and even Assyria's assault on Judah. Assyria itself, Isaiah said, was Yahweh's rod, staff, and saw. Yahweh Himself "commissioned" Assyria (v. 6; שָׁלַח) against the "godless nation," the people who were no longer the people of the Passover and exodus but the people of wrath (v. 6).[7] Isaiah's imagery assured Judah of Yahweh's goodness. Yahweh used Assyria as a rod and staff, but the people of Judah who had sung Psalm 23 knew that the Lord uses His rod and staff to comfort and to guide and that He is the good shepherd of Israel.[8] Imperial expansion even of the most vicious kind was Yahweh's dread tool. The Lord commissioned and raised the Assyrian empire to discipline and do His work at Zion and Jerusalem (v. 12; cf. Isa 29:1–8). When that was completed, the king of Assyria's time was done.[9] The Assyrians entered Judah, marched as far as Jerusalem, besieged Jerusalem, but could not take the city. Jerusalem was the limit of Assyrian *imperium*, as Yahweh overruled Assyrian ferocity for His purposes.

Part I: Empires in Scripture

After seven woes (5:8–23; 10:1–4), Yahweh pronounced an eighth woe, but this time on Assyria (10:5). "Eight" is the number of rebirth in Scripture. When Yahweh's wrath had been filled to a seven, He renewed His people by striking Assyria.[10] Yahweh had many reasons to judge Assyria. Assyria did not humbly acknowledge that it was only an instrument, but proudly boasted of its own power (vv. 7, 12–14). The king of Assyria was very impressed with the power of his own hand. His hand reached to the kingdoms of the idols. With his hand, he came to the nests of the nations and gathered in their riches; it was as easy as gathering eggs, and none of the cities fought back; they did not even let out a chirp. My hand, my hand, my hand; I, I, I, I.[11] The arrogance is more than Yahweh can take. As Yahweh revealed Himself to Pharaoh, so He would do with Assyria (v. 12). Another exodus was coming. Egypt struck Israel with the rod, but eventually the rod was turned against Egypt. Yahweh used the Assyrian rod, but He was ready to turn against Assyria. They had come to drown Judah, but they would end up floundering in a flood of Babylonians, sinking into the depths of the sea like Pharaoh and his strength (vv. 24–27). When Yahweh broke the strength of the Assyrians, the burden of Judah would be removed, the yoke broken from her neck.[12] In fact, the fire that could consume Assyria was the spark from Israel stoked to a fire (v. 17). When the Assyrians crashed against the people of Judah, Judah burst into a flame that consumed the Assyrians.[13] Because Judah is the empire of Abraham, it was dangerous for Assyria to attack Judah; cursing Judah brought down curses on them.

Isaiah's warnings to Ahaz fell on deaf ears, but they had an effect on his son Hezekiah. When the Assyrians actually invaded, the king did not turn to Egypt or bribe Sennacherib with temple treasure. Instead, he turned immediately to the prophet and took the boasting letter of Sennacherib into the temple to present before Yahweh.[14] Hezekiah learned what Ahaz never did, that in any contest between Israel and a great power, there is always a third party, Yahweh, the Lord of all.[15] The woe pronounced over Assyria was effective. After the angel of death chased away the Assyrians in another Passover, the Assyrians disappeared from Isaiah's prophecy (never mentioned after 38:6). After Yahweh had disciplined His son Israel with His rod Assyria, Assyria's curtain fell.

Elsewhere, the Bible provides another perspective on the Assyrian empire. In Jonah, the Assyrian capital of Nineveh repented, like the sailors on Jonah's ship, when Israel's prophet preached to them (Jonah 3). Instead of judgment, Jonah mediated salvation and grace to the Assyrians. Jonah also depicted Assyria as a guardian of Israel. The great fish that swallowed the prophet is analogous to the "sea monster" Assyria that swims in the ocean of nations devouring smaller nations. Jonah is an allegory of exile (swallowing) and return (vomiting), and the allegory suggests that the fish of Assyria will swallow but not digest Israel. Nahum is a companion book to Jonah and denounces the Assyrians for their mistreatment of Israel and for their cruelty. Though once penitent, Nineveh had become a "bloody city" (Nah 3:1), like Jerusalem later (Ezek 24:6, 8).[16] At one time, the rising city-state of Nineveh heard the voice of God through Jonah; at one time, Nineveh was like a protecting vine overshadowing the people of God. Perhaps at one point Assyria was Yahweh's willing rod. They did not remain so, and so were judged for their arrogance and apostasy.

REFUGE (DANIEL 2)

The exile of Judah into Babylon matches and inverts the original pilgrimage of Abram from Chaldea. The Abrahamic people who were detached from the imperial orders of Babel and Egypt were sown back among the nations. This was certainly a judgment, but at a deeper level it fulfilled Israel's original calling. Israel was scattered, as were the men of Babel.[17] As the *goy* of Abram, Israel replicated the history of the nations, but Israel did not remain in exile. Their regathering to Zion was a pledge of the reunion of the peoples of the earth at God's holy mountain.[18]

Babylon was renewed Babel, associated with the original program of imperial rebellion, false eschatology, sacrifice, and tyranny. As Isaiah said, Babylon was ultimately even more arrogant than Assyria. The king of Assyria merely boasted about his conquests, but the king of Babylon claimed even more: "You said in your heart, 'I will ascend to heaven; I will raise my throne above the stars of God, and I will sit on the mount of assembly in the recesses of the far north. I will ascend above the heights of the clouds; I will make myself like the most high'" (Isa 14:13–14; cf. Daniel 4). The unnamed king of Babylon was a self-idolater, a rival to the Most High God who sits enthroned in the far north, at the governing pole of the celestial sphere. Yahweh would not tolerate Babylonian arrogance any more than Assyrian. Instead of climbing to the top of

Part I: Empires in Scripture

the world, the king of Babylon would fall like a star (v. 12), all the way down to Sheol (v. 15). His corpse would lie unburied (v. 19) because he trampled and ruined his own country (v. 20). His fall would leave the rest of the world amazed: "Is this the man who made the earth tremble, who shook kingdoms?"(vv. 16–17).

Babylon was, like Assyria, Yahweh's creation. Yahweh had given the world into Nebuchadnezzar's hands. The same could be said of Assyria in its time, but Jeremiah's description of Nebuchadnezzar's dominion is richer, more Adamic, more Christological even:

> I have made the earth, the men and the beasts which are on the face of the earth by My great power and by My outstretched arm, and I will give it to the one who is pleasing in My sight. And now I have given all these lands into the hand of Nebuchadnezzar king of Babylon, My servant, and I have given him also the wild animals of the field to serve him. And all the nations shall serve him, and his son, and his grandson, until the time of his own land comes; then many nations and great kings will make him their servant. And it will be, that the nation or the kingdom which will not serve him, Nebuchadnezzar king of Babylon, and which will not put its neck under the yoke of the king of Babylon, I will punish that nation with the sword, with famine, and with pestilence, declares Yahweh, until I have destroyed it by his hand. (Jer 27:5–8)

Yahweh's conferral of authority to Nebuchadnezzar was not grudging. He gave the earth into the hand of "the one who is pleasing in My sight" (לַאֲשֶׁר יָשַׁר בְּעֵינָי),[19] and this pleasing one was Nebuchadnezzar.[20] Yahweh reinforced His commendation of Nebuchadnezzar by calling him "My servant," a title reserved for some of the great heroes of biblical history (Gen 26:24; Num 12:7–8; 14:24; Josh 1:2, 7; 2 Sam 3:18; 7:5) and never used elsewhere for anyone outside of Israel. In 1–2 Kings, "My servant" is used almost exclusively of David (cf. 1 Kgs 11:13, 32, 34, 36, 38). Jeremiah used the title only for Nebuchadnezzar (25:9; 43:10) and two others—Jacob (30:10; 46:27, probably understood corporately) and David (33:21–22, 26). By calling Nebuchadnezzar "My servant," Yahweh assigned him a Davidic role. Like David, a new-Adamic king, Nebuchadnezzar ruled wild animals as well as nations. It is no wonder that he was given the imperial title "king of kings" (Ezek 26:7; Dan 2:37), a title that not even Yahweh receives in the Old Testament. Nebuchadnezzar was also a Mosaic figure, leading a remnant out of the

"Egypt" of corrupted Jerusalem into the "wilderness" of Babylon, where they awaited a second entry and "conquest."

Because of Yahweh's gift of dominion to Nebuchadnezzar, Jeremiah advised that the Jews of Jerusalem surrender to Nebuchadnezzar. "Come out of her" is a biblical exhortation to exiles in Babylon (Rev 18:4), but Jeremiah urged the opposite: He did not call Judah to "come out" from Babylon, but to "go in" *voluntarily. False* prophets were the ones who counseled resistance to Nebuchadnezzar and assured Judah that their exile would be brief (Jer 28:1). The ones who surrendered to the empire survived into exile, whereas those who resisted were summarily executed. Some who surrendered rose to high positions within the empire, as Joseph had in Egypt. Jeremiah insisted that the people should expect to be in Babylon for some time. The exile would *not* be brief, so the Jews were to make themselves at home: "Build houses and live in them; and plant gardens, and eat their produce. Take wives and become the fathers of sons and daughters, and take wives for your sons and give your daughters to husbands, that they may bears sons and daughters; and multiply there and do not decrease. And seek the peace of the city where I have sent you into exile, and pray to Yahweh on its behalf; for in its peace you will have peace" (Jer 29:5–7). Yahweh laid a Deuteronomic choice before Judah, a way of life and a way of death: Resistance to the encroaching Babylonian empire was death; submission to Nebuchadnezzar was the way of life because it was, at the time, the form of submission to Yahweh (Jer 21:1–7).[21] A new Jeremiah political stance, consistent with an imperial phase of history, thus replaced the political ethic of Israel's monarchical period.[22]

Daniel provides details about Nebuchadnezzar that support the Jeremian portrait of an emperor who qualified as Yahweh's servant. The king of Babylon took some of the youth of Israel into exile, but instead of enslaving them, he trained the best young men for the Babylonian civil service (Dan 1:1–7). Nebuchadnezzar aimed to co-opt Judah's elite into the Babylonian cause, of course, but the Jewish heroes were treated with remarkable deference. When Daniel and his friends objected to the food they were served, the Babylonian commander gave them leave to test their own diet (Dan 1:8–16). In his first interview with Daniel, Hananiah, Mishael, and Azariah, Nebuchadnezzar concluded that they were ten times wiser than all the other wise men of Babylon (1:17–21). When Daniel interpreted his dream, Nebuchadnezzar treated Daniel as

Part I: Empires in Scripture

a god, bowing to him and offering incense and a sacrifice (2:46). The king became enraged when the Three refused to bow to his image, but when he saw how they were miraculously preserved in the fiery furnace, he praised Yahweh: "Blessed be the God of Shadrach, Meshach, and Abed-nego, who has sent His angel and delivered His servants who put their trust in Him" (3:28). He followed up his confession with a decree that no one should speak "anything offensive against the God of Shadrach, Meshach, and Abed-Nego," on pain of being torn limb from limb and having his house reduced to rubble (3:29). Like the king of Babylon in Isaiah 14, Nebuchadnezzar became proud of his achievements, and Yahweh humbled him by taking away his reason and turning him into a beast (Dan 4:1–33). When he humbled himself and came to his senses, he made one of the Bible's great confessions of the sovereign rule of Yahweh over the nations: "His dominion is an everlasting dominion, and His kingdom endures from generation to generation. . . . I, Nebuchadnezzar, praise, exalt and honor the King of heaven, for all His works are true and His ways just, and He is able to humble those who walk in pride" (Dan 4:34–37).

This is hardly a life of unwavering loyalty to the God of Israel, but it is a life marked by regular and sincere confession of Yahweh's dominion, also over Nebuchadnezzar and Babylon. Nebuchadnezzar was Yahweh's servant largely because he displayed consciousness—sporadic though it may have been—of being exactly that. Unlike Pharaoh, he blessed Abraham's seed and reaped political blessings as a result. More importantly, by resisting at crucial moments, Daniel and his friends broke the uniformity of neo-Babelic worship and created fissures in the homogeneous political structure of neo-Babel. Shemites who once cooperated in building Babel staked out a space of independence. Nebuchadnezzar was forced to make a choice—kill his favored young men, or tolerate the God of Israel. Yahweh scattered citizens of His empire among the nations for a reason, not just to teach Israel a lesson but to begin forming a martyr-people whose faithful resistance would remake Gentile empire. Neo-Babel was one city, and high-placed Israelites helped administer the city. But because of faithful Israelites, neo-Babel failed in its ambition to construct a single tower.

Nebuchadnezzar's confession of Yahweh and respect for Israel's wisdom was not a personal peculiarity. Instead, the formation of new Babel marked a new phase in the history of Israel and empire, a new stage of maturity for the people of Abraham. Like Joseph before him, Daniel went before to prepare a place for the Israelites who submitted to Yahweh's servant Nebuchadnezzar and settled in Babylon. Israel's monarchy was in ruins, but Yahweh's imperial experiment was not stopped or even slowed. Through the monarchy, Yahweh trained Israel to be scattered again into the world, now as a faithful people, resistant to the gods of the Gentiles, resistant to the gods of empire while simultaneously promoting the city's welfare. Babylon's cordial reception of the Israelites initiated Israel-in-Empire—the geopolitical system that the New Testament describes as the οικουμηνη. The geopolitical organization is portrayed in Nebuchadnezzar's dream in Daniel 2 in which Nebuchadnezzar saw a statue made up of various metals. It had a head of gold, a torso of silver, thighs of bronze, lower legs of iron, and feet of iron and terra cotta. A stone cut without hands hit the feet of the statue, and the whole crumbled to powder, while the stone grew into a mountain that filled the entire earth. Daniel interpreted the dream as a portrayal of four "kingdoms" that would dominate the world from the time of Nebuchadnezzar until a fifth kingdom, the kingdom of God, displaced the rest. These were the four great Mediterranean empires of late antiquity—Babylon, Persia, Alexandrian Greece, and Rome. Nebuchadnezzar's dream portrayed what the Lord would do in the "end of days" (Dan 2:28).

Echoing Jeremiah, Daniel told Nebuchadnezzar that he was the head of gold "to whom the God of heaven has given the kingdom, the power, the strength, and the glory" (Dan 2:37–38). The materials of the statue are temple materials.[23] Solomon's temple had an inner sanctuary of gold, silver in the outer sanctuary, and a bronze altar, sea, and water chariots in the courtyard. The movement from "top" (Most Holy Place) to "bottom" (courtyard) was from gold to silver to bronze, just like the sequence of metals in the statue of Nebuchadnezzar. The statue represented a sanctuary for Israel, an imperial temple in which Israel, God's *imperium*, would find asylum during the period from Nebuchadnezzar to the coming of the kingdom, the whole period of the "end of days." In this imperial sanctuary, Israel was to practice the disciplines of Torah—the disciplines that they had been taught for centuries and had not learned well. In Israel's temple, there was no image of Yahweh, and Israel was forbidden to bow to images of any kind. In the imperial sanctuary, too, they were to have no other gods "before the face of" Yahweh. For

Part I: Empires in Scripture

centuries, Israel had been trained to refrain from unclean meats and impurities of all sorts. They were being trained to resist the seductions of the Gentile world, so that when they were housed in the imperial sanctuary they would remain clean.

Israel looked ahead to a series of empires that would rule over the known world. Rather than try to subvert these empires, they were to seek the good and prosperity and become good citizens within the empire, all the while refraining from eating the food and worshiping the gods of the empires. This program not only preserved Israel through a national disaster of enormous proportions, but also raised Israelites to a prominence that they had never before achieved. Joseph went to Egypt alone and rose to become second only to Pharaoh. During the exile, the Israelites could boast not one but a handful of Josephs. Daniel was trained for service in the court of Nebuchadnezzar and, after interpreting the king's dream, he became the ruler over the province of Babylon and the prefect of the Babylonian wise men (Dan 2:49). Daniel and his friends resisted imperial culture at crucial points, but they resisted imperial culture and worship from *within* the empire, from their very high places in the royal court. As with Joseph, we have here a fulfillment of the promise to Abraham, and a sign that God's empire was being established as a fifth column (or fifth monarchy) in the midst of Babylon's. Daniel (like Joseph!) was forgotten in the reign of Belshazzar (Daniel 5), but when the Persians conquered Babylon, Daniel again rose to a high position as one of the three commissioners ruling the satraps of the Persian empire (Dan 6:1–2). Despite the opposition of other officials, Daniel survived the lion's den and impressed Darius so much that he decreed that "in all the dominion of my kingdom men are to fear and tremble before the God of Daniel" (Dan 6:25–28).

Daniel was the most Josephine character in the exilic period, but he was far from the only one. In the book of Esther, Mordecai had some standing in the court of Ahasuerus, sitting at the king's gate (Esth 2:21). Yet when he instructed Esther to hide her identity, all the Jews were placed in danger. As a result of Esther's courage and cunning, the Jews turned on their enemies, and Haman, the enemy of the Jews, was hung from the gallows that he prepared for Mordecai. Mordecai was raised up, not on a gallows, but to a position at court. When he wrested power from Haman, Ahasuerus gave it to Mordecai: "The king took off his signet ring which he had taken away from Haman, and gave it to

Mordecai. And Esther set Mordecai over the house of Haman" (8:2). Mordecai wore "royal robes of blue and white, with a large crown of gold and a garment of fine linen and purple" (8:15), resembling the décor of Ahasuerus' feast that begins the story (1:6). Mordecai replaced Ahasuerus' palace; while faithfully serving in the "temple" of Persia's empire, Mordecai had become the Persian emperor's "temple." Esther ends with a reminder of the extent of Ahasuerus' kingdom, but the real novelty was the fact that Ahasuerus now had a Jewish advisor at his side:[24] "And all the doings of his authority and strength, and the full account of the greatness of Mordecai to which the king advanced him, are they not written in the Book of the Chronicles of the Kings of Media and Persia? For Mordecai the Jew was second only to King Ahasuerus, and great among the Jews and in favor with the multitude of his kinsman, one who sought the good of his people and one who spoke for the welfare of the whole nation" (10:2–3). Israel's Kings were written in the Chronicles of Judah and Israel. Mordecai got an entry in the Chronicle of the Medes and Persians.

As "cupbearer to the king," Nehemiah too had a high position in the court of the Persian emperor (Neh 1:11). Nehemiah served the king wine (2:1–2) but held authority beyond the activities of a butler. When the king asked him what he needed, he boldly requested safe passage to Jerusalem, the use of timber from the king's own forest, and personnel to help him prepare the timber for the temple (2:7–8). Nehemiah depended on the king's protection and royal patronage to finish the work of rebuilding Jerusalem. This is the Israel-in-Empire system of the οικουμηνη in action—a Gentile emperor giving aid and support to Jewish projects and people who, in turn, rise to high positions in the empire.

Something had happened to Israel. In Egypt, Israel turned to Egyptian gods and had to be wrenched away with a mighty hand. In Babylon, Jews resolutely refused to bow before idols, and they rose and rose until there was virtually nowhere higher to go. Between Babel and neo-Babel, something had also happened to empire. Empires and emperors had become responsive to the witness of the Jews, respectful of Jews, sometimes reverent toward the God of the Jews. Yahweh's counter-Babel Abrahamic empire advanced, transforming both Israel and the Gentiles.

Part I: Empires in Scripture

Messianic Empire (2 Kings 25; Isaiah 44–45)

To lamenting Jeremiah, Judah's exile was an unmitigated disaster. It left Jerusalem a bereft widow, a princess reduced to tearful servitude (Lam 1:1–2). Yahweh Himself had turned His strong arm on His own people, destroying His booth, causing forgetfulness of His feasts and Sabbaths, rejecting His altar. He gave His sanctuary to the Babylonians, who filled it with noisy triumph, a terrible parody of the appointed feasts of old (2:5–7). Despite the glimmers of hope at the center of Lamentations, the book ends in chaotic sorrow, as even the acrostic poetic form falls to pieces. The only hope was that the Lord would restore His people, but that hope was overshadowed by the impossible possibility that Yahweh's rejection might be final: "Unless You have rejected us, and are exceedingly angry with us" (5:21–22). Jeremiah's "How lonely sits the city" was the key signature of the dirge that concluded the history of Israel's monarchy.

The end of Kings seems to be equally dismal (2 Kings 24–25). Nebuchadnezzar burned the great houses, the palace, the temple; he broke the walls of the city, and removed leaders in all walks of life. Just at the end, though, comes an episode—the elevation of Jehoiachin—that modulates into what may be a delicate, discordant gesture toward hope. In my end is my beginning: That tonal shift encourages us to reconsider the entire conclusion of 1–2 Kings, or even the entirety of 1–2 Kings. A narrative that ends with Jehoichin's elevation may not be quite the kind of tragedy it seems to be, which means that Judah's exile might not be the kind of exile it appears.[25] The close of Kings is a narrative rendering of Jeremian political theology. Jehoiachin was the one ruler who followed the prophets' instruction to submit to Nebuchadnezzar (Jeremiah 27, 29).[26] He alone entrusted his future to Babylon's sanctuary, and, implicitly, to Daniel, who had already prepared a soft landing for the exiles in Babylon.[27] And Jehoiachin was the one ruler who survived to reappear in the narrative. He remained an acknowledged king, though his kingship was subordinate to the imperial kingship of Babylon. With the exile, Davidic kingship was absorbed into the Babylonian orbit, just as the royal chronology of Judah's kings gives way to the regnal chronology of Nebuchadnezzar. A new epoch began, but in Jehoiachin the Davidic dynasty, and with it Davidic hope, became embedded in the times of the Gentiles.[28] Under the οικουμηνη, Israel-in-Empire includes Davidide-in-Empire.

First–Second Kings does not end with anything like a restoration of Davidic glory, nor even an explicit statement that Jehoiachin's elevation fulfills Yahweh's promise.[29] The Davidic line survived the destruction of Jerusalem, but the question was not simply survival. First–Second Kings describes the *form* that survival would take now that Nebuchadnezzar had conquered Jerusalem, taken the Davidic king into exile, dismantled Solomon's temple, and absorbed Judah into Babylon. Echoes of earlier Scriptures in the closing verses of 2 Kings fill out the picture. Evil-merodach "lifted the head" of Jehoiachin (2 Kgs 25:27), as Pharaoh once "lifted the head" of his baker and cupbearer (Gen 40:13, 19–20). The echo of the Joseph narrative reinforces the fact that, like Joseph and Daniel before him, Jehoiachin received a place of honor above all the conquered kings in Babylon, a throne at the right hand of the emperor (2 Kgs 25:28).[30] Jehoiachin is implicitly compared to Mephibosheth, son of Jonathan son of Saul, a descendant of a fallen royal house fed at the table of the generous king who supplanted his dynasty.[31] The analogy should be pressed: Evil-merodach is to Jehoiachin as David is to Saul's grandson. First–Second Kings casts Jehoiachin as a Saulide, the last of a dying dynasty. David's dynasty ends with a Saul-like sigh and whimper. More importantly, if Jehoiachin is Mephibosheth, then 1–2 Kings casts Evil-merodach as the new David, the Lord's anointed who shows Davidic generosity to a fallen royal house.

The closing verses of Kings go even further, again tracking the instructions of Jeremiah. Gedaliah insisted that if the Jews "served" Babylon, "it shall be well with you" (v. 24). According to Deuteronomy, Israel is called to serve King Yahweh and Him alone (Deut 10:12, 20), but now they serve Babylon's king. When Israel serves Yahweh, things go well (Deut 4:40; 5:16, 33; 12:28), but now the king of Babylon promises to ensure that "all is well." Evil-merodach spoke "good things" to Jehoiachin (v. 28), as Yahweh had earlier spoken "this good" to David (2 Sam 7:28). In all these ways, Babylon occupies the place earlier reserved for Yahweh.[32] That might indicate that Judah is falling into imperial idolatry, and there is little doubt that the conclusion of Kings is pro-Babylonian. In the light of Jeremiah's prophecy that Yahweh had given "the earth, man and beast" to Nebuchadnezzar to serve him (Jer 27:5–11), however, these echoes instead indicate that Babylon and the empires to follow are Yahweh's chosen agents for preserving His people. Submission to Babylon is submission to Yahweh. The rehabilitation of Jehoiachin helped "to bring the legacy of the promissory covenant with David into line with the new historical reality effected by the events of 587 B.C.E and with the novel social and political situation of the continuing Diaspora." But there is also a theological dimension to this. Yahweh sent Judah into exile to teach his people the habits of covenant fidelity and submission, in a situation where Gentile emperors stood in as Emperor Yahweh's regents.[33] Not only was the Davidic dynasty *preserved* under the imperial system; the Davidic task, and much of the Davidic hope of Israel, was absorbed into empire. Evil-merodach, King of neo-Babel, was dressed in the robes and crown of David, son of Yahweh.

Meanwhile, Solomon's temple dissolves before our eyes. Pots, shovels, snuffers, spooks, vessels, firepans, and basins were collected and taken off to Babylon. According to verse 13, the Chaldeans "broke" (שָׁבַר) the larger bronze furnishings of the temple and carried the bronze away to Babylon. The fixtures of the temple did not go into exile intact but were reduced to their base materials, reverting to the bronze from which they were made. "Breaking," further, was just what Israel was supposed to do to the idols of the land (שָׁבַר is used in Exod 23:24; 24:13; Deut 7:5), and it was what faithful kings did to the idols that popped up around the land (2 Kgs 18:4; 23:14). By prophetic reckoning, Solomon's temple had become a den of brigands, no better than the Baal temple, and so it was fitting that Nebuchadnezzar, like a new Joshua, like a Babylonian Josiah, "broke" the temple furnishings in pieces. The pillars originally made by the half-Tyrean craftsman Hiram were sliced in pieces by the Babylonian King. Nebuchadnezzar treated the great pillars of the temple as if they were no better than the idolatrous סְבוֹתָם that covered the land.

The same verb "break" is used at each of the major junctures of the book of Kings. In 2 Kgs 11:18, the people of the land went to the house of Baal in Jerusalem and destroyed it, "breaking" its idols and images and killing the priest of Baal, and in 2 Kgs 23:14 Josiah "broke" sacred pillars and Asherim before defiling the place with human bones. Solomon's temple seemed as thoroughly vanquished as the temple of Baal or the bull shrine at Bethel.

Faintly, all but unheard, comes the whisper of another melody. The list of temple furnishings in 2 Kgs 25:14–16 begins with the large bronze furnishings that were broken in pieces for transport to Babylon. Then we learn that smaller utensils were packed up and transported intact. When the text returns to the pillars, sea, and stands at the end of the passage, however, there is no mention of their destruction. Instead, verse 15 reminds us that Solomon *made* these items for Yahweh's house and also reminds us that the bronze was so abundant that it could not be weighed—precisely what was said when the bronze implements were built (1 Kgs 7:47).[34] There is a further and more global oddity. Second Kings 25:17 describes the bronze pillars as if they were still standing. It records their height, the height of the capitals, and briefly describes the network and pomegranates that adorned the capitals. In short, the text is written upside down. Logically, the description of the size, materials, and decorations of the two pillars better fits at the beginning of the passage. In that position, the description of the pillars' size and shape would mean: "This is what the bronze pillars once *were*, but now they are in pieces in the royal treasury in Babylon." Instead, the text begins with the pillars being dismantled and ends with them erect. At the beginning of the list the bronze pomegranate trees have been chopped down, but at the end they are replanted. It is not simply that the list includes a few discordant notes of hope; the melody flows backwards. It is an un-dirge.[35] By dismantling the pillars, Nebuchadnezzar removed king and priest from Israel, but by writing the list so that the erect pillars come at the end, the author hints that king and priest will one day be restored to their place in Yahweh's house. But more: The text is written in a way that suggests that the pillars of Solomon's temple are re-erected *in Babylon itself*. Israel-in-Empire will, someday, include a new temple, a temple-in-empire. As the empire becomes quasi-Davidic by becoming the protectorate for the Davidic survivors, so the empire becomes quasi-priestly by absorbing the temple and preserving its materials until the house and its pillars rise again.

All the hints entwined in the closing narrative of 1–2 Kings come to explicit expression in Isaiah's astounding prophecy of the Persian Cyrus, Yahweh's shepherd and His "anointed" (Isa 44:24—45:4).[36] In part, this passage merely reiterates Isaiah 10's message about Yahweh's political Lordship over nations and kings, as Isaiah substitutes Yahweh for Marduk in a palimpsest of a Persian myth in which Marduk confers *imperium* on Persian kings.[37] As the richly resonant language suggests, though, Cyrus's conquest of Babylon and imperial reign was not a product of Yahweh's general providential orchestration. It is a vocation, an election:

> Thus says the Lord, your Redeemer, and the one who formed you from the womb, "I, the Lord, am the maker of all things, stretching out the heavens by Myself and spreading out the earth all alone, causing the omens of boasters to fail, making fools out of diviners, causing wise men to draw back and turning their knowledge into foolishness, confirming the word of His servant and performing the purpose of His messengers. It is I who says of Jerusalem, 'She shall be inhabited!' and of the cities of Judah, 'They shall be built.' And I will raise up her ruins again. It is I who says to the depth of the sea, 'Be dried up!' And I will make your rivers dry. It is I who says of Cyrus, 'He is My shepherd! And he will perform all My desire.' And he declares of Jerusalem, 'She will be built,' and of the temple, 'Your foundation will be laid.'"
>
> Thus says the LORD to Cyrus His anointed, whom I have taken by the right hand, to subdue nations before him and to loose the loins of kings; to open doors before him so that gates will not be shut: "I will go before you and make the rough places smooth; I will shatter the doors of bronze and cut through their iron bars. I will give you the treasures of darkness and hidden wealth of secret places, so that you may know that it is I, the Lord, the God of Israel, who calls you by your name. For the sake of Jacob My servant, and Israel My chosen one, I have also called you by your name; I have given you a title of honor though you have not known Me.

Cyrus was not a mere tool, as Assyria was, but a servant chosen by the Redeemer and Creator of all things. By incorporating Judah and by entering a covenant with the king of Judah, Babylon (and the successor empires) became a quasi-Davidic polity.[38] The connections between Cyrus the servant of Yahweh and the redeeming Servant of Yahweh later in Isaiah are not fortuitous. Cyrus the Anointed Emperor, heir to the Davidic task of ruling Israel and building a house for the Lord's name, became a type of the future Davidic World Ruler who would bring *Yahweh's* imperial project to its climax.[39]

In Cyrus's empire, the fissures and cracks that opened up in homogeneous Babelic empire, due to the witness of Daniel and others, opened into chasms. Persia was at base an ethnically dual rather than a uniform empire, a *Medo*-Persian polity. In Scripture, the contrast between Babel and Persia is dramatic. Babel demanded a single confession, one lip; Cyrus spoke to Jews in the name of the God of heaven,

Israel's God. Babel gathered and confined; Cyrus scattered Jews (and others). Babel constructed a single tower; Cyrus provided the materials for the construction of a second temple in Jerusalem, and the work continued in spite of warnings that rebuilding would threaten Persian power (Ezra 4–6). Babel had only "one set of words"; whatever Persian emperors decreed was proclaimed "to every province according to its script, to every people according to their language" (Esth 8:9).[40] After a neo-Babelic effort to consolidate tongue and lip, Persia represented "scattering" and a harmonious "babble" of tongues.

The original Babel was an abortive imperial project. Shemites, Joktanites, assisted in building Babel's tower. With Cyrus's decree, the tables turned. The tower/temple was no longer Babel's but Israel's. Instead of Shemites sacralizing a Hamite project, Gentiles built the house of Yahweh. Yahweh sent Israel into exile so they could be under the protective wing of Gentile emperors. In the event, Gentile empires came partly under the wing of Zion. With the exile and restoration, Israel was placed in a position to achieve Yahweh's imperial design, where Yahweh presides as King of kings over the Jew-and-Gentile, Israel-and-Empire project of building Yahweh's house.

Beast (Daniel 7)

Empires may be towers and cities raised in rebellion against God, rods that crush, or sanctuaries and saviors for the faithful. Persia's first emperor was an anointed one who carried on the work of the Davidic kingdom, building the temple and governing the *imperium* of God.

Empires can also be beasts.

Early on in Daniel, we have a glimpse of the imperial beast, when the Lord humbled the pride of Nebuchadnezzar by taking away his reason and sending him to live among the cattle (Daniel 4). Pride turned the emperor bestial, and this incident anticipated a later portion of Daniel when the prophet himself saw a vision of four beasts arising from the wind-stirred Gentile sea:

> Four great beasts were coming up from the sea, different from one another. The first was like a lion and had the wings of an eagle. I kept looking until its wings were plucked, and it was lifted up from the ground and made to stand on two feet like a man; a human mind was also given to it. And behold, another

> beast, a second one, resembling a bear. And it was raised up on one side, and three ribs were in its mouth between its teeth; and thus they said to it, "Arise, devour much meat!" After this I kept looking, and behold, another one, like a leopard, which had on its back four wings of a bird; the beast also had four heads, and dominion was given to it. After this I kept looking in the night visions, and behold, a fourth beast, dreadful and terrifying and extremely strong; and it had large iron teeth. It devoured and crushed, and trampled down the remainder with its feet; and it was different from all the beasts that were before it, and it had ten horns. (Dan 7:3–7)

Eventually, Daniel saw a heavenly courtroom, where the Ancient of Days passed judgment on the beasts and in favor of one like a Son of Man, who ascended to receive the dominion of all the beasts (7:9–14). The Son of Man is the new Adam, the beast tamer. He will be a new Nebuchadnezzar, a king of kings into whose hands the Lord gives even the wild beasts.

In Daniel's vision, the first beast is Nebuchadnezzar himself, the emperor turned into a beast then restored. The other beasts represent the same three kingdoms that Nebuchadnezzar saw in his dream (Daniel 2): Persia, Greece, Rome.[41] What does a bestial empire do? On the one hand, the composite beasts resemble the cherubim of the temple.[42] Cherubim have four faces—ox, lion, eagle, man—and wings, like the sphinxes and griffins of ancient and medieval iconography (cf. Ezekiel 1–3). Like the cherubic guardians of God's house, the empires are powerful beasts tamed by God to guard His people. At their best, Nebuchadnezzar and the kings of Persia were as ferocious as lions and leopards toward the *enemies* of the Israelites.

Yet, Daniel 7 does not simply repeat Nebuchadnezzar's dream, but shows the advance, or degeneration, of imperial rule. The empires of the οικουμηνη were called to form a protective sanctuary and to be guardian cherubs for the people of God, but by the time we get to Daniel 7, at the moment when the first empire is about to fall (cf. 7:1, the first year of Belshazzar), Daniel foresaw that these empires had the potential to produce something else entirely. From among the ten horns of the fourth beast emerges a little horn rising that uproots three of the other horns and begins speaking boastfully (7:8). That horn boasts great things and attacks the saints (7:21). In later visions as well, Daniel foresaw a future of suffering at the hands of various imperial and semi-imperial powers.

The hosts of heaven—Israel as the Abrahamic stars (cf. Genesis 17)—will be cast from the sky, and sacrifice will cease for a time (8:9–11). After Alexander, the "Beautiful Land" of Israel would become a pawn in conflicts between the Syrian Seleucids and the Egyptian Ptolemies (Daniel 11). The king of the North would seduce "to godlessness those who act wickedly toward the covenant" (11:32). Some would resist the compromise, but they too would fall (11:34–35). Bestial empires would one day turn on the masters they are called to guard.

Since Cain, political structures had been erected on sacrificial blood. Blood was the mortar that held the wall of Babel in place. The Bible condemns violence, but bloodthirsty injustice is not, in itself, enough to make an empire a beast. Empires turn bestial when they begin to eat the people of God and drink their blood. Empires become predatory when they adopt a regular diet of *sacred* flesh. Sacrificial banquets on the flesh of saints always turn out badly for the banqueters. Through their witness, Daniel and his friends opened up a space of free worship in neo-Babel, and when the saints witness to the point of shedding blood, they are beginning to reduce the foundations of empire to rubble. Empires that bless the Abrahamic people, who acknowledge God's Abrahamic *imperium*, are blessed. Those who eat the Abrahamic people gulp down curses. In this ironic fashion, bestial empires play a central role in the redemption of Israel. Instead of providing material and protection for the Jews who rebuild the temple and the city, bestial empires slaughter the saints. But the blood of saints is the wine-wrath of Yahweh, and it can only intoxicate empires until they reel, stagger, and fall.

Conclusion

The struggle of the Old Testament is not empire versus non-empire, but between rival imperialisms,[43] rival visions for the political salvation of a human race divided linguistically, culturally, and religiously in the wake of the rebellion at Babel. This is why empire is always a seduction for Abraham's children. For Israel, looking at Babel is like looking in the mirror. Israel is a parody of Babelic empire, and empires counterfeits of Israel.

CHAPTER 3

The Good News of Empire

First-century Rome was the last of the four beasts of Daniel's visions, the fourth empire of the Israel-in-Empire οικουμηνη.[1] In continuity with Babel, it was a religious-political unit, a tower and a city.[2] *Roma* was a goddess, and emperors were increasingly given divine honors. Yet like the Persians before them, the Romans permitted conquered peoples to retain their own systems of patronage and power, their own religious traditions, their own cultural customs. The Romans were adept at using regional and local elites for their own purposes. Herod styled himself "king of the Jews," but everyone knew he was a Roman lackey, and that created suspicion about the legitimacy of his pious projects like the temple. The Sadducees who made up the temple elites were cozy with Rome, in sensibility sometimes more "Hellenic" than "Hebraic." Other Jews frequently agitated against the Roman occupation, sometimes in the quiet of Jerusalem's back alleys but sometimes in open acts of civil disobedience that could turn violent.[3] Zealous Jews who fought Roman oppression with violence betrayed an unwitting brotherhood with their Roman enemies; for both, the most important form of power was naked force. Zealous Jews hated collaborating Jews, and the collaborators feared the Zealots. First-century Judea was divided not simply between Jew and Roman, but between collaborating Jew and resistant Jew. Few Jews maintained the Jeremian stance within and over against the οικουμηνη; resistance to idolatry and compromise subtly combined with compliant pursuit of the good of the city of exile.

God's *Imperium* at Hand

Into this volatile political situation came Jesus, herald of the "kingdom" or "empire" (βασιλεια) of God.[4] It was not a new message. From the beginning, Abraham's seed had constituted God's *imperium*, Yahweh's challenge and alternative to Babel. Jesus simply announced its long-awaited fulfillment, and this entailed opposition to some of the foundational claims of Rome. God's fifth monarchy, not Rome's fourth, was the mountain that would fill the earth, the *imperium sine fine*. Jesus' entire life challenged Roman pretensions. Jesus was proclaimed "king of the Jews" at his birth, a title that Herod rightly saw as a challenge to his own kingship (Matthew 2). Jesus proclaimed Jubilee and the casting-down of elites (Luke 4), taught His disciples to renounce the honor-shame instincts of dominant Greco-Roman-Jewish culture (Matthew 5), denounced the Jewish leadership who had cozied up to the Romans (Matthew 23–24), and gave cleverly evasive answers to questions about paying tribute taxes to Caesar. He became a folk hero for besting both the collaborating and the resisting Jewish leaders in every verbal *agon*.[5]

Jesus, a victim of a conspiracy among threatened Jewish leaders, died on a Roman cross.[6] Babel put Jesus to death: City and tower, Jew and Gentile, Shem and Japheth, the whole οικουμηνη, joined forces to kill the true Emperor.[7] To the Jewish temple elites, Jesus threatened the delicate balance with Rome. As He gained a following, it became more and more likely that the Romans would come to take away "our place and our nation" (John 11:48). *It was expedient that one man die for the people.* Jesus threatened resistant Jews because He favored Judea's untouchables and flouted the rules of purity. His movement was a contagion that could infect all of Judaism and prevent Yahweh's advent to redeem Israel. He had to be expelled. *It was expedient that one man die for the people.* For the Roman procurator, Jesus was another Jewish nuisance, innocent perhaps but not worth protecting at the cost of a riot. It was defensible to execute Him, since He called Himself a king, talked about an empire other than Rome, set Himself as rival to Caesar. *It was expedient that one man die for the people. . . .* or, it was convenient to offer a scapegoat to protect one man's dead-end post in the fetid backwaters of the empire. Pilate's utilitarian calculus unmasked the brutality just underneath the shiny surface of Roman justice. Roman *iustitia* cracked forever at the cross of Jesus. And Jesus' unmasking of Roman power advanced a crucial step in the resurrection, the Father's own verdict regarding Jesus, His "justification" or "vindication" (Rom 4:25; 1 Tim 3:16). The resurrection made public what was hidden in the cross, that Jesus is the Righteous One. If that is true, then the alliance of Jews and Romans to execute Jesus was unjust. Before the cross, Jew and Gentile, partners in building Babel, stand exposed.

Yet Jesus was a prophet in the mold of Jeremiah and Daniel. His stance toward Rome was the stance of the faithful exiles in Babylon. He had cordial conversations with Roman soldiers unimaginable to many Jews, and complimented one Roman centurion on his faith (Matt 8:10–13). He associated with hybrid imperial patsies like tax collectors. He instructed His disciples to cheerfully over-accept[8] the abuse of Roman soldiers who requisitioned them to carry luggage or demanded their cloaks. Though He shared some of the tactics of the powerless,[9] He went beyond the foot-dragging and petty subversions of peasant resistance. He taught disciples the difficult way of love toward enemies, and for Jesus love was not another name for ironically veiled cooperation. Love meant doing good to persecutors and haters. This was revolution, but it was, as N. T. Wright has well put it, a "revolutionary way of being revolutionary."

Even His death on an imperial cross was not merely an exposure of Roman brutality. Jews needed not a man from heaven to tell them about Roman cruelty. Pontius Pilate made his way into the early creeds because he was an instrument for the reconciliation of the world to God (2 Cor 5:19), and the reconciliation of the world with itself. Pilate unwillingly used Roman power to break the wall between Jew and Gentile, which tipped the dominos and broke down the walls between slave and free, Roman and subject people, Greek and barbarian. Because of Pilate's, and Rome's, role in the cross of Jesus, God "brings the pagan *oikoumene* into an integral relationship with the 'fullness of time,'" and thus "the Roman Empire is no longer just an instrument of God's purposes, but is now itself subject to the Gospel."[10] Rome was not yet saved, but for much of the first century, Rome served as an agent for the spread of the gospel, a station on the gospel's progress toward the "ends of the earth," the Gentile sea that it has always been God's purpose to pacify and unify.

Imperial ambitions and concepts were "reinscribed"—or, better, always already inscribed—at the heart of Jesus' teaching. Though He refused the kingdoms offered to Him by the devil, He proclaimed an empire of His own, acknowledged His imperial status, and after the resurrection claimed a dominion that surpassed Cyrus's (Matt 28:18–20; cf. 2 Chron 36:22–23).[11] He was the greater Cyrus, a new Nebuchadnezzar into whose hand all the peoples of the world have been given. No matter how fine the critical scalpel, this is a layer that cannot be cut away from the historical Jesus. Nothing is more characteristic of Jesus, whether in the canonical gospels or the fantasy-text of Q, than Jesus' self-identification as "Son of Man." The phrase has multiple sources in the Old Testament Scriptures, from the new Adam of Psalm 8 to the prophet Ezekiel, who is identified as "son of man" dozens of times in his prophecy. Daniel 7 is a key passage in the background, a classic passage of counter-imperial imperialism. After the bestial empires are tamed, the dominion, power, glory, and riches of those empires are handed over to the Son of Man and the saints (Dan 7:13–14, 23–28). One of the few Old Testament passages that speak of the kingdom of God, Daniel 7 identifies the kingdom of the "Highest One" with the dominion of the saints (v. 27). Daniel 7 pervaded Jesus' self-consciousness and preaching. Every time Jesus spoke of Himself as "Son of Man," He claimed to be the heir of imperial authority, the Emperor who fulfills God's original anti-Babel imperial promise to Abraham. When Jesus announced "the kingdom of God is *near*," He meant the kingdom of Daniel 7 (with, of course, all its rich Zion context). By adopting the role of the Son of Man, Jesus fulfilled the hopes of Zion's prophets, because through Him Zion's light would spread out to the borders of the Gentile sea.

This is the gospel of Jesus, the good news of empire: The time has come for God to defeat the principalities and powers, take His throne, and deliver the dominion of the nations to the Son of Man—*and His saints*. In the fullness of time, the God of Israel brings His imperial project to completion in the life, death, and exaltation of Jesus. The good news is that the Davidic Emperor has come and taken the throne, and is now King of kings and Lord of lords. If Jesus is the heavenly King of kings, it seems reasonable to expect some actual kings will assume the genitive position in submission to him. Andrew Perriman puts it with disarming modesty: "I wonder whether it is too fanciful to suggest that this apocalyptically conceived hope [of Daniel 7] . . . found fulfillment in the victory of Christ over the gods, represented historically—and therefore *ambiguously*—by Constantine's adoption of Christianity as the religion of the empire."[12] Calling Constantine the "fulfillment" of Daniel 7 may overstate the case, but no one reading Daniel 7 would be surprised by the Roman confession of Jesus as King.

Pentecost inverted Babel: Not in a tower reaching heaven but in an upper room, the apostles and their associates received the heavenly Spirit, and in Acts this is immediately followed by a "table of nations" (cf. Genesis 10) and a de-confusion of tongues. At Pentecost, God advanced His post-Babelic purpose of reuniting nations. The pneumatic church became God's renewed *imperium*. The Spirit-filled church became the new Zion, the mountain from which Israel's God rules and from which He reaches out to the Romans and barbarians. It is anti-Babel at nearly every point: Many tongues, not one; scattering, not gathering; built on the blood of a willing victim; Jew and Gentile united in God's work, not in opposition to Him. Yet the ecclesial *imperium* is at certain points a mirror image of Babel: All tribes, tongues, nations, and peoples confess with one *lip* that there is one Lord, Jesus. Jesus sends His Spirit to enliven the church as a multilingual, multiethnic, multinational empire.

Paul's parodic reuse of imperial propaganda was also pervasive and integral to his message.[13] For Paul, Jesus is ο κυριος, a common title for Caesar; Jesus is "Son of God," another imperial epithet. Jesus, not Rome, establishes justice (δικαιωσυνη) and peace (ειρηνη), which are realized through the goods news (ευαγγελιον) of His imperial victory (σωτηρια). Jesus, not the Emperor, qualifies as the Blessed and Only Sovereign, King of kings and Lord of lords, whose liberating παρουσια believers await in hope (1 Tim 6:15).[14] When Paul preached the gospel of the Lord Jesus and called everyone to acknowledge that Lordship, he was unsurprisingly suspected of trying to undermine the Roman system. He preached another βασιλευς, one Jesus, and began to turn the οικουμηνη upside down.

The *imperium* Paul preached fulfilled Yahweh's promise to David, a promise held in trust by Gentile emperors during the post-exilic period. Romans begins with a brief summary of his gospel, which concerns a Davidic scion declared Son of God by the resurrection (Rom 1:2–4). Paul preached this gospel to bring about the "obedience of faith among the nations" (1:5). According to Paul's gospel, Jesus is the Son of God of Psalm 2, "begotten" in the resurrection (cf. Acts 13:33) and given authority over the raging nations: "The promise . . . entailed in the metaphor of *begetting* is that Israel's king will have victory over the nations that oppose him. [Psalm 2] concludes with a warning to the kings of the earth not to conspire against the God of Israel but to fear him, or they risk being destroyed by his wrath. . . . the thought is not that the Gentiles are being included in the people of God but that the one who has been appointed Son of God in power will eventually conquer and rule over the nations." The apostle did not expect an invisible heavenly reign, but hoped for "future political-religious outcomes."[15]

Thus Paul's theology and preaching had a sharp "apocalyptic" element. Wrath is poured out already against the οικουμηνη, and neither Gentiles nor disobedient Jews will escape the coming day of wrath (Rom 1:18–32; 2:1–16). Paul's gospel would be vindicated when God demonstrated through some historical catastrophe that He is as superior to the emperor and gods of Rome as He is to Pharaoh and the gods of Egypt (Exod 12:12). Directly or indirectly, Paul learned from Jesus that such a catastrophe was just over the horizon.[16] Jesus predicted that the world would collapse within "this generation" (Matt 24:34; Mark 13:30; Luke 21:32). Jesus' prophecy included a warning about the unraveling of the heavens (Matt 24:29), an allusion to Isaiah's prophecy about the collapse of the political universe of neo-Babylon (Isaiah 13). Rome would fall from the circle of heaven as surely as the king of Babylon did (Isaiah 14). Neither Jesus nor Paul was wrong. The Romans destroyed Jerusalem and its temple in AD 70, and the Julio-Claudian line of Roman emperors ended at the same time. That conflagration was the end of the world of the οικουμηνη. Though Rome retained political power for centuries, Rome ceased to play its special divine role as a refuge for the people of God. By the end of the first generation, the old Israel-in-Empire world was gone for good.[17] A counter-imperial message allied with an apocalyptic expectation that the οικουμηνη would fall and be replaced by Jesus' Abrahamic empire: That is the core not only of Paul's political theology but very near the core of his gospel.

Nor is this merely a proclamation, an idea. Israel was the first political form of God's empire, nurtured in Palestine until He scattered the seed of Israel among the empires. Planted in Babylon, Persia, then Greco-Rome, Israel had already begun to flourish as an international shadow-empire, and the church, constituted initially as a network of synagogues, inherited and expanded that empire. As Paul proclaimed Jesus as the true κυριος to Jew and then Greek, as he witnessed to the omnipotent weakness of Jesus by his suffering in Spirit, he established outposts of Jesus' empire, concrete communities of broken and redeemed people, throughout the realm claimed by Caesar. The church surpassed Rome's best aspirations with its international scope, multicultural peace, impartiality toward Jew and Greek, slave and free, male and female. In its Mediterranean-wide network of charity, the church constituted a cooperative "welfare state" of unprecedented scope.

Cain built his city on the blood of Abel, and Babel was "covered" with the blood of innocents. Even Israel had its sacrificial beginning, and her conquest of Canaan was a sacrifice that purged the land of idols and altars. Yahweh remained in Israel on the condition that His palace and throne room—the temple and Most Holy Place—were annually cleansed with blood. Assyria, Babylon, Persia, Alexandrian Greece, and Rome all had their sacrificial foundings, their animal sacrifices, and their sacrificial wars protected the borders of the empire and refreshed the imperial mission. The fulfilled Israel of the church, by contrast, was founded by the victim not the victimizer. It was a city founded by crucified and risen Abel rather than Cain. Its ritual center was not a repetitive round of bloody sacrifices, but the memorialization of the sacrifice-ending sacrifice of Jesus, celebrated with wine rather than blood. With this founding and this ritual, ecclesial imperialism was sure to be a peculiar conquest. The establishment of the ecclesial *imperium* did not immediately end war. It did not even end war for Christians. But it brought a decisive end to holy war, the sacrificial prosecution of war, the legitimation of imperial regeneration through violence. The church's sacrificial practice imitated that of Jesus, as willing martyr-victims mixed their blood with His. Renewal came through violence suffered, not violence enacted. Force continued to be used, and could be used justly; but force was de-sacralized because de-sacrificized.

Paul's gospel challenged Rome at a fundamental level, yet Paul adopted the same Jeremian stance toward Rome that Jesus did.[18] Romans 13 contains Paul's "defense of Roman government," and Romans 12–16 is characterized by one scholar as Paul's program for "upholding the Roman Empire and making it last." Paul's political thought was consistent with Hellenistic political thinking of his time in his exhortation to obey the powers, and the theology basis for this exhortation—the fact that God establishes the powers that be—is the "very framework for his political vision." The apostle "understood the advantages of Christianity and used them to strengthen the Roman political system, which he admired and endorsed."[19] Bruno Blumenfeld, whom I have quoted here, overstates the case, but there is no getting round Romans 13 and similar Jeremian exhortations to seek the peace of Rome's imperial city.

Paul did not "come out" from empire, nor did he call the churches he established to do so. Paul used his rights as a citizen to escape punishment that would have inhibited his ministry as an apostle, but his appeal to Caesar was not merely self-protective, nor a mere tactic to protect his preaching. He appealed to Caesar "to oblige the authorities to do their duty and maintain justice."[20] This is a symptom of the change that had occurred in empires between the time of Egypt and Rome. Moses did not "appeal to any tradition or consciousness of justice on the Egyptians' part." He simply demanded Israel's freedom and warned of the consequences if Pharaoh refused. When Nebuchadnezzar was restored to human sense, by contrast, Daniel urged him to take the opportunity to change his policies and repent of his oppression: "break away from your sins by doing righteousness and from your iniquities by showing mercy to the poor" (Dan 4:27). Like Daniel, Paul had "confidence in the ability of the Roman authorities to maintain justice and order and to ensure the freedom necessary for evangelization." In his appeal to Caesar, Paul "witnesses to the fact that Jesus is now Lord over the pagan world" and that the Roman pagans are liberated from darkness and can do justice.[21]

The Jeremian complexity of Paul's stance toward Rome is evident in his *being* as much as his words or his actions. Paul was a Jew and a Pharisee who wrote and preached in Greek and who was self-consciously a citizen of the Roman empire. Such an apostle was hardly an ideal candidate to be a straightforward rebel. He was not merely a subversive. What Paul *was* is what he preaches: He was a living enactment of the reunion of the nations announced by the gospel.

Imperial Protectors (Acts)[22]

Acts makes it evident that the apostolic gospel was viewed as a threat to the Roman way of life. The Philippians were not amused by the apostles,

Part I: Empires in Scripture

who urged new customs and a novel ethos (εθη) contrary to the accepted way of life of the Romanized city (Acts 16:21). In Thessaloniki, Paul and his companions were accused of acting contrary to the "decrees [δογματα] of Caesar" by preaching an alternative king (βασιλεα ετερον), Jesus (Acts 17:7). No wonder the Thessalonians denounced the apostles as men who turned the world upside down (οι την οικουμενην αναστατωσαντες, 17:6). The disruptions they caused were an inevitable consequence of their gospel. They announced that God made Jesus κυριος and Christ (2:36), hardly a proclamation to endear them to Rome or to Rome's willing subjects.

During the church's first generation, Rome still functioned as a protector, sponsor, and patron of the people of God. If Rome was a beast, it was still a cherubic beast. Instead of sponsoring the Jewish community and its temple project, as Cyrus the anointed did, the Romans became providential protectors of the Christian community. The early Christians were not well placed in the empire like Daniel, Nehemiah, Esther, or even Jeremiah (whose preaching Nebuchadnezzar endorsed, Jer 39:11). But early Christians relied on Roman power to advance the gospel, gathered the citizens of God's *imperium*, and began building God's city and tower. Paul asserted his citizenship rights to gain the upper hand in tense situations or to deflect persecution (Acts 16:35–40; 21:37–40; 22:22–29). He used Roman transport to get to Rome. Though he went to Rome as a prisoner, Paul saw it as an opportunity for carrying his ministry to the center of the empire. Rome itself provided him the forum to declare the Lordship of Jesus to Caesar, the pretended lord of the earth. Rome gave him the chance to challenge Rome. Acts climaxes not with Paul's martyrdom, but with Paul as the *de facto* pilot of a Roman ship heading toward the capital (Acts 27–28). One is more than a little tempted to find in that an allegory of future apostolic direction of the empire.

During the first generation, persecution arose mainly from fellow Jews. Peter and John were dragged before the Sanhedrin more than once (4:1–22; 5:17–42). Paul's former Jewish allies plotted to kill him soon after his conversion (9:23–30). Jealous Jews opposed Paul in Pisidian Antioch and incited prominent citizens to drive the apostles from the city (13:42–52). "Jews" from Antioch and Iconium chased Paul to Lystra, turned the people against Paul, and stoned him nearly to death. Like the Crucified Lord he served, Paul refused to stay dead, arose, and moved on (Acts 14:19-20). In Corinth, Jews brought Paul before the proconsul (18:12). When some Jews saw Paul in the temple, they seized him (21:20-21). Jews formed a conspiracy to kill Paul, taking a vow to fast until they eliminated him (23:12-30). Paul summarized what Luke depicts when he reminded the Ephesian elders of his tears and trials that came "through the plots of the Jews" (20:19).

Roman officials meanwhile protected Paul and the apostles from their attackers. At Philippi, the Romans threw Paul and Silas into prison, but when the Lord freed them in the night (a symbolic "Passover" and resurrection), the magistrates let them go (Acts 16:35-40). When the Jews arraigned Paul before Gallio, proconsul of Achaia, the Roman official dismissed the Jewish complaint: "If it were a matter of wrong or of vicious crime, O Jews, it would be reasonable for me to put up with you; but if there are questions about words and names and your own law, look after it yourselves" (18:14-15). Gallio drove the Jews away, while his guards "took hold of Sosthenes, the leader of the synagogue, and began beating him in front of the judgment seat. But Gallio was not concerned about any of these things" (18:17). In Ephesus, Paul aroused the ire of pagans who hastily summoned the city εκκλησια to hear charges of blasphemy against Artemis of the Ephesians. The town clerk was able to calm the assembly, enabling Paul to depart for Macedonia (19:23-41). In Jerusalem, the Romans mistook Paul, chained him, and prepared to torture him until he revealed that he was a citizen. The commander let Paul go, and prepared for an orderly trial (22:22-29). When the commander received a tip about the assassination plot, he sent Paul to Felix with a message: "When I was informed that there would be a plot against this man, I sent him to you at once" (23:30).

The Roman officials before whom Paul testified gave him a fair hearing that the Jews typically denied. Like Herod with John the Baptist, Felix kept bringing Paul to court to peach about "righteousness, self-control, and the judgment to come" (24:24-25). In Acts, Romans have better moral discernment than the Jews. Festus recognized Paul's innocence and passed him up the Roman judicial ladder only because he had already appealed to Caesar (25:6-12). Agrippa and Bernice listened to Paul's testimony at length (25:13—26:29), concluding like Festus that Paul was innocent (26:30-32). Paul was under Roman house arrest in Rome, but it was loosely applied and gave him ample opportunity to continue preaching the gospel (28:16-31). To be sure, "Luke's portrait of Roman officials reveals them to be indifferent to violence in the streets (Achaian proconsul Gallio, 18:12–17), willing to torture to gain evidence (an anonymous chiliarch, 21:24), seeking to be bribed (Judean procurator Felix, 24:22–27), and beholden to the patronage system (Judean procurator Porcius Festus, 25:1–9). These portrayals are hardly designed to lead readers to be impressed with the representatives of Roman justice."[23] All true, and yet Luke shows that the Roman officials, intentionally or not, purely or not, continued to play the role that God assigned to empire in the days of Nebuchadnezzar.

Some Roman officials converted. At the beginning of Paul's first missionary journey, Sergius Paulus, a proconsul, converted (Acts 13:4–12) as Cornelius, centurion of the Italian cohort (Acts 10:1), had done before. Jesus' *imperium* has Roman soldiers and officials in its ranks, Romans who convert without being called to "come out" of empire. They left behind imperial loyalties and certain imperial practices. Perhaps like Daniel they eventually faced crucial choices that forced them to serve God and not Caesar. Paul would certainly have expected them to dare to be Daniels. Yet for the time being they remained part of Caesar's empire even as they became citizens of Jesus' empire. The conversions of Sergius Paulus and Cornelius were portents of the future: If they can believe, why *not* the emperor? Why can the whole Roman empire not enter into the shade of the *imperium* of Jesus? Why can Rome not come to Zion to be instructed in God's law and to learn to beat swords into ploughshares? Is that not what the prophets would lead the early Christians to *expect*?

BESTIAL ROME AND HARLOT BABYLON (REVELATION 13–14)

The Roman empire eventually turned from protector to persecutor, from a cherubic to a predatory beast. Jesus warned the first generation of Christians to expect this shift. The apostles knew from Jesus' own testimony that the Israel-in-Empire system was not going to last beyond the apostolic generation. He prophesied that the temple would be so demolished, that there would not be "one stone left on another which will not be torn down" (Luke 21:6). He also described the collapse of the political universe of the οἰκουμηνη and the fall of Jerusalem to the Gentiles, using typical "apocalyptic" language about falling stars, an eclipsed moon, a darkened sun (Luke 21:25–26). The coming of the

Son of Man and of God's empire (Luke 21:27, 31) would mean the end of the world, the οικουμηνη that had organized the ancient Near East and Mediterranean world for more than half a millennium. Before this catastrophe took place, Jesus predicted, "they will deliver you to tribulation and will kill you, and you will be hated by all nations on account of My name" (Matt 24:9). This would be the "great tribulation, such as has not occurred since the beginning of the world until now, nor ever shall" (Matt 24:21), the birthpangs of a coming new world order. It is no wonder that emperors beginning with Nero made the Christians scapegoats for disasters in Rome and the empire. Christians talked incessantly about the approaching doom of the empire, and to Roman ears this sounded subversive: If Christians talked like that, they must be plotting arson and worse.[24]

The latter half of the book of Revelation describes the process by which Roman emperors turned against the church and allied with the harlot Jerusalem who had already developed a taste for the blood of the saints.[25] It also tells the story of the collapse of this final stage of the Israel-in-Empire οικουμηνη. It elaborates the details of the "great tribulation."

After Satan the Dragon unsuccessfully attempts to kill the child born to Mother Israel, he is cast from heaven to earth, where he assaults the woman, again unsuccessfully (Rev 12:1–17). Enraged at his failure (12:17), the Dragon stands by the sea and summons up a monster, a composite of the beasts of Daniel 7: "like a leopard, and his feet were like those of a bear, and his mouth was like the mouth of a lion" (13:2). Coming from the sea, the beast is a Gentile and imperial beast. His power is the power of the Dragon (v. 2), and with that power He begins to "make war with the saints" and to overcome them (v. 7). Another beast rises from the earth, the "land" of Israel, and through signs and portents deceives the Jews into worshiping the beast from the sea (13:11–16). After his unsuccessful direct assaults on the Mother and Child, the Dragon attempts an indirect assault on the saints through the combined agency of Rome and Israel. The entire οικουμηνη unites against the saints as it had conspired together against Jesus.

Killing saints proves as counterproductive as crucifying the Lord of glory. John sees "one like the Son of man" (14:14) riding a cloud and harvesting the grain and grapes from the earth. Grain and grapes are the raw materials of Eucharist, and in this vision the Son of Man harvests the eucharistic people. Once gathered, the grapes are pressed until blood flows from the winepress of God (v. 19). This vision of harvest repeats the vision of Revelation 13. From the ground, it looks as if the Dragon-inspired beasts overcome saints, as Romans and Jews join forces to slaughter Christians, burn them as human lanterns, flay them, roast them like human barbeque. From John's perspective in heaven, the same events look like harvest, the Son of Man's gathering of His people. From either perspective, the beasts spill the blood of saints, and the wine-blood of the harvested grapes is gathered in seven vials to be poured out on the city (Rev 16:1–21).

The harlot-city is a new character. From the beginning, Hamites and compromised Shemites collaborated in the Babel project. The οικουμηνη represented a positive alliance of Jew and Gentile in the building of God's house, but Revelation envisions the corruption and disruption of the alliance. The harlot-city of Revelation is not Rome, but Jerusalem, the city where the Lord was crucified (11:8), the city that drinks the blood of all prophets (18:24; cf. Matt 23:35, 37).[26] As in the Old Testament (cf. Ezekiel 16, 23; Hosea), Jerusalem has turned harlot, engaged in adultery, fornication, and bestiality (Exod 22:19; Lev 20:15–16). Like the priest's daughter that she is, she is punished with burning (17:16; cf. Lev 21:9).[27] Placed at the center of the οικουμηνη as a witness to the Creator, called to communicate God's wisdom to the Gentiles and to lead the nations toward worship of God, Jerusalem instead entices the nations into idolatrous πορνεια and teaches the Romans the delights of drinks mixed with the blood of the witnesses to Jesus. Jerusalem was supposed to be the locus of God's Abrahamic *imperium*, but in Revelation she has become so thoroughly Babelic that she is named "Babylon the great, the mother of harlots" (17:5). Jerusalem's apostasy is the beginning of the end of the οικουμηνη. Drunk with holy blood, Babylon the great city stumbles and falls, and the two beasts are dispatched into the lake of fire (Revelation 17–18; 19:19–21).

Revelation describes the fall of a world order that had once been a very different order. Nebuchadnezzar became a beast and recovered; Cyrus was always a cherubic imperial beast. Rome protected the church for a generation, but in time turned wholly bestial. Revelation does not depict eternal essence of empire. John sees the destruction of a specific empire (which serves as a type of future empires). He describes the latter history of the Israel-in-Empire οικουμηνη of late antiquity. *That* order kills the saints, and becomes so drunk on holy blood that it can no longer stand. This is the victory of the saints: They topple venerable and invincible superpowers because they witness to Jesus and do not love their lives even to death (Rev 12:11). This is the strategy of conquest for the empire of Jesus.

AFTER THE οἰκουμηνη

No book "reinscribes" empire more insistently than Revelation.[28] In no other is it clearer that empire is not *re*inscribed but inscribed in the gospel from the beginning.

Revelation is a series of four visions, each of which begins with the phrase "in the Spirit" (1:10; 4:3; 17:3; 21:9–10; εν πνευματι).[29] John moves from Patmos to heaven to the wilderness to the mountain. The first two visions focus on Jesus: He stands unveiled before John (Revelation 1), then He appears as the slain Lamb opening the seals (Revelation 5). The final two visions are feminine: the civic whore Jerusalem/Babel burned and devoured by the beast (Revelation 17–18), then the purified bridal city of gold (Revelation 21–22). John's visions move from the male Christ to the feminine Church, recapitulating the creation account that progresses from the formation of Adam from the dust to the building of Eve from Adam's bleeding side.

John first sees Jesus while in Spirit on the Lord's day. A voice like a trumpet calls him from behind (1:10). When he turns, he first sees lampstands (1:12), then the clothing of the "one like a son of man" (1:13), and finally the Person Himself in the midst of the lampstands (1:14–16). The inward movement resembles the progress of a high priest through the veils into the inner sanctuary to see the glory of the Lord. Jesus is the glory in glorified flesh. As seen by John, the glorified Jesus is a mosaic constructed from overlapping and interlocking biblical fragments. As a human figure among the lampstands (1:12), Jesus is both a priest and a new Adam among the golden trees of a glorified garden.[30] Like a priest, too, he wears a robe girded across the middle with a golden belt (1:13). Jesus is also a vertical human temple (vv. 14–16). His head is white with glory like the cloud of Yahweh's presence in the Most Holy Place; his right hand is in the location of the *menorah* and holds stars like the lamps of the lampstand; his feet are glowing bronze like the bronze altar of the temple court. Jesus is a cosmic figure with a face like the sun and with stars in his hand.

The Song of Songs and several visions of Daniel form the major part of the background of John's description. Twice in the Song of Songs, Solomon sings an ecstatic head-to-toe hymn of praise to the bride using a form that, because of its resemblance to Arabic love poetry, biblical scholars have come to call a *wasf* (Song 4:1–6; 7:1–9).[31] Between these, the bride describes the attractions of her man to the daughters of Jerusalem in a similar style (5:10–16). While she desperately searches the streets for her absent lover, her companions ask, "What kind of beloved is your beloved?" (5:9). In its shape, John's description of Jesus resembles the *wasf* of Song of Songs 5, and this formal parallel is sufficient of itself for us to begin to surmise that the first unveiling of Jesus is the unveiling of a Lover. That is as it should be, since the book is moving toward the unveiling of a Bride who joins with her Lover in an eternal marriage supper.[32] The Gospel of John is a love story. Jesus is identified early as the Bridegroom (John 2:1–11; 3:29), and after His resurrection He appears as the new Adam in a garden with Mary (John 20:1–18). Jesus is the Bridegroom who gives His life for His beloved. Revelation continues the love story, only here the focus is on the dowry Jesus bestows on the bride.[33]

Even before Jesus appears to John, the trajectory of the Apocalypse has been set by a quotation from Dan 7:13: "Behold, He is coming with the clouds" (Rev 1:7). John reinforces the link with Daniel 7 in the vision scene later in Revelation 1 when he describes Jesus as "one like a Son of Man" (1:13; ομοιον υιον ανθρωπου; the LXX of Dan 7:13 has ως υιος ανθρωπου). As John's vision penetrates to see Jesus Himself, Jesus resembles not the Son of Man but the Ancient of Days. According to Daniel, that figure wears a "vesture like white snow" and has a head of hair "like pure wool" (Dan 7:9; το τριχωμα της κεφαλης ωσει εριον λευκον καθαρον), and at the beginning of his *wasf* John sees a Jesus with "head and hair . . . white like white wool, like snow" (Rev 1:14; η δε κεφαλη αυτου και αι τριχες λευκαι ως εριον λευκον, ως χιων). Jesus is the Son of Man, but in glory He has "aged" into the Ancient of Days. In the light of Daniel 7, that means that Jesus is not only the *Recipient* but a *Giver* of kingdoms. Thus, the conflation of characters from Daniel 7 in Jesus anticipates the scene in Revelation 20. After the Dragon is sealed up like the beasts of Daniel, thrones are set up, "they" sit on them, and judgment is rendered in the saints' favor (v. 4). At the end of Revelation 20, God sits on His great white throne and opens His books to render judgment on the "small and great" that gather before Him (vv. 11–14). By the end of the book, the saints and martyr-witnesses of the Highest One receive dominion that once belonged to the Dragon and his bestial associates.

That Jesus has feet like burnished bronze not only links Him with the gold-and-ivory lover of the Song of Songs but also with the metal men of Israelite prophecy. In Daniel 2, Nebuchadnezzar dreams of a metal statue that Daniel later interprets as a preview of the succession of empires that will follow Babylon: After the Babylonian head of gold comes the Persian torso of silver, the Greek thighs of bronze, and the Roman legs of iron.[34] The bronze figure that Daniel himself sees in 10:5–6 resembles the glorified Jesus even more closely:[35] "I lifted my eyes and looked, and behold, there was a certain man dressed in linen, whose waist was girded with pure gold of Uphaz. His body also was like beryl, his face had the appearance of lightning, his eyes were like flaming torches, his arms and feet like the gleam of polished bronze, and the sound of his words like the sound of a tumult." Daniel, like John later, falls before the metal man in a deep sleep until the man touches him and instructs him to record his words (Dan 10:17–21). The parallels with Revelation 1 are evident. The One John sees before him is the embodiment of empire, the *imperium*-in-Himself that is Jesus. As Son of Man, Jesus receives the kingdoms of the earth; as Ancient of Days, He confers the kingdoms on His disciples; as the Metal Man, Jesus incorporates the empires of late antiquity as the heir of all their glory and dominion. All of the treasures of the nations have become components of the body of Jesus. As lover, Jesus gives Himself to His bride; being the *imperium-in-se*, He therefore also grants them the kingdom.[36] The Roman emperor issues his edicts from the capital to the provincial governors, and Jesus, as heavenly Emperor, issues edicts to the "angels"[37] who preside over the provincial capitals of His alternative imperial system, commending the faithful, correcting abuses, warning of His approaching Parousia. The messages to the churches are love letters, but letters from an Imperial Lover.

Jesus already rules the kings of the earth at the outset (1:5), but His holy ones do not yet share His rule. Through the events of the Apocalypse, the βασιλειαι of this world become the βασιλειαι of the Lord and of His Anointed One, the Son of Man (Revelation 11). Revelation envisions the delivery of the kingdoms of the world to the victors who overcome by faithful witness to death, the victors who follow Jesus-Victor to victory. As the empire of God is founded in the death of innocent Jesus rather than in the death of His enemies, so it is furthered when the blood of saints is mingled with the blood of Jesus.

The rhetoric of empire *is* embedded in the text, and Revelation does promise that the people of God will constitute "an empire." This "anti-language" is not a sign of the church's capitulation to the first-century Roman *Zeitgeist*. John views Jesus as the fulfillment of the hopes of Israel, including her political hopes, and the political hope of Israel from the time of Daniel was not merely that the imperial order would end, but that the power and glory and dominion of the imperial order would be given over to a Davidic emperor and to the saints of the Most High, the servants of the Son of Man. The hope of Israel was that the Lover would yet again come bounding over the mountains of spices like a gazelle or a young stag to raise His Bride to her throne. Early Christian martyrs died in the same hope: They looked to the time when headless martyrs and those who resisted Roman sword and fire would be not only vindicated but enthroned with Christ for a thousand years. This is the political message of Revelation: Jesus the Imperial Lover, the Son of Man glorified into the Ancient of Days, confers a kingdom upon His saints. He gives the nations with all their treasures to His Bride as a wedding gift.[38]

Conclusion

Revelation—the Bible!—ends with a vision of the fulfillment of Yahweh's imperial order. When the city-bride descends from heaven to replace the destroyed harlot-city, John sees that "nations shall walk by its light, and the kings of the earth shall bring their glory into it." Gates will be permanently opened, since "they will bring their glory and the glory of the nations into it" (Rev 21:24–27). The hopes of Israel's prophets, inspired by the promises to Abraham, are fulfilled in the heavenly bride that descends to earth. Jesus is acknowledged as King of kings, the Emperor of nations that enter through the gate of God into the empire of God (cf. Psalm 72; Isa 2:1–4; 49:14–26; 60:1–14).

The Mediterranean world began the first century AD organized by an Israel-in-Empire structure. Through the cross and resurrection of Jesus, and the witness and martyrdom of His saints, that system was brought to a crashing end in the destruction of Jerusalem by Roman armies and the collapse of the Julian line. Though the apostles shared the prophetic hope that Gentile nations and kings would acknowledge the God of Israel as God, they did not envision that another empire or series of empires would fulfill the role played by Nebuchadnezzar, Cyrus, Alexander, or the early Roman emperors. The statue of Daniel 2 is demolished; there are only *four* beasts in Daniel 7. The statue is replaced by the mountain that grows to encompass the earth, the imperial mountain that is the kingdom and empire of God. Augustine was right to "secularize" Roman imperial order.[39] After the first century, the Roman empire plays no essential, sacred role in the history of the church, nor does any other empire. Cyrus was an "anointed" one, but that Davidic title now belongs to Jesus alone. Kings and emperors like Constantine can act in ways analogous to Nebuchadnezzar and Cyrus, but it is analogy only. What replaced the ancient system was not a new church-in-empire system, but simply the church, the fulfilled Abrahamic empire. Beast and harlot are cleared away to make room for the Bride. Kings and empires are no longer chosen to shelter the church. Instead, the church as the fifth empire keeps its doors open day and night so that kings from across the sea will be able to enter and pay homage to the Son who reigns from Zion.

Conclusion to Part I

We can now draw together some threads from the preceding three chapters and summarize the biblical portrait of empires and imperialism.

- In response to the rebellious imperial project at Babel, Yahweh initiates His own imperial project. Through Abraham and Israel, He begins to form a family of tribes, tongues, nations, and peoples. He establishes Zion as the land in the midst of the sea of nations, and begins to bring Zion's light to the farthest islands. The full emergence of this empire is inherent in the gospel of the kingdom. It *is* the gospel of God's *imperium*.

- God's empire is founded on the self-sacrificial death of Jesus and of the firstfruits of His people. It is renewed by ritual commemoration of Jesus in Eucharist, which forms a community readied for martyrdom.

- God's empire is not a transhistorical aspiration, an ideal, or a sentiment of fellow feeling among nations. It takes concrete form in a catholic church, where rival rulers and emperors, rival nations and empires, become table fellows and, under the church's discipline, are to learn the Lord's ways of peace and justice. Under Jesus and filled with the pentecostal Spirit, the ecclesial empire is a historical form of international community. The church is the eschatological empire already founded.

- God's empire coexists with and interpenetrates other political structures of the world. Citizens of God's empire may serve the kings and rulers of this world, and may fight for kings and rulers of the world. Citizens of God's empire must be ready always to

Conclusion to Part I

be martyrs when the demands of Caesar conflict with discipleship to Jesus.

- Empires differ. One of the key distinguishing marks is how they treat the people of God. Those that bless Abraham's seed, acknowledging the Abrahamic empire, are blessed; those that curse, are cursed.

- For a time, God called a series of empires to be a refuge for Israel. Since the first century, no empire has filled that role. Constantine and Charlemagne are similar to David and Cyrus in some respects. Neither is a "Messiah."

- Babelic empires build a city and tower against God; Cyrian or cherubic empires endorse and support the building of God's temple. Babelic empires impose a uniform culture and religious confession; Cyrian empires are multicultural and multi-confessional, and in particular leave space for the saints to worship God. Babelic empires gather; cherubic empires scatter and leave subjects relatively free to be themselves. Babelic empires arrest history; Cyrian empires remain open to disruptions and rearrangements in history. Babelic empires sow confusion; cherubic empires bring order.

- Babelic empires are founded on the blood of innocents. Bestial empires are founded on the blood of the *saints*. Ironically, bestial empires get tipsy in the very act of drinking the blood of saints.

PART II

Americanism

CHAPTER 4

Heretic Nation

"American" is a new kind of human being. First there was Francis, then a new brand of humanity known as "Franciscan"; first Luther, then "Lutherans." America has no single founder, but it too has "forced itself upon man's plasticity" and remade humanity in its own image.[1] Today everyone is, or aspires to be, American. Even our worst enemies wear our sneakers and eat our burgers and envy our freedoms.

The American was a long time coming. Conceived by Luther, gestated by Calvin, he was born of the Puritan parents who begat America. It took three labors to bring him finally to birth—the English Civil War from which American Puritans escaped, the American Revolution, and the American Civil War.[2] From these emerged a new character type, distinguished by a boundlessly optimistic sense of possibility and inventiveness, an extraordinary willingness to try, fail, and try again that has been the astonishment and envy of the world. He is generous, always ready to help. He is sentimental; even American warriors have a soft side. The American is fiercely independent; don't tread on him, because he won't be pushed around. He is often willing to extend the same independence to others, to live and let live. The American has a dark side: He is utterly confident of the rightness of his every cause, infatuated with violence, insatiably hungry for novelty, not greedy for stuff so much as greedy for *new* stuff. He assumes that if the world were rightly ordered, it would look like a global America, and he is bewildered by people who resist this utopia. Like most people, the American's virtues and vices are sometimes hard to distinguish.

American Christianity, like everything American, is new, a fresh Christian experience and form. It is Christianity unhaunted by a Catholic past, Christianity detached from Christendom, the "first experiment in Protestant social formation."[3] The virtues formed by America are the hardy Weberian virtues of hard work, thrift, restraint, inner-worldly asceticism—aggressively moralistic virtues expressed in Prohibition and anti-smut campaigns—but not only those. Every renewal of American Protestantism has blossomed in remarkable efforts to serve the poor, the stranger, the orphan and widow.[4] Americans give more of their income to more charitable causes than any other people on earth, and we have a lot of surplus to give away. For nearly three centuries, most human beings of the American type have professed to believe in Jesus and the tenets of Christian faith. What he really believes is not Christianity but another creed, which the versatile David Gelernter has identified as "Americanism," the "fourth biblical world religion."[5]

"America" is a new type of political community, and being an American entails commitment from the heart to this particular form of political community, an assurance that the Declaration of Independence and the U.S. Constitution establish the best political order the world has ever seen, the last best hope of mankind. It is a polity devoted above all to liberty. America is the firstfruits of the polity of the end of time, but it is not the full harvest, and Americans and America will never feel content, or quite secure, until the inner American that dwells within every human being, and the splendid inner America that is the *telos* of every political order, struggles free of his chrysalis. America is the already of an American global order not yet formed, but Americans are here to help. The "Americanism" in which Americans, including American Christians, believe is a religiously charged faith in American liberty as the hope of mankind. Our national self-consciousness is a "Messianic consciousness."[6]

In this chapter I try to make theological sense of this extraordinary character and this extraordinary country and the novel religion that animates both. I have not abandoned the question of empire. If we are to assess American power, if we are to determine whether it is Babel or Beast or something else, we need to pay some attention to the inner dynamics of the American character and American polity.

THE METAPOLITICS OF CHRISTENDOM

Different as they are, Western Christendom and Byzantine civilization shared a fundamental political-theological framework. Without ever developing a "political theology" per se, the church renewed politics simply by pressing its own claims about reality. Christian convictions about Jesus, His death, the church, the Eucharist, and the future established a "metapolitical" framework within which Western political life took a new shape.

Sheldon Wolin has argued that by the early part of the Roman empire, political thought had become exhausted.[7] Aristotle's systematic treatment of politics was applicable within the bounded space of the Greek *polis*, but the Roman imperial system had stretched the categories of Aristotelian political thought to the breaking point. Hellenistic and Roman theorists attempted to give cosmological grounding to political order, and by doing so raised politics into the realm of metaphysics. It did not work: "The reconstruction of political thought . . . was a process that began in paradox and ended in irony." Christianity appeared in this exhausted intellectual world, and "it fell to Christianity to revivify political thought."[8] Christianity did not aim in any direct way to revive antique political thought and life. On the contrary, the early Christians were, by contemporary standards, almost apolitical, and many of the leaders of the early church boasted of the church's freedom from the polluting effects of involvement in politics. Yet, Christianity revived political thought and life because of practices and ideas that were inherent in Christian faith: "Christianity succeeded where the Hellenistic and late classical philosophies had failed, because it put forward a new and powerful ideal of community which called men to a life of meaningful participation. Although the nature of this community contrasted sharply with classical ideals, although its ultimate purpose lay beyond historical time and space, it contained, nevertheless, ideals of solidarity and membership that were to leave a lasting imprint, and not always for good, on the Western tradition of political thought."[9] The church revived political thought because she was a church, a quasi-political yet apolitical community, soon as international as the empire itself yet lacking an earthly homeland, an army, or a visible emperor. As the fulfilled Abrahamic empire, the church was an unprecedented social and political form, and it burst the bonds of all prior political categories.

Part II: Americanism

The sheer existence of the church and notions of church memberships revolutionized the "idea of political obligation." Classical political thought had insisted that human beings reached happiness, the good life, the *telos* of human existence, in political life, and that this was so strong that even perverse regimes or unjust laws could not raise doubts "about membership in political society per se." Stoics claimed "allegiance to a universal society of rational beings" but never imagined "a genuine alternative to the political order." Christians, however, "could entertain meaningful doubts about political obligation and membership," and they did not face "a hard choice between membership in a political society and membership in no society at all." The Christian could choose "because already he belonged to a society that surpassed any existing one in the things that mattered most." For the first time, "the politically uncommitted [previously restricted to the odd Cynic or Stoic] had been gathered into a determinate society of their own." For the first time, political disengagement "went hand in hand with the rediscovery of community, albeit one pitched to a transcendent key."[10] Christians were not faced with the Socratic choice between compromise or exile. It was not for nothing that Roman emperors and their subordinates came to regard Christians with suspicion. Peaceable as they were, they were a subversive force in ancient political life.

At the center of this political community was a new ritual, the quasi-sacrifice of the Eucharist. Through participation in the Eucharist, the members of the church were formed into a more-than-human community. It was a human society constituted by its common participation in the living God-man, Jesus Christ. Christian belief in "a mystical body cohering around a godhead" was unprecedented in Western political thought, and by this concept "Christianity helped father the idea of a community as a non-rational, non-utilitarian body bound by a metarational faith, infused by a mysterious spirit taken into the members; a spirit that not only linked each participant with the center of Christ, but radiated holy ties knitting each member to his fellows." By this concept, "The Christian community was not so much an association as a fusion of spirits, a pneumatic being."[11] Eucharist was seen as the sacramental embodiment of the fulfilled project of divine *imperium* that began with Abraham. The community gathered at the eucharistic meal "crossed all ethnic borders" and achieved a "unity that was not abstract, nor was it made by coercion or force," yet constituted a depth of "political allegiance" that had never before been achieved. In the Eucharist the church ritually enacted "a transcendent vision that not even the most expansive understanding of 'empire' could have competed with."[12]

When Constantine gave permanent legal recognition to the church, he was implicitly, more or less consciously, acknowledging that the church was a true and independent *imperium* in the midst of the Roman empire. Not the empire, but the church was the true city, an outpost of a heavenly *imperium*. Constantine simultaneously suppressed traditional Roman sacrifice, and (again, more or less consciously) placed the Christian eucharistic sacrifice at the center of Roman order.[13] Sacrifice is an inescapable feature of political order, and the relocation of sacrifice, the public recognition of the Eucharist as the one true sacrifice, is one of the foundations of Western Christendom and Byzantine order. Public acknowledgment of the eucharistic sacrifice went hand in hand with the early medieval notion that loyalty to the church, as well as to local communities and families, transcended loyalty to the state.[14] Where your sacrifices are, there will your heart be also. By the regular remembrance of Jesus' sacrifice, the church celebrated the end of sacrifice, the end of sacralized politics and sacralized war.

Even before Constantine, Christians had been laying a novel sacrificial groundwork for God's *imperium*. "Jesus is Lord," said the early Christians in opposition to Roman claims that Caesar was Lord, and their verbal witness was backed up with the enacted witness of martyrdom. The sacrificial deaths of the martyrs, intended by the Romans as a sacrificial prophylactic for and renewal of the *pax Romana*, instead exposed the naked power of Rome in all its pathetic weakness: "The martyr [like Jesus] denies the state power, while yielding to its violence. . . . This is not a kind of quietism in the face of the state, but a faith imbued with an idea of resistance from the very beginning." In this sense, "Resistance to the state is built into the fundamental tenets of Christianity."[15] Even after Rome reconciled to Christianity, "the threat of martyrdom is always a dangerous power that the religious can wield against the state. It is the means by which the religious claim an indefeasible power: if defeat means martyrdom, then the state's victory is always precarious."[16] In her regular eucharistic celebrations, the church refreshed its collective memory not only of Jesus' sacrificial death, but also of the sacrificial deaths of those who suffered as Jesus did. In refreshing her collective memory, the church also refreshed her collective determination to resist rulers or politics that claimed authority that belonged to her Lord. The faithful resistance of martyrs, resistance like Daniel's, opened fissures in the foundations of Rome. Rome had either to tolerate Christians and acknowledge the competitive *imperium* of the church or to kill peaceable believers and risk exposure as fearful bullies. Up through Diocletian, Rome's emperors more or less followed the latter course, and the blood of saints rose to haunt them. Constantine wisely chose the former.

The church's perception of her political form grew from typological or allegorical readings of the Scriptures, especially of the Old Testament. There was some diversity in approach to the political import of the Bible. Eusebius, for instance, tended to view the Christianized Roman Empire as the fulfillment of ancient prophecies and wrote his *Life of Constantine* to bring out analogies between Moses and the Roman emperor.[17] For a time, Augustine did something similar.[18] What emerged as the mainstream mode of reading linked Israel with the *church*, as promise and fulfillment, or as distinctive stages of the single history of the *imperium* of God, or both together. On this reading, the fulfillment of God's imperial project through Jesus forms an empire as odd in its constitution as exilic Israel, a polity-within-worldly-polities. Kings like Constantine might be typified by David and Solomon in a very attenuated sense, but strictly speaking, the antitype of David is Jesus and Jesus alone. Before emperors can be construed as David-like, they must become subjects of the *imperium Dei*.

At least for modern Orthodox theologians, eschatology has a prominent place in the metapolitics of Byzantium. According to Alexander Schmemann, there was in Byzantine thought no static or spatial division of church and state, but a temporal–eschatological dualism of church and world. The world with all its structures and institutions is good, but it becomes demonic when it is disconnected from its source and end in God. To treat the world as "secular," as an end in itself, is the very definition of original sin. But the world is not condemned to remain imprisoned within its own cramped eschatological horizon forever. The church is in the world as a *presence*, as the sacrament of the coming kingdom, and the gospel that the church proclaims aims at the redemption of the world, which is to say, its reorientation toward that kingdom.

This eschatological perspective was the foundation of Byzantine political theology: "as everything else in 'this world,' the state may be under the power of the 'prince of this world' . . . yet, by 'accepting' the Kingdom of God as its own ultimate value or 'eschaton,' it may fulfill a positive function." The state can be Christian just insofar as it recognizes "its limit"; the Christian state refuses to become an absolute value, an end, *the* end, and acquires genuine value in subordination "to the only absolute value, that of God's Kingdom."[19] A Christian state refuses the Babelic illusion that it can arrest history.

Though Byzantine *symphonia* involved the church's administrative and juridical "surrender" to the empire, the church made its peace with the empire when, and only insofar as, the empire began to care for the church and submitted to the Lord Christ and His Kingdom. Even after peace was made, the church continued to fulfill its vocation as a presence "to reveal, manifest, and communicate the Kingdom of God." Byzantium was not the kingdom of God on earth. Yet, over time, the church's submission to the empire turned inside out to become the empire's submission to Jesus. The world, also the Byzantine state, was "Christianized" since, with the conversion of Constantine, the empire acknowledged that the "ultimate goal of creation" was "anticipated in the mysteries of the church."[20] Despite their differences, Western theologians shared this eschatological perspective. Politics could be just, Augustine argued, only if it were imbued with the graces that come only from Christ and only if it were ordered to the city of God.[21] In acknowledging Jesus and His church, Constantine was subordinating his empire to God's imperial project, and placing his conduct of state under the judgment of the High King.

In Christendom and Byzantium, then, "political order" in the narrow sense was founded on central metapolitical convictions. At the heart of the project was the "state's" recognition of the church as an independent polity or order of its own, the civil order's (often grudging) acceptance of the quasi-civic order of the church in its midst, the acknowledgment of the Eucharist as the sacrificial center of a polity—a sacrificial center *not* controlled by the state—and civil government's embrace of the church's end, the kingdom of God, as its own end. Christendom in the West and Byzantium in the East took shape within the metapolitics of christological and ecclesial typology, a political ecclesiology, eucharistic practice that nourished the spirit of martyrdom, and eschatology.

Already in the medieval period, the metapolitical framework of Christian politics was beginning to shift and crack.[22] Following Henri de Lubac,[23] Wolin points to the shifting meanings of *corpus mysticum* as a marker of seismic changes. The term was a Christian invention, first used in the ninth century. Initially, it described the eucharistic body of the incarnate Son who offered Himself in Christian worship and so formed His corporate body around His table. After the controversy with Berengar in the ninth century, "mystical body" came to be seen as an inadequate description of the reality of Christ's presence in the Eucharist, and the eucharistic body came to be viewed as the *corpus verum*. By the High Middle Ages, *corpus mysticum* was transferred to the corporate body itself, and by the end of the Middle Ages, it was used to describe political communities other than the church. "By the middle of the thirteenth century [a secular writer] defined a people as 'men assembled into one mystical body,'" and John Forescue used "the phrases *corpus mysticum* and *corpus politicum* indiscriminately to designate a people or a state." For later nationalists, a nation was not merely united by territory or governing institutions but "a fellowship of free and equal men bound together in a brotherly concord of labor towards a single end . . . The country . . . is the sentiment of love, the sense of fellowship which binds together all the sons of a territory."[24] The sacredness of the *corpus mysticum* migrated[25] from the Eucharist to church to the state, which came to be viewed as a suprarational, *geistliche* community, an ethnic group with the soul of the church.

Not surprisingly, this migration affected the way Christians thought about and conducted war. Defending Israel's wars against Faustus the Manichean, Augustine had made room for the possibility of a war of extermination carried out in obedience to the command of God, but for Augustine the possibility was theoretical. Holy war could be just only if commanded directly by God, and that prospect was unlikely to say the least.[26] During the Middle Ages, war was gradually re-sacralized. By the tenth century the church was consecrating weapons, and by the following century, Christian knights were assured that they could in some circumstances fight under a sacred banner, blessed by the church. As the Pope's voice became increasingly identified with the voice of God, Augustine's theoretical possibility became realizable in practice: "Gregory VII revolutionized the Christian view of warfare and . . . he was the principal inventor of the holy war idea in medieval Christendom," and he "seems to have entertained the notion that those who died in battle on behalf of righteousness were automatically and deservedly freed from their sins." In the end, "By the pontificate of Urban II Western churchmen had in principle embraced the concept of holy war and viewed warfare as a positive value in the Christian life."[27] A sacredness that once attached to Jesus' self-sacrifice commemorated in the Eucharist became attached to the knightly sacrifice of enemies. Christian concepts and biblical terms were twisted to justify a pre-Christian conception of warfare.

State-building kings of the early modern period had learned well the lessons in centralization and power-formation that medieval Popes had taught them. They developed administrative structures to collect the taxes that paid for their wars, centralized judicial processes, and asserted their headship over the church.[28] By the beginning of the fourteenth century, "loyalty to the state was stronger than any other loyalty."[29] French readers of Scripture began to see France, not the church, as the fulfillment of Israel, as English readers had done before them.[30] Notions of national destiny began to form in France and, most relevantly for our purposes, among the post-Reformation English. National identities were forged in exclusion, by opposition to rival nations and churches. British nationality was in significant measure a product of an anti-Catholicism that was simultaneously anti-Spanish, fostered by a particular reading of the Bible and the wildly popular Foxe's *Book of Martyrs*.[31]

The Reformation had, after all, inadvertently assisted in the migration of the mystic community from church to nation that began in the late Middle Ages. The Reformation obviously divided the church, and on the heels of that ecclesiastical revolution came a political revolution. Prior to the Reformation and the wars that followed,[32] the church could reasonably present herself as the *imperium* to which the kings and princes of Christendom were vassals. After the Reformation, in the absence of a single church throughout Europe, the church's authority was diminished and diffused. The church was transformed from a Europe-wide or even worldwide body into a national entity, in many cases a department of state. The formula of the Peace of Augsburg (1555)—*cuius regio, eius religio*—became the new order of church and politics, as the hundreds of principalities and duchies that made up sixteenth-century Europe were slowly consolidated into the twenty-odd national states of the nineteenth century. Even where the powers of the state were limited by representative assemblies, a unitary and totalitarian "society" absorbed the varieties of independent subcommunities that had characterized the medieval *universitas* of *consociationes*.[33] The notion that the church was God's overarching *imperium* was no longer believable.

The Reformation produced martyrs aplenty, but they were mostly Christians put to death for heresy by other Christians. The church utterly lost its eucharistic center. No longer did the Eucharist function as a locus of union of all nations and peoples. It was no longer even the locus of union for all *Christians*. The sacredness of the Eucharist was increasingly co-opted by the state, which demanded absolute, sacrificial loyalty.[34] Kings were quick to seize on the relatively new ideology of holy war: If the state is a sacred community, and war endowed with a mystic aura, then kings might well think they have the right to demand that their soldiers sacrifice themselves and their enemies for the fatherland.

The church's role in Western political life had come full circle. When the church first appeared, it was a surd, a novelty that upset the balance and equilibrium of Roman political life. After the Reformation, the church became in the rising national states what the civic religions of the ancient *polis* or the Roman empire had been. The church had been domesticated, and the holiness of the *corpus mysticum* was slowly, often deliberately, transferred to the state. Modern politics is unimaginable without the metapolitical contributions of Christian ecclesiology, eucharistic practice, and eschatology, but modern political order is no longer organized by the metapolitics of Christendom.

Just as these twists on Christian political theology were gelling into political form, a boatload of white martyrs docked near the shore of Massachusetts to start afresh, inspired by a post-Christendom vision of Christian polity.

American Israel

"Americanism" was initially constructed from the misshapen fragments of the metapolitical outlook of Christendom. The Puritan Founders of New England were orthodox Christians in all their theological beliefs, but they laid the foundations for Americanism because of their tendency toward a nationalist, *an-ecclesial*[35] reading of Scripture, their enthusiasm for nationalistic eschatology, and their privatization and individualization of the Eucharist. As Americanism developed, these tendencies settled into habits, and the result was the fourth great biblical religion.

a. American Typology

"God's American Israel." If the phrase no longer comes readily to Americans, it was a fundamental paradigm to help early American settlers understand their role in God's history. The Puritans who settled Massachusetts Bay Colony believed that God had providentially guided them to the new land and that He had great intentions for them. The parallels with Israel's history were too numerous and too precise to be accidental. They had faced persecution and oppression of various sorts in Europe, now characterized as an old Egypt.[36] The Lord had led them across a dangerous and deadly sea to get to the Americas, as Israel passed through the Red Sea. America was an uninhabited and uncivilized wasteland, the desert of Israel's testing, where the Puritans would pursue their "errand into the wilderness."[37] Alternatively, the new world was new Canaan, not a land of cities and cultivated vineyards, but a raw natural world that lay before the colonists for their conquest and dominion. Of course, this placed the Indians in the unfortunate and unenviable position of latter-day Canaanites, their sins filled up until the coming of the English Joshua to cleanse the land. The American colonists were a chosen people who had relived the history of God's earlier chosen people.[38]

It is true that the earliest American Puritans continued to read Scripture in a traditionally typological fashion within a traditional orthodox eschatology. They were right to use biblical categories to understand the meaning of their settlement and to anticipate its future. Following the metapolitical eschatology of Christendom, they believed that their settlement existed to serve the kingdom of God and advance the purposes of the gospel, not to advance its own interests. The tremendous sacrifices they had made to emigrate were not for the sake of New England but in order to establish New England as a beacon of the gospel, and of the evangelical organization of community, to Europe and to the rest of the world. They often read the history of Israel as a type of the history of the church, just as Christians had done for centuries.

From the beginning, though, Puritan reading of Scripture tilted in a "nationalist" direction,[39] so that the colony, rather than the ecclesial *imperium*, became the fulfillment of biblical types.[40] In his inspiring programmatic plan for Massachusetts Bay, John Winthrop described the settlers as "a Company professing our selves fellow members of Christ" who had all "entered into Covenant with him for this worke."[41] At the

Part II: Americanism

time, the members of the Company would also have been members of the church, but the same equation of New England colonists with Christians persisted long after the identification was true or obvious.⁴²

In his *Wonder-Working Providence*, Edward Johnson applied the history of Israel's rebuilding of the temple to the founding of New England:

> as Israel met with many difficulties after their returne from Captivity, in building the Temple and City, so [did] these N. E. people. In a desolate and barren Wilderness, exceedingly weakened with continued labour, watching and hard diet, [they suffered] such distresses, as to appearance of man seemed to be both hopelesse and helplesse. . . . But Christ was resolved to fight for them; wherever with bold resolvedness these Soldiers of Christ set forth . . . to rebuild the most glorious Edifice of Mount Sion in a Wildernesse, know[ing] this is the place where the Lord will create a new Heaven, and a new Earth, in new Churches and a new Common-wealth.⁴³

There was typically a reserve, a recognition that, however closely they might be allied, the church and colony were not identical. Yet Puritan readers easily slipped back and forth between the two, with the effect that the church took a typological back seat to the colony.

New England's dissenters raised their protests in terms of an alternative typology. Roger Williams argued that Israel was a figure "of the Spiritual State," and insisted that America as such "lyes dead in sin," just like the European peoples that have been left behind. "Nature knows no difference between [men] . . . in blood, birth, bodies" or geography. To see the prophecies of Scripture fulfilled in a "new found land of Canaan" or in a "people, naturally considered" amounts to pulling "God and Christ and the Spirit out of heaven, and subject them unto naturall, sinful, inconstant men."⁴⁴ Mainstream Puritans disagreed both with the hermeneutics and the political theology that resulted. Despite appearances, for the Puritan colonists, America was not "just another plot of ground in a fallen world." Rather, "The New World, like Canaan of old, belonged wholly to God."⁴⁵ American missionaries have likewise long struggled to sort out the Christ-and-America problem, frequently stressing the independence of the church.⁴⁶

Yet, insofar as the ecclesial focus of traditional typology is set aside, the political result of the conflicting typologies was virtually identical.

Mainstream Puritan readers could so identify Israel with the Puritan community that the church disappeared as a political entity. Williams so spiritualized the antitype of Israel that the church became invisible and weightless. What is crucial for my purposes is to notice that this Puritan hermeneutics, and the political theology and eschatology that grew from it, were an-ecclesial. The Puritans were not anti-ecclesial in principle. There was certainly more than a little anti-clericalism in Puritanism, and in the outlook of the Revolutionary generation, but it was not nearly so strong as the anti-clericalism of the French Revolution. American political theology was an-ecclesial because it offered little space for an independent and public church to take hold.

Though it is often believed that this biblical paradigm had given way to an Enlightenment, secular outlook by the time of the Revolution, the notion that America is "God's New Israel" persisted into the Founding period, as did the typology that went with it.[47] In a sermon preached in East Haven, Connecticut, in 1777, Nicholas Street reviewed the recent history of British oppression in the light of Israel's history with Egypt: "We in this land are, as it were, led out of Egypt by the hand of Moses. And now we are in the wilderness, i.e. in a state of trouble and difficulty, Egyptians pursuing us, to overtake and reduce us. There is the Red Sea before us, I speak metaphorically, a sea of blood in your prospect before you, perhaps."[48] The typological understanding of American experience was not intended as flattery. With great blessing came great accountability, and Street's main aim was to warn his hearers not to become proud or complacent now that the colonies have broken free from Pharaoh.[49] Jeremiads were the natural flip side of chosen status.

Street was a preacher and got paid to talk like that. Political leaders did not have a professional obligation to talk Bible, but they resorted to the same imagery and typology as well. The day after his election to the presidency, George Washington wrote in a letter: "May the wonder-working Deity, who long since delivered the Hebrews from their Egyptian oppressors, planted them in the promised land, whose providential agency has lately been conspicuous in establishing these United States as an independent nation, still continue to water them with the dews of Heaven."[50] Just before the Continental Congress concluded its business on July 4, 1776, the group discussed the design of a seal for the newborn United States. John Adams, Franklin, and Jefferson formed the committee to propose a seal, and Franklin proposed as a motto "Rebellion to

Tyrants is Obedience to God," which would be reinforced by this image of "Moses [in the Dress of High Priest] standing on the Shore, and extending his Hand over the Sea, thereby causing the same to overwhelm Pharaoh who is sitting in an open Chariot, a Crown on his Head and Sword in his Hand. Rays from a Pillar of Fire in the Clouds reaching to Moses, to express that he acts by [the] Command of the Deity."[51]

Biblical paradigms for American history persisted into the nineteenth century. "What is Zion?" Brigham Young asked in one of his *Discourses*, and answered, "It is the land that the Lord gave to Jacob, who bequeathed it to his son Joseph, and his posterity, and they inhabit it, and that land is North and South America. That is Zion, as to land, as to territory, and location. The children of Zion have not yet much in their possession, but their territory is North and South America to begin with."[52] A more mainstream American religious leader, Henry Ward Beecher, resorted in an 1861 sermon to exodus typology when attempting to understand the impasse that had led to civil war. After reviewing the history of Israel's liberation from Egypt, he observed that "in the history which belongs peculiarly to us, over and over again the same thing has occurred." Luther struggled against popish tyranny, as did the Protestants of the Netherlands. So too "the Puritans were enveloped in darkness. Their enemies were more than their friends" and they struggled until, "wearied and discouraged . . . they fled away to plant colonies upon these shores." Two centuries later, and America again faced an exodus: "Right before us lies the Red Sea of war. It is red indeed. There is blood in it. We have come to the very edge of it, and the Word of God to us to-day is, 'Speak unto this people that they go forward!' It is not of our procuring. It is not of our wishing. It is not our hand that has struck the first stroke, nor drawn the first blood. . . . We have yielded everything but manhood, and principle, and truth, and honor, and we have heard the voice of God saying, 'Yield these never!'"[53] More famous than these are the observations of Herman Melville: "We Americans are the peculiar, chosen people—the Israel of our time; we bear the ark of the liberties of the world."[54] Even more well known is Abraham Lincoln's chastened version of this theme: "this almost chosen people." America as Israel-of-exodus is one of the continuing threads of American political theology from the beginning to the twentieth century.[55] America's sense of providential election, her sense of uniqueness, her exceptionalism, has biblical roots that trace back to the Puritans who originally settled New England.[56]

Americans are today biblically illiterate, but biblical cadences continue to echo in our political rhetoric, setting the terms of our national purpose and mission. It was no accident that President Bush memorialized the first anniversary of 9/11 with a Statue of Liberty speech full of intertextual links with the opening verses of John's Gospel. "Ours is the cause of human dignity," he said, identifying this cause as "freedom guided by conscience and guarded by peace." This American ideal is "the hope of all mankind," the hope that "drew millions to this harbor." Even after 9/11, he declared, "That hope still lights our way. And the light shines in the darkness. And the darkness will not overcome it." He ended with "May God bless America."[57] In John, the light that shines in the darkness is the Word who becomes flesh to display the glory of the Father, but in Bush's hands that image of light is transferred to the "American ideal" of "freedom," which is the hope of the world. If America is the light, all that is not-America is darkness. Bush, an evangelical believer, would acknowledge that it is Jesus who brings light, but that admission only makes the point more sharply: Bush, like many American Christians, has so instinctively and viscerally identified Jesus with the spread of American-style liberty that he can hardly distinguish them. Ignorant as we are of the Bible, we are all heirs of nationalist typology.[58]

Insofar as its civic religion twists Scripture in a nationalist direction and thereby marginalizes the public role of the ecclesial *imperium*, America is a heretic nation in the literal sense. G. K. Chesterton famously observed on a visit to the United States that ours is a nation "with the soul of a church." That is true mainly because Americanism leaves so little room for a church body.[59] It is also heretical in a related sociological sense. Etymologically, "heresy" means "choice," and for Peter Berger, "heresy" is the condition of the modern age. Unlike traditional societies, where settled pathways of religion, culture, class, even vocation are laid out from birth, modern society affords every individual a choice at every point.[60] America is a heretic nation because it is, and has always been, a pro-choice nation.[61]

Nationalisms are not all equal, and Americanism has mutated over time. For the orthodox Christian Puritans, being chosen was no guarantee of favor or worldly success, since chosen people are under more intense divine scrutiny than other peoples. As Americanism was

Part II: Americanism

filled with republican content, America became an agent not of God's kingdom but an instrument for the spread of American institutions and American culture, and there was a tendency to see America "basking in [God's] permanent favor." France became an object of overt veneration after the French Revolution, as did Germany under the Nazis. Throughout American history, orthodoxy has been strong enough to check the danger of deifying America itself—check, but not eliminate. But the intellectual structure is in place for Americanists to think those who worship America are offering service to God.[62]

b. American Eschatology

Puritans gave the American and Americanism its first birth by giving Americanism a nationalist typology that infused American rhetoric and poetics. Americanism's second birth came with the Revolution, which bequeathed a refined sense of national destiny and a freshly stated American Creed.

By the time of the Revolution, the residual ecclesial sensibility among the original Puritans had nearly vanished. A sense of national unity was strengthened by the Great Awakening and the French and Indian Wars,[63] and the possibility that the church might function as a counterweight to national sentiment or state power was drowned in waves of revivals, each of which further damaged the catholicity of American Christianity.[64] The ambiguities of Puritan typology eroded, as America and her heroes more firmly took the place normally reserved for Jesus and His church. Israel's constitution provides a model for American political life, America is the people of the exodus, and Washington the great conqueror who leads the people from the wilderness across the river into the promised land.[65]

Allegories imply anagogies: If Israel was a figure of America, it was also a figure of an eschatological American destiny. So sober an exegete and careful a theologian as Jonathan Edwards suggests that "it is not unlikely that this work of God's Spirit, so extraordinary and wonderful, is the dawning, or at least a prelude of that glorious work of God, so often foretold in Scripture, which, in the progress and issue of it, shall renew the world of mankind." From all signs, it appears that "the beginning of this great work of God must be near," and Edwards found reasons "that make it probable that this work will begin in America."[66] By the time of the French and Indian Wars and the Revolution, nationalist typology had given birth to fervent nationalist eschatology. America is the "last act" in the great drama of redemption.[67] The battle with the French was nothing less than the last battle, "the commencement of the grand decisive conflict between the lamb and the beast." Once the French were defeated, Americans would witness the arrival of "a new heaven and a new earth."[68] "Let your faith be strong in the divine promises," said Samuel Sherwood during the Revolution, because "although the daughter of Zion may be in a wilderness state, yet the Lord himself is her Light" and "Jehovah will dry up the rivers of her persecuting enemies" to bring the "Ransomed of the Lord" home. Timothy Dwight saw the Revolution as the final result of an exodus from England "on eagles' wings," proof "that this great continent is soon to be filled with the praise of the Millennium."[69] The fervor was not limited to preachers.[70] It was not even limited to orthodox believers. Thomas Paine of all people whipped up millennial frenzy in his 1776 tract *Common Sense*. He compared the American resistance to tyrannical monarchy to Israel's "national delusion" in requesting a king. By resisting George III, Americans were opening up the possibility of a new beginning for the human race: "We have it in our power to begin the world over again. A situation, similar to the present, hath not happened since the days of Noah until now. The birthday of a new world is at hand."[71] Jefferson was more restrained: America is the "best hope" of mankind.[72]

In the first third of the nineteenth century, Lyman Beecher observed that "it was the opinion of Edwards, that the millennium would commence in America," an idea Beecher first thought "chimerical." But "providential developments since, and all the existing signs of the times, lend corroboration to it."[73] For Harriet Beecher Stowe, the blessings bestowed on early New England foretold a "glorious future of the United State of America," which "must be commissioned to bear the light of liberty and religion through all the earth and to bring in the great millennial day" when wars cease and day dawns.[74]

By Beecher's and Stowe's time, the content of the American Israel's hope has shifted. Instead of widespread conversions, Beecher pointed to other signs that the United States was remaking humanity and the world through the spread of its political institutions: "the march of revolution and civil liberty . . . experimental knowledge of free institutions . . . such facilities of communication, obstructed by so few obstacles."[75] Instead of Puritan righteousness, the spread of Christian charity, or the coming of the kingdom of God, the American Israel was to be the bearer of the American values of liberty and republican institutions. America's vocation was to "prove the virtues of republicanism, to assert the rights of Man, and to make society better," said David Ramsey already in 1794.[76] By the time of the Revolution, the content of the Puritan vision had faded, but the rhetoric of American mission was still alive, and the energy that the Puritan vision provided had, if anything, increased. Puritanism thus lent the American system a religious impulse that elevated it beyond the run of normal nations and placed it in the center of world history. Even if the concept of "redemptive" history was not as lively in the eighteenth as in the seventeenth century, the instinct to believe that America had a redemptive role for the world persisted, rooted in the New England hermeneutics of Israel. America was chosen to be the bearer of freedom and also of Christianity, and distinguishing the two was no longer easy to do.[77] Americanist typology pulled the biblical props holding up the metapolitical canopy of Christendom. The result is that Americanist typology has no *meta*politics, since the creed it confesses is the truth and power of its own political institutions.

This mission has taken a number of different practical forms over the centuries. Sometimes, Americans have thought it best to encourage freedom and justice from a distance, or to be a shining example of the possibility of free political order. At other times, Americans have turned crusader. But no American leader has ever shrunk from the Puritan vision that America has a destiny of sometimes literally biblical proportions. America will "allure the world to freedom by the beauty of its illustration," George Bancroft said. Timothy Dwight before him had declared that the United States had been "by Heaven designed, th' example bright, to renovate mankind." On America, Washington said, depended "the preservation of the sacred fire of liberty and the destiny of the republican model of government," and for Lincoln, the Declaration of Independence provided "hope for the world for all future time."[78] The American version of already–not yet eschatology is expressed on every dollar bill: We are the *novus ordo saeclorum*, and we exist to bring mankind to share in the new creation that has begun here in America. This is a Babelic aspiration to remake the world in our image, one city, one tower, one lip confessing one democratic American creed.

Anagogies thus entail tropologies: If America is the fulfilled Israel, and her creed of liberty the "hope for the world for all future time" (as Lincoln had it),[79] then Americans were obligated to carry this creed and this system to the corners of the world. America had a mission—not the original Puritan mission to advance the kingdom of God, but the American mission of advancing American ideals. America is the already of the *novus ordo saeclorum*; the rest of the world is the not yet. And our vocation is to shine our light into the surrounding gloom. If America is a religious community, and if it is a biblical religious community with eschatological aspirations, then America is an inherently globalizing, universal nation. It cannot remain to itself and be itself. It must, no matter what, strive to fulfill its role as God's New Israel. America is founded on, it *is*, an ideal of liberty; and America exists to promote this ideal throughout the world. It is difficult to see how this is anything more than a sacralization of national interest: America exists to promote Americanism. One might argue, with some justice, that the ideals of liberty transcend America; they are universally human, and even America is judged, and sometimes found wanting by their measure (cf. the end of slavery and the Civil Rights movement). Even so, America is the first and chief embodiment of this ideal. We know how it's done, and measuring everyone else by the standard of American liberty easily slips into measuring everyone by America. Thus does our commitment to global liberty become a version of what Augustine regarded as Rome's "splendid vices." It collapses into a Babelic program of one city, one word, one lip—one confession of the Americanist Creed. Guided by Americanist heresy, even genuine virtues get misdirected.

This is not to say that Americanism produces no virtue. American order cultivates American virtues, the economically successful virtues of a secularized Puritanism, but more. American eschatology sounds wildly overblown, and most especially sounded overblown when "America" consisted of a few struggling towns in rocky New England or thirteen raucous colonies barely united by the Articles of Confederation and surrounded by colonies of Europe's great powers. Yet many of the wildest predictions in fact came to pass. As Gelernter points out, "I believe in America" really *is* a global confession of faith, often a yearning confession of the oppressed of the earth. Something must have gone right.

Part II: Americanism

American eschatology implies the vocation to be a haven for the tyrannized and abused. From the start, America has been an asylum. William Penn intended his colony to be a refuge from "anxious and troublesome solicitations, hurries, and perplexities of woeful Europe." Poor Richard claims that the colonies provided a place "where the sick Stranger joys to find a Home, / Where Casual Ill, maim'd Labor, freely come, / Those worn with Age, Infirmity, and Care, / Find Rest, Relief, and Health's returning fair." Thomas Paine called America "an asylum for the persecuted lovers of civil and religious liberty from every part of Europe." No poem expressed this sentiment so potently as Emma Lazarus's "The New Colossus," its words emblazoned on a bronze plaque in the pedestal of the Statue of Liberty: "Give me your tired, your poor, / Your huddled masses yearning to breathe free, / The wretched refuse of your teeming shore. / Send these, the homeless, tempest-tost to me."[80] America has fulfilled the vision of John Winthrop, and has been a model of Christian charity. If America wrongly and dangerously regards herself as God's New Israel, she is at least an Israel that has not neglected the weightier matters of the law. Even heretics do works of charity and mercy. So do heretic nations.

c. Sacrifice, American Style

Puritanism in both Old and New England had a bias against the churchly faith of the Church of England, and this was particularly evident in the problematics of Puritan sacramental theology and practice. At times an anti-sacramental mood was evident among New England's Puritans, but they wrote and preached and thought about Christian rites a good deal. Given their insistence on forming pure communities of believers, they were bound to have difficulties with the baptism of "unbelieving" infants and the admission of "merely professing" believers to the Lord's Table. These problems came to a head in New England, where Puritans hammered out a compromise between their convictions about infant baptism and their insistence on personal conversion in the Halfway Covenant. The debate between Samuel Stoddard and Increase Mather brought similar problems to the fore in eucharistic theology.[81]

The political stakes in all of these debates were enormous, though largely unrecognized. In both the Halfway Covenant discussions and the debates over access to communion, the political question had to do with the relationship between colony and church. Did they coincide entirely? Was the church, like the community, an intergenerational project, or did the church require a discontinuous outpouring of converting grace in every generation? Beneath these was the more subtle question of the public weight of the church: Was the church viewed as an independent *imperium* to itself, as a private voluntary association, or as the nation at prayer? Despite church establishments in many colonies, and despite the interest in sacramental theology evident in various debates, Puritanism leaned toward the second alternative, the notion that the church was a private association, and this leaning was established as the law of the land by the Constitution and as the heartfelt faith of Americans by revivalism.[82] Such a church could not play the role that the church had played in Western or Eastern history, whether before or after Constantine. The sacramental debates were debates about whether American Christianity would come up with a Protestant reorganization of the metapolitical framework that had guided Christendom, or would become something else. In the end, it became something else, something consistent with Americanist typology and eschatology. It has been a long time since a sizable proportion of American Protestants have viewed the Eucharist as a gift of the *corpus mysticum* that forms individual participants into a pneumatic body in Christ, and it is thus a long time since American Protestants have thought that the Eucharist would do much to form God's Abrahamic *imperium* in America. American Eucharists have done little to nurture an alternative empire of martyrs ready to resist the unjust demands of the nation. By the early nineteenth century, more traditional Protestants were alarmed at the spectacle of American Protestantism—a creedless, clergy-less, sacramentless affair in the main.[83] Augustine, Calvin, and Luther would have had a hard time identifying American churches *as* churches at all.

Given the pressure of American typology and eschatology, it was inevitable that a new form of nationalist sacrifice would take the place of the eucharistic sacrifice of martyrdom, a sacrifice not for Christ but for kin and country. That notion of sacrifice came to its earliest explicit expression during the Civil War, the third and most agonizing birth of the American and Americanism. During that conflict, "sacrifice and the state became inextricably intertwined."[84] Fallen leaders were honored as martyrs. In the South, Stonewall Jackson was declared a "Martyr for our country's cause."[85] Lincoln even more: "He has been appointed . . .

to be laid as the costliest sacrifice of all upon the altar of the Republic and to cement with his blood the free institutions of this land," said a group of ministers after his assassination. That he was murdered on Good Friday sealed the Christlike character of the one Whitman called the "Redeemer President." "It may be almost impious to say it," wrote James Garfield while a Congressman, "but it does seem that Lincoln's death parallels that of the Son of God."[86] Ordinary soldiers were decked in the wreaths of martyrs too. Jefferson Davis said that though the South may "mourn the loss of the martyrs whose lives have been sacrificed in their defense," they still accept "this dispensation of Divine Providence with humble submission and reverend faith."[87] Editorialists at the *Independent* encouraged the martyrs: "blood is not worth the having which is not worth the shedding."[88] These were not martyrs who died for their witness for Christ, but martyrs to the religion of America.

Focusing on the individual martyrs, however, misses the larger sacrificial significance of the Civil War. Many historians have pointed out the many ways that the American colonies were forged into a single national unit by the war.[89] Prior to the war, the States had few institutions or symbols of national unity. After the war, we had both in abundance.[90] Not only martyrs, but sacred ground consecrated by their blood (Gettysburg), totem flags[91] that embodied the hopes and losses of the nation (Union and Confederate), rousing battle hymns ("Battle Hymn of the Republic" and "John Brown's Body" and "Dixie"), sacred texts (the Gettysburg Address and other speeches of Lincoln), heroes and diabolical villains (Lee, Jackson, Davis, Lincoln, Grant, Sherman, John Brown).[92] Few churchmen stopped to ponder whether a U.S. flag planted in a church represented a hostile takeover. Most were content to consider their churches territory of the American nation.

The Civil War created a nation by a massive effusion of blood, a total war of shock and awe carried out against fellow Americans. Both sides quickly abandoned traditional just war principles and the gentlemanly "West Point" ethos and prosecuted war on unarmed civilians—civilians who only a few years before had been *fellow* citizens. Even what many regard as the moral high point of the war—the Emancipation Proclamation—was arguably a brief for total war, "employed by Lincoln and the Northern Republicans as a 'lever' (Lincoln's term) for total war on the Confederacy that deliberately targeted civilian farms, cities, and—in at least fifty thousand instances—civilian lives."[93] The North offered this massive sacrifice to realize a vision of America's future. "The contest on the part of the North is now undisguisedly for empire," wrote a British journal in 1862. No matter what the South conceded, the North would refuse, "provided only that the seceding States would re-enter the Union" and reconsolidate the American system.[94]

Given our confidence in American Israel, no American war can be anything but a cosmic battle of good and evil. If the Confederacy were to undercut Northern manufactory and trade, the consequences for the North would be apocalyptic: "Northern industry was to be paralyzed; Northern looms were to be stopped; Northern merchants and banks were to suspend payment. . . . Universal bankruptcy and general impoverishment would break up the foundations of social order. Anarchy would reign in Northern cities, and grass would grow in their streets."[95] A satirist, Tim Shay Arthur, claimed that Southern traitors have "united to destroy our beautiful fabric of civil liberty," and warned darkly that if the South were victorious, "who can tell under what iron rule we might have fallen."[96] The South had launched an attack on the North; the North claimed to be acting in self-defense in this "clash of civilizations." And the response had to be savagely decisive.[97]

Some few Americans discerned what was happening, and lamented. Most famously, Lincoln spelled out the logic of sacrificial retribution in his Second Inaugural Address, where he speculated that God might want the war to continue until every drop of slave blood is atoned for by the blood of a Union or Confederate soldier.[98] Philip Schaff was dismayed by the "very baptism of blood" that Americans hoped would give "hope for a glorious regeneration."[99] One John Cruickshanks recognized that the war continued with such ferocity because America had been erected as America's idol: "In a word, the army is the people's God. They idolize it—they worship it."[100]

In general, the war's terrors and injustices were valorized by reference to Americanist typology and eschatology: "Mine eyes have seen the glory of the Coming of the Lord," trampling, trampling, trampling, fighting and dying like Christ not to make men holy but "to make men free." As the war continued, both sides seemed to lose whatever moral compass and insight they started with: "On all sides—clerical, political, journalistic, military, artistic, and intellectual—the historian searches in vain for moral criticism directed at one's own case." Writers wrote incessantly about the war, talkers talked, preachers preached, but "few directly addressed the question of what constitutes a just war, and what limitations ought to be observed in the unpleasant event of the war."[101] According to Harry Stout, there was "one simple reason" for the moral failure of America's leaders during the war—"nationalism." Our word is *Americanism*. The cult of America blinded leaders on both sides to norms of justice that might transcend the nation. For the participants, "something mystical and even religious was taking place through the sheer blood sacrifice generated by the battles." The Revolutionary War had never "shaped a coherent sense of the *nation* as the prevailing object of fealty, over and against local communities and regions.... Before the Civil War, Americans would routinely say, 'The United States *are* a republic.' After the war they would instinctively come to say, 'The United States *is* a republic.'" As a result, as the war continued, "the grounds of justification underwent a transformation from a just defensive war fought out of sheer necessity to preserve home and nation to a moral crusade for 'freedom' that would involve nothing less than a national 'rebirth,' a spiritual 'revival.'" Out of the carnage "a national religion was born," a fresh commitment to the Union that Americans would defend to the death. Americans came to be convinced that this was the only way the Union could be saved: "it absolutely required a baptism of blood to unveil transcendent dimensions of that union."[102]

The national devotion that blinded American leaders was consistent with the ecclesial tradition of American Christianity. Churches reduced to voluntary societies or cheerleaders of republicanism had few resources to resist overheated war fever. They did not have the critical distance or independence to say no. Pulpits became propaganda arms for the Union or Confederacy. On the other hand, more traditional preachers refrained from addressing politics at all. Convinced of a typically Southern Presbyterian view of the "spirituality" of the church, Richmond's Rev. Moses Hoge lamented the division, but was determined, along with his associate T. V. Moore, not "to introduce anything political into our sermons, but wish to direct the minds of the people from man to God."[103] A noble sentiment, but the effect was to leave the laity without moral compass or guide, and to leave the state to its own reasons of state.

Outside the metapolitics of Christendom, founding sacrifices do not stop with the founding. They need to be repeated regularly. The connections between the Civil War and America's future wars were at times quite direct. If we bombed towns without regard to women and children, Gen. Sheridan asked Sherman after the war, then why should we play nice with savages?[104] America invented total war, and we have been among its most effective practitioners. Since the Civil War, we have sacralized all our wars, transfigured all soldiers into Americanist martyrs. Lincoln spoke at Gettysburg of the "unfinished business" of the war, and if the business completed so far required bloodletting on a numbing scale, what would the future hold? How, Stanley Hauerwas asks, can we validate the sacrifices of our forefathers if we do not offer a sacrifice of our own?[105]

In a brilliantly myopic essay written in the aftermath of 9/11, Jody Bottum applied Girardian theories of sacrifice to the combat with Islam. He assessed radical Islam as a pagan system that depends on blood, and urged the Bush Administration to do whatever it could to prevent "a new culture from being founded on the mythological value of the blood of six thousand dead American scapegoats. We must not allow the return of that ancient logic, that satanic solution, that other scapegoating answer to the question of what violence is for." Bottum says there are only two solutions to violence—scapegoating versus "Christ's positive solution," and if he thinks America's job is to prevent the expansion of satanic order, he must assume that we have adopted the Christian solution.[106] He never asks the obvious question: What if America is herself locked in the ancient logic, the satanic cycle? What if Americanism, increasingly detached from the checks and balances that orthodox metapolitics provides, has left us prey to the same sacrificial dynamics as Islam? What if we do not embody the Christian solution, but represent another, less conscious version of the antique system of perpetual sacrifice, dressed up in Christian rhetoric?

Sacrifice American style can only go on and on. For in Americanism, this fourth great biblical religion, there is no final sacrifice, no end to bloodshed until we have rid the world of evil, until the American creed becomes the creed of humanity. In this, too, we are a heretic nation.

Conclusion

In the midst of the horrors of the Civil War, Methodist minister George S. Phillips was still bullish about America's future. The American "mission . . . should only be accomplished when the last despot should be dethroned, the last claim of oppression broken, the dignity and equality of redeemed humanity everywhere established, and the American flag . . . should wave over every land and encircle the world with its majestic folds. Then, and not till then, should the nation have accomplished the purpose for which it was established by the God of heaven."[107] At the end of the century, while the United States was herding Filipinos into concentration camps, Americanist fervor was undiminished among our leaders—one of whom, Senator Albert Beveridge, said that

> God has . . . made us the master organizers of the world to establish system where chaos reigns. He has given us the spirit of progress to overwhelm the forces of reaction throughout the earth. He has made us adept in government that we may administer government among savage and senile peoples. Were it not for such a force as this the world would relapse into barbarism and night. And of all our race He has marked the American people as His chosen nation to finally lead in the regeneration of the world. This is the divine mission of America, and it holds for us all the profit, all the glory, all the happiness possible to man.[108]

America is exceptional. It has exceptional resources and strength, and an exceptional track record of political and economic success. It is exceptional as the first post-Christendom Christian political order. It is exceptional in cultivating certain virtues, including some Christian ones.

But it is not exceptional in the ways that Americanist typology and eschatology suggest. We are not the new Israel, nor the last best hope of mankind, nor the *novus ordo saeclorum*. Insofar as Americans have believed and acted on these convictions, we have been quite literally a heretic nation.

We are a great power, better than many, worse than some. What is perhaps most exceptional about the new human type called "American" is our dogged attachment to our national religion, which impels us to evangelize the world, teaching the Gentiles to observe our Creed. For, if Americanism is what I have suggested, we cannot keep it to ourselves. It is an ideology of expansion, a faith that in the right circumstances readily lends itself to imperialism of one sort or another. Americanism is the monstrous Nephilim that people the earth when the sons of God intermarry the daughters of men. Americanist Christians are Joktanites who uncritically join Nimrod in building Babel. Americanism is ideology with the mythical power to bewitch a Babel into thinking it is Persia, a distorting mirror that might fool a predator into believing he sees the reflection of a cherub.

CHAPTER 5

Chanting the New Empire

George W. Bush expressed an article of American faith when he declared during the 1999 presidential campaign, "America has never been an empire" and added, "We may be the only great power in history that had the chance, and refused—preferring greatness to power, and justice to glory." Newt Gingrich agrees: America has "no interest in conquering territories," he has stated, though we do have "every interest in getting people to believe in their freedom and getting people to govern themselves."[1] This reading of American history cuts across the political spectrum: We were born out of resistance to empire, President Obama has reminded hostile audiences.

According to this notion, the United States, founded in resistance to an overweening British empire, swore off the intoxications of imperialism and pursued a policy of blissful isolation for the first century and a half of our existence. Only in the early twentieth century, when we were dragged into World War I, did we make our marks on the international stage, and even then it was with great reluctance. If we resemble an empire today, it was not our plan. We hold our international power "reluctantly," and we are, if an empire, an "inadvertent" one.[2] Late and inadvertent: That is the story we tell ourselves about America's global reach.[3]

Washington's Farewell Address was memorized and recited by generations of American schoolchildren as the summary of American views of international relations. "The great rule of conduct for us, in regard to foreign nations," said the father of all American fathers, "is in extending our commercial relations, to have with them as little political connection as possible. Europe has a set of primary interests, which to us have none, or a very remote relation. Hence she must be engaged in frequent controversies the causes of which are essentially foreign to our concerns. Hence, therefore, it must be unwise in us to implicate ourselves, by artificial ties, in the ordinary vicissitudes of her politics, or the ordinary combinations and collisions of her friendships and enmities." Jefferson declared in 1791 that the United States had renounced classic forms of imperialism: "If there be one principle more deeply rooted than any other in the mind of every American, it is, that we should have nothing to do with conquest." As president, John Quincy Adams famously proclaimed that, while the United States "is the well-wisher to the freedom and independence of all," she is "the champion and vindicator only of her own." The United States "goes not abroad, in search of monsters to destroy."[4] In his 1823 address to Congress, James Monroe articulated what later came to be known as the Monroe Doctrine. He reiterated Washington's insistence that the United States avoid embroilment in European conflicts: "In the wars of the European powers, in matters relating to themselves, we have never taken part, nor does it comport with our policy, so to do. It is only when our rights are invaded, or seriously menaced that we resent injuries, or make preparations for our defense."[5] The president then formulated a policy for the Americas consistent with "isolationist" principles:

> With the movements in this hemisphere we are of necessity more immediately connected, and by causes which must be obvious to all enlightened and impartial observers. The political system of the allied powers is essentially different in this respect from that of America. This difference proceeds from that which exists in their respective Governments; and to the defense of our own, which has been achieved by the loss of so much blood and treasure, and matured by the wisdom of their most enlightened citizens, and under which we have enjoyed unexampled felicity, this whole nation is devoted. We owe it, therefore, to candor and to the amicable relations existing between the United States and those powers to declare that we should consider any attempt on their part to extend their system to any portion of this hemisphere as dangerous to our peace and safe-

ty. With the existing colonies or dependencies of any European power we have not interfered and shall not interfere. But with the Governments who have declared their independence and maintain it, and whose independence we have, on great consideration and on just principles, acknowledged, we could not view any interposition for the purpose of oppressing them, or controlling in any other manner their destiny, by any European power in any other light than as the manifestation of an unfriendly disposition toward the United States.[6]

The United States might have to intervene in South America, but only defensively, to protect our interests in the Western Hemisphere in ensuring that our nearest neighbors had stable governments. Isolationism is "woven into the DNA of the American character."[7]

The myth of isolationist America has enough basis in reality to gain plausibility. One can string together quotations from prominent American leaders and thinkers, and events from American history, to make the case. If, however, Americanism—the heretical blend of American typology, ecclesiology, eschatology, and sacrificial practice that is the foundation for our sense of national identity, vocation, and mission—is embedded in the American character and American culture, isolationism *cannot* be the whole story. It cannot even be the main story. But Americanism distorts our self-image: If we see ourselves as God's gift to the world, we will have a hard time acknowledging our blemishes. The myth of American isolationism is part of the reason we have so much trouble reconciling our national self-image with the rest of the world's view that we are a "dangerous nation." Robert Kagan is right: "On balance, Americans would be better off if they understood themselves, their nation, and their nation's history better."[8]

AMERICAN AND THE WORLD: THEORY

America's Founding Fathers were not anti-empire.[9] Quite frequently, they stated the opposite. Washington described America in 1783 as a "rising empire," and later predicted that the "infant empire" that was born from the Revolutionary War would one day "have some weight in the scale of Empires." In Hamilton's opinion, expressed in *Federalist* #1, America was "the most interesting" empire in the world, and in *Federalist* #11 he looked ahead to "a great American system, superior to the control of all trans-Atlantic force of influence, and able to dictate the terms of connection between the Old and the New World." The language was not a Federalist monopoly. "Empire for Liberty" is from Jefferson, who also described the United States as an "Empire *of* Liberty."[10] Jefferson "cherished an imperial vision for the new American nation."[11]

"Empire," of course, has meant different things in different contexts. Originally, *imperium* meant "the legal power to enforce the law," though even in the writings of Caesar and Cicero it came to mean "a territorial and administrative whole." To speak of Rome's *imperium* was often simply to speak of Rome's dominance.[12] By the time of America's founding, the word had taken on much of its current meaning: "When George Washington used the word *empire*, he meant a polity that exercises sovereignty over and was responsible for the security of a large expanse of territory that, composed of previously separate units now subordinate to the metropolis . . . included many peoples of diverse 'races' . . . and nationalities." Washington assumed that "not all the people within the heterogeneous population could qualify as citizens, not all were equal, not all could or would assimilate, and not all consented to the rule of the sovereign." Far from eschewing empire, many of the Founders aspired to build a "particular 'genre' of state that would grow in size, strength, and prosperity, exercise influence over populations that either considered themselves autonomous or resided beyond America's political boundaries . . . and possess a centralized government."[13] What the Founders did reject in principle was *colonization*, annexation and government of foreign peoples or settlement of foreign nations by Americans. American foreign policy was guided by a vision of "imperial anticolonialism."[14]

Not only did the Founders aim for an empire, at least a territorial empire that stretched between the Atlantic and the Pacific, they theorized about how such a vast tract of territory and a vast population could be ruled according to republican principles. Jefferson and Madison agreed, against Montesquieu, that republican government could be extended to a large territory. Madison argued that the American system was more suited to a large than to a small territory. For Madison, extending American territory was of a piece with cultivating competing interests and preventing any single interest from dominating the whole: "This form of government, in order to effect its purpose, must operate not within a small but an extensive sphere. Extend the sphere, and you take in a greater variety of parties and interests; you make it less probable that a majority of the whole will have a common motive to invade the rights of other citizens; or if such a common motive exists, it will be more difficult for all to feel it . . . to act in unison with each other."[15] The logic is the same as the logic of the First Amendment and *Federalist* #10: Permit a proliferation of sects so that sect cancels sect and none is able to master the national government.

A year before he articulated his "Doctrine," Monroe offered a similar perspective in an address to Congress, though with a different rationale: "The greater the expansion, within practical limits, and it is not easy to say what are not so, the greater the advantage which the States individually will derive from it. . . . It must be obvious to all, that the further the expansion is carried, provided it be not beyond the just limit, the greater will be the freedom of action to both Governments, and the more perfect their security; and, in all other respects, the better the effect will be on the whole American people."[16] It was no accident that the proposal to limit the western boundary of the original states was turned down before it ever reached the convention drawing up the Articles of Confederation. From the outset, the Founders envisioned a republic that would encompass what later came to be called North America.

a. Benjamin Franklin

No early American devoted as much energy and attention to American expansion as Benjamin Franklin. In the aftermath of the third French and Indian War, Franklin had responsibility for protecting the interests of Pennsylvania. British colonists were fearful of French encirclement, and Pennsylvania, which did not have formal claims to western territories, was more vulnerable than other colonies. In 1751, Franklin produced his *Observations Concerning the Increase of Mankind and the Peopling of Countries,* which provided one of the earliest visions of the future of the American frontier. He believed that the British American population would continue to grow and would demand more territory. Americans marry early and were highly fertile, a fact that led Franklin to conclude that the American population would double every two decades. As long as Americans could move into the frontier, though, "the supply of labor would not outstrip the demand for it." From these two assumptions, Franklin drew the conclusion that Britain should promote "continental expansion" and should revise its mercantilist policies to make the colonies an equal partner in empire, a model advocated by Adam Smith and Edmund Burke from the English side. If the mother country were to feed American's desire for land, the results would be beneficial to both Britain and America: "The Prince that acquires new Territory, if he finds it vacant, or removes the Natives to give his own People Room; the Legislator that makes effectual Laws for promoting of Trade, increasing Employment, improving Land by more or better Tillage; providing more Food by Fisheries; securing Property, etc. and the Man that invents new Trades, Arts or Manufactures, or new Improvements in Husbandry, may properly be called *Fathers* of their nations, as they are the Cause of the Generation of Multitudes."[17]

Franklin suggested that the standard mercantile model be inverted. Instead of thinking of the colonies as providers of raw materials for domestic manufacturers, the British should think of colonies as "a glorious Market wholly in the Power of *Britain*, in which Foreigners cannot interfere, which will increase in a short Time even beyond her Power of supplying, tho her whole Trade should be to her Colonies." If Britain worried about the periphery becoming a competitor to the metropole, that problem could be solved by territorial expansion: "So vast is the Territory of North America, that it will require many Ages to settle fully." Working together, Britain and her American colonies could become the dominant force of the world: "What an Accession of Power to the *British* Empire by Sea as well as Land! What Increase of Trade and Navigation! What Numbers of Ships and Seamen!" Were the British to play their cards right, they could make "this Side of our Globe reflect a brighter Light to the Eyes of Inhabitants in Mars or Venus."[18]

Thus far Franklin in 1751. Things changed, of course, with the outbreak of war, and Franklin had to give up his vision of a symbiotic British-American empire. Yet he did not give up his conviction that the United States ought to expand across the continent. He supported the Federalist argument that permitted a "diverse, geographically immense political community to be held together without creating a sovereign power that would threaten the liberties and rights the Revolutionary War had been fought to preserve." He supported the Northwest Ordinance of 1787, which formed the Great Lakes states into a territory, because it helped realize his dream of "indefinite expansion" of "self-governing republics, immune to the possibility of despotic rule from the center."[19] Empire was not a threat to American liberty. It was the means for ensuring liberty's preservation against the threatening world.[20] Franklin's empire was not as a means for aggrandizing power or property, but a "defensive" imperialism, an imperialism of security. It was an imperialism born, in part, of fear.

b. John Quincy Adams

John Quincy Adams, the anti-crusader who warned about pursuing monsters, was another early American leader who established the contours of American empire. He accepted Madison's argument for an expansive "republican empire" that would preserve freedom by increasing the number of competing interests and factions. Unlike other Federalists, Adams supported Jefferson's Louisana Purchase, partly out of a conviction that in expanding across the continent and even into the Caribbean, Americans were only following the dictates of nature. He considered Spain's holdings in the Americas to be contrary to nature. Other great powers of the world should become accustomed to America's expanding "dominion" across the continent since "from the time when we became an independent people it was as much a law of nature that this should become our pretension as that the Mississippi should flow to the sea." America's right to control the Pacific Northwest was absolute, "pointed out by the finger of Nature." Cuba and Puerto Rico were "natural appendages to the North American continent," and this could only mean that they would be drawn into the orbit of the United States; "laws of political as well as of physical gravitation" were at work: as an apple cut from a tree "cannot choose but fall to the ground," so "Cuba, forcibly disjoined from its own unnatural connection with Spain, and incapable of self-support, can gravitate only towards the North American Union, which by the same law of nature cannot cast her off from its bosom."[21] That Cubans might choose otherwise did not occur to Adams, and he conveniently forgot that the colonies that became the United States had, not long before his time, been as "unnatural" as Spanish America.

With his stress on "natural" domination of the continent and the hemisphere, Adams tended toward a homogeneous, "Babelic" vision of empire:

> Adams anticipated [the] rhetoric of Manifest Destiny by proclaiming that the continent was America's "natural dominion." No people or nation could stand in the way of Americans transforming "howling deserts into cultivated fields and populous villages." The acquisition of and settlement of the trans-Mississippi region was necessary but not sufficient for fulfilling the nation's destiny. Believing, as did Jefferson, that Divine Providence destined the continent to "be peopled by one nation, speaking one language, possessing one general system of religious and political principles, and accustomed to one general tenor of social usages and customs," the territories had to be organized as states and "associated in one federal union" committed to life, liberty, and the pursuit of happiness. Otherwise, Adams eerily warned, "America like the rest of the earth [would] sink into a common battlefield of conquerors and tyrants."[22]

Adams backed up his theory with practical political activity. He publicly criticized Jefferson and Madison for not being ambitious enough about American expansion. When they proposed the "Two Million Act" that sought to induce "Spain to recognize that Florida and Texas were territories belonging to the United States," Adams objected that Jefferson was willing to "renounce all our claims upon the western boundary [of Louisiana, i.e., Texas] and pay several millions to get the Floridas." It was wholly unnecessary: "West Florida I consider as our own," since with the Louisiana Purchase, "we have bought and paid for it."[23] Between 1815 and 1817, Adams was the American minister in Britain, and "initiated the process of Anglo-American reconciliation that almost a century later provided the framework for the replacement of the Pax Britannica by Pax Americana."[24] As secretary of state in the Monroe administration, Adams initially opposed Andrew Jackson's invasion of East Florida. Ambitious for the presidency himself, he saw in Jackson a potential rival, and he embarked on a diplomatic effort with Spain to resolve tensions. Once Jackson invaded and took the territory, however, Adams argued that "there was no real, though an apparent, violation" of President Monroe's instructions and that "his proceedings were justified by the necessity of the case, and by the misconduct of the Spanish commanding officers in Florida." He convinced Monroe that rebuking Jackson for his unilateral decision would be seen as "a confession of weakness" and would set a bad precedent that would diminish the power of the executive branch.[25] He also worked out a deal by which Spain ceded all lands north of the forty-second parallel from the Rockies to the Pacific to the United States, an event that Adams rightly saw as "a great epocha [sic] in our history."[26]

Adams' vision was a political version of the Americanist eschatology that had been given new impetus by the revivals of the early nineteenth century. He viewed his plans for national improvement and expansion as a program inspired and directed by Providence: "Progressive improvement in the condition of man is apparently the purpose of a superintending Providence." The system of road and other improvements that he proposed in his First Message to Congress was no mere pragmatic effort. It was "a sacred duty" to elevate American civilization. Moving to the metric system would fulfill "the trembling hope of the Christian," and through these various improvements, America would see "the unity of humanity, the binding of Satan in chains, and the promised thousand years of peace."[27] Adams' ambitions were somewhat tempered in old age, as he opposed Jackson's plan for Indian removal as a plan for "extermination."[28] But even late in life, as he debated Polk's plans for the Oregon Territory, he argued that the Bible promised the United States title to all of the continent: "I want the country for our western pioneers," he told Congress, quoting Psalm 2's promise of "the uttermost parts of the earth for thy possession."[29] With a heady mix of political analysis of American eschatology, it is no wonder that Adams could issue this challenge: "Who shall dare to set limits to the commerce and naval power of this country?"[30]

c. Monroe's Doctrine (1823)

It was Adams, too, who was largely responsible for the paragraphs concerning European colonialization that appeared in Monroe's 1823 address to Congress, which came to be known as the Monroe Doctrine. As noted, Monroe's speech is frequently cited as evidence of American isolationism. In its original context, the speech was something quite different. Monroe echoed Washington's famous Farewell Address by reiterating American policy to leave European politics to Europeans insofar as these political battles "relat[ed] to themselves," but he added that "circumstances are eminently and conspicuously different" in the Western Hemisphere. The United States must protect her own interests, and Monroe warned that these interests reached beyond our borders. America could not remain indifferent if European powers attempted to "extend their political system to any portion of either continent." European meddling would threaten the "peace and happiness" of the United States. With independence movements erupting in Latin America, Monroe stated that the United States regarded any European effort to subdue those new governments as "the manifestation of unfriendly disposition toward the United States."

The American Revolution inspired independence movements in South America and throughout Europe. Many in the United States feared that Spain would intervene in Latin America to suppress democratic rebellions and set up new Spanish colonies. In response to European democratic revolutions, Russia, Austria, and Prussia formed the Holy Alliance to defend monarchy against revolution, democracy, modernism—in a word, against Americanism. Monroe's speech warned the members of the Holy Alliance, as well as Spain and other Catholic powers, that the United States would not look kindly on their efforts to impose a system hostile to America within their hemisphere.

Monroe's speech was intended for international consumption, but it was also an intervention in a roiling debate within the United States over how it should respond to the Holy Alliance and to the American-style democratic movements. Americans such as Daniel Webster argued that it was America's duty to "come forth, and deny, and condemn" the absolutism embodied in the Holy Alliance. Greece's revolt against the Turks (1821) in particular captured the American imagination. Americans were sympathetic to the Greek struggle to recover her ancient democratic roots. Groups collected funds for the Greek resistance while newspapers heated public opinion with reports on Turkish atrocities. Webster observed that "we have as much Community with the Greeks, as with the inhabitants of the Andes." He admitted that the United States could do little practical good for Greece, yet he hoped that America could at least "assure them of public regard." Monroe initially wanted to intervene aggressively in the debate about Greece. In his first draft of his State of the Union speech, Monroe explicitly recognized Greek independence and attacked the Holy Alliance for trampling down reform efforts in Europe. Alarmed at the aggressive tone, Secretary of State

Part II: Americanism

John Quincy Adams warned that Monroe's speech would "have the air of open defiance to all Europe" and pick a "quarrel with all Europe." Adams convinced the president to soften his rhetoric, but even in its final form, Monroe's speech expressed "strong hope" that Greece would achieve independence and condemned attacks on republican freedom by European autocrats.

In the very speech that stands as a monument of American desire to stay close to home, Monroe expressed American sympathy for republican revolutions half a world away. Like most Americans of his time, Monroe viewed the struggles in Europe from an ideological not a geopolitical perspective. He saw a threat to American ideals, and therefore to America's experiment in liberty, in the rise of organized absolutism. Though an ocean (and more) separated Monroe's America from the Holy Alliance, the latter was a threat to America because it was a threat to the *idea* of America. (Americans still share Monroe's perceptions of the great geopolitical struggles of our time.) Europeans understood that Monroe aimed to nudge Europe in an American direction. This upstart nation, Metternich observed, wanted to "foster . . . revolutions wherever they show themselves" and gave aid and comfort to "the apostles of sedition."[31]

Monroe's speech did not lay out a doctrine or establish American foreign policy forever and always. To begin with, it did not work. The United States did not have the power to enforce Monroe's warning, and Monroe knew it. He cleverly sidestepped that problem by refusing to explain what the United States would do if Europeans ignored Monroe's warning.[32] They did ignore it: "The British established the colony of British Guiana (now Guyana) out of the three formerly Dutch possessions in 1831 and continued blithely to colonize north of the forty-ninth parallel as if oblivious of Monroe's great declaration. In 1839 they seized the island of Ruatan off the coast of Honduras; in the 1850s they briefly occupied the nearby Bay Islands; in 1862 they turned Belize into the colony of British Honduras. The French too ignored the Monroe Doctrine."[33] Insofar as it was enforced at all, Monroe's policy was enforced by the British, whose eventual alliance with America greatly limited what *other* Europeans powers dared in the Western Hemisphere.

By 1923, Mary Baker Eddy could declare ecstatically, "I believe strictly in the Monroe Doctrine, in our Constitution, and in the laws of God." It is an interesting list, in an interesting order. Both before and after its centenary, however, Monroe's speech was less a binding or even settled doctrine or declaration than it was a site of controversy. James Polk invented it as a "doctrine" in the context of disputes about slavery and American expansion, and Monroe's claims were given anti-slavery interpretations as well. Pro- and anti-imperialism ideologies, pro- and anti-interventionist policies—all were defended by appeal to Monroe. As every American leader—left, right, center, margins—pays lip service to the Declaration and the Constitution and adapts them to his political ends, so too everyone has to genuflect before the Monroe Doctrine.[34] Whatever it means, the Monroe Doctrine's main role has been to give political expression to Americanism.

d. "Peace or War": Washington's Speech (1796)

Though later generations of Americans have a difficult time believing it, Washington was a political leader not an oracle, engaged with the problems of his own day rather than making apodictic pronouncements for all time. The 1790s were a period of intense debate within the United States. Though the Constitution had passed, the meaning of the Constitution was still very much up for debate. On the one side were the Federalists, led by the progressive nationalist Alexander Hamilton, who advocated a nationalist and expansionist program for the federal government, believed that there should be a national bank, and encouraged tariffs to protect domestic industries. Republicans like Jefferson and Madison worried that the gains of the Revolution would be lost if the Federal government were to become too powerful. Each side interpreted the Revolution and Constitution in a way that supported its political predilections (though which supported which is open to debate). Jefferson saw the Revolution as a break with the British past and the formation of a *novus ordo saeclorum*, while Hamilton insisted that the Revolution aimed to preserve and recover the colonists' preexisting liberties as Englishmen. The debate had an international component as well: Francophile Jeffersonians were enthused by the French Revolution, while Hamiltonians were so enamored of America's ties with Britain that many feared (or pretended to fear) that Hamilton wanted to revive the monarchy. Hamilton's real intentions were more prosaic. He discerned that American prosperity depended on ties to the British commercial empire, which was underwritten by the Royal Navy. Renouncing

Britain would be disastrous for America's future. Hamilton had his own paranoia: He feared that the republicans might bring French Terror to America.[35] Both sides believed they were fighting for the soul of the American experiment.

At the time of Washington's address, these debates had come to a head in the debate over the Jay Treaty with Great Britain. Too pro-British even for Hamilton, the Jay Treaty fired up republicans in the United States and enraged France, which began harassing American ships. Washington worried with Hamilton that some in the United States wanted to turn it into a French colony, and his main theme in the speech was domestic, an effort to ward off the danger of secession plots inspired by France. With Britain and France at war, the United States could not afford to pursue alliances with France. If France defeated Britain, the French would overrun the nascent and still very vulnerable United States. "No entangling alliance" did not mean "No alliance ever with anyone," but, for Washington, "No alliance with France." His administration had, after all, just concluded a controversial treaty with Britain. For Washington, "Nonentanglement was a selective tactic, not a grand strategy."[36]

Washington did articulate a principle of American foreign affairs in his speech, though it was a much less famous one than the warning against alliances. "If we remain one people," he said, "under an efficient government, the period is not far off when we may defy material injury from external annoyance; when we may take such an attitude as will cause the neutrality we may at any time resolve upon to be scrupulously respected; when belligerent nations, under the impossibility of making acquisitions upon us, will not lightly hazard us provocation; when we may choose peace or war, as our interest, guided by our justice, shall counsel."[37] "Peace or war"—determined by "our interest, guided by our justice." This was an enduring grand strategy, a strategy of American greatness, or what might be called the strategy of getting strong enough to do whatever you damn well please. For the Founders, it was a strategy of liberty, for the stronger America became, the more sure she was to preserve her own liberty as a beacon to the benighted world and the more capable she became of assisting others in securing the same liberties for themselves. It was a strategy perfectly consistent with the heresy of Americanism.

AMERICAN EMPIRE: PRACTICE[38]

America's power has expanded throughout the world in numerous ways: American missionaries spread over the globe, as did American businessmen; troubled or endangered nations have appealed for American help, and we have helped; American food has fed the hungry and American money has rebuilt homes and cities for victims of natural and man-made disaster; American technologies and styles are today imitated everywhere. Over the past several decades, the United States has not controlled "a stable territory" so much as "global finances and naval, air, and electronic spectrum space."[39] Every historian who studies America's ascent comments that it is an unusual, if not unique, great power.

For all our reliance on soft power, we have resorted to the hard kind more often than we like to admit. Military engagements have not been rare. For most of the first two centuries of our history, we were periodically at odds with Britain. Public opinion regularly favored war with Britain and France, and nearly every president between Washington and Wilson sent American troops abroad or had to deal with a crisis with some European power.[40] Between 1800 and 1934, the United States Marines conducted 180 landings, many of them during our period of blissful innocence and isolation.[41] Prior to 1850, U.S. Marines landed in the Dominican Republic (1800), Tripoli (1804, 1805), the Marquesas Islands (1813–1814), Puerto Rico (1824), the Falkland Islands (1831–1832), Sumatra (1832), Argentina (1833), Peru (1835, 1836), Sumatra again (1838, 1839), Fiji (1840), Samoa (1841), and Liberia, West Africa (1843).[42] By the middle of the nineteenth century, American forces were scattered throughout the world. We had a force in the South Pacific, and a permanent Mediterranean squadron. As early as 1822, we had a squadron in the West Indies and the Pacific, one in the South Atlantic by 1826, an East Indian squadron by 1835, and an African squadron by 1843. In short, "during the period of American innocence and isolation, the United States had forces stationed on or near every major continent in the world; its navy was active in virtually every ocean, its troops saw combat on virtually every continent, and its foreign relations were in a permanent state of crisis and turmoil."[43]

"Intervention is not now, never was, and never will be a set policy of the United States." Herbert Hoover's denial was cleverly stated: Even dozens of interventions might be *ad hoc* responses to particular

Part II: Americanism

situations rather than part of a "set policy." Still, the world had reason to be skeptical. Teddy Roosevelt was more honest and accurate: Our entire history, he observed, has been a history of expansion.[44] It could hardly have been otherwise for a nation imbued with Americanist eschatology and forged in the sacrificial conflagration of the Civil War.

a. Commercial War: Barbary Pirates

No one sings it anymore, but the original version of what became our national anthem drew its inspiration not from the War of 1812, but from an earlier American conflict.

> In the conflict resistless, each toil they endured,
> 'Till their foes fled dismayed from the war's desolation:
> And pale beamed the Crescent, its splendor obscured
> By the light of the Star Spangled flag of our nation.
> Where each radiant star gleamed a meteor of war,
> And the turbaned heads bowed to its terrible glare,
> Now, mixed with the olive, the laurel shall wave,
> And form a bright wreath for the brows of the brave.[45]

Neither the "turbaned heads" nor the "Crescent" is British. In 1805, Francis Scott Key wrote the poem "Song" to celebrate the American victory in North Africa. It is a fantastic and largely forgotten story, and worth recalling briefly not only for its sheer drama but also for the light it sheds on early, and later, American foreign affairs.

Not long after achieving independence, the United States faced "its first acute foreign threat."[46] Three American merchant ships had been captured by pirates off the North African coast, and hijackings and hostages were just beginning. John Paul Jones complained that "the Algerians are cruising in different squads of six and eight sail, and extend themselves out as far as the western islands." It was standard procedure for the North African client states of the Ottoman Empire—Tunis, Tripoli, Algiers. They had long profited from piracy in the Mediterranean by capturing ships and seizing plunder or by extorting large fees from European and American ships for the right to pass in safety. Many European powers swallowed hard and paid the bribes, knowing that extortion was cheaper and safer than war. Until 1776, American ships plowed the Mediterranean under the aegis of the Royal Navy. With British protection gone, the United States had to decide what to do for the one hundred American expeditions being made to the Mediterranean annually with the purpose of trading fish, flour, lumber, sugar, and other goods for lemons, oranges, figs, olive oil, and other Middle Eastern commodities.[47]

Stories of atrocities trickled home. Captured while a sailor aboard the *Polly* in 1793, John Foss recounted tortures of more than oriental cruelty: "Slaves found guilty of malingering could expect up to 200 . . . whacks on the feet with a five-foot cane. A slave who spoke disrespectfully to a Muslim could be roasted alive, crucified or impaled."[48] Americans were appalled. John Adams argued that it would be less expensive for the United States to pay the tribute and move on. Tribute was expensive—bribes to Algiers came to $1,000,000 at its peak, 1/6 of the federal budget[49]—but most Americans did not object because of the money. Washington chafed under a disgraceful system that made Westerners and Americans "tributary to such banditti who might for half the sum that is paid them be exterminated from the earth."[50] Jefferson too knew that Americans would prefer to "raise ships and men to fight the pirates into reason than money to bribe them." Shock and awe directed at the pirates would not only put Barbary in its place but also send a message to the rest of the world: "It will procure us respect in Europe, and respect is a safeguard to interest."[51]

When the attacks began, the United States suffered from a structural weakness. Under the Articles of Confederation, there was no legal and constitutional basis for the states to coordinate efforts to fight back. "America cannot retaliate," said Lord Sheffield in England. It was too difficult to get the states "to act as a nation." This was one of the motivations for the replacement of the Articles with the Constitution, which provided a mechanism for the formation of a navy: "Though downplayed during the Constitutional Convention, the connection between the Middle East and the American federation figured prominently in the impassioned state-level debates on ratifying the proposed Constitution."[52] By the time Jefferson became president in 1800, the United States had a Navy sufficient to resist piracy, and Jefferson made full use of America's sea power. Between 1801 and 1805, the United States Navy engaged in a seesaw war with a variety of North African powers. Daring heroes emerged from the conflict, none more colorful than Stephen Decatur. Disguised in Maltese costume, Decatur sailed the *Intrepid* (itself captured from pirates) into Tripoli's harbor, within range of Tripolitan

Part II: Americanism

cannon, to burn and disable the *Philadelphia*, a captured American vessel. When Decatur learned after a battle that the captain of an enemy ship had killed his brother, he gave chase, boarded the ship, and killed the offending captain in hand-to-hand combat.[53] Decatur was celebrated and lent his name to many towns across the United States. He was America's first superhero, and the mythology of Decatur was one of the factors that coalesced the thirteen former colonies into a single nation.[54]

Almost completely forgotten are the exploits of William Eaton, an American T. E. Lawrence. While serving a diplomatic post in Tunis in 1804, he learned that the reigning pasha had exiled his older brother, Hamid. With permission from Jefferson and Secretary of State James Madison, Eaton embarked on a clandestine plan for regime change. He gathered a ragtag army of Americans, Tripolitans, European mercenaries, and Bedouin in Egypt, and marched across the desert to the city of Darna on the way to Tripoli. Eaton's forces were able to take the city and fly the American flag on its fortress, but he soon learned that the reigning pasha sent reinforcements to take the city back. Eaton repelled the attack, but before he could secure his victory, an American ship, the *USS Constellation*, arrived. Eaton was ordered to withdraw and informed that Jefferson had concluded a treaty with the government of Tunis.[55] Madison's defense of the coup could have been pulled from George W. Bush's diary: "Although it does not accord with the general sentiments or views of the United States to intermeddle in the domestic contests of other countries, it cannot be unfair, in the prosecution of a just war, or the accomplishment of a reasonable peace, to turn to their advantage, the enmity and pretensions of others against a common foe."[56]

The Barbary Wars ended in 1815. Adams had been right: War *was* more costly than extortion. The sum eventually came to $3,000,000 for the war, not to mention the hundred or so American casualties.[57] But Jefferson was right, too: The United States had won admiration and respect from the world. It was on its way to fulfilling Washington's aim of being able to choose peace or war as interest, guided by justice, dictated.

America's first Middle Eastern war anticipates several features of later American wars. The Barbary Wars could have been avoided with tribute and bribes, but they *were* defensive wars, protecting American lives and interests. As has frequently been the case since, the American navy was deployed to protect business, the freedom of commerce on the seas.[58] Just as importantly, the wars protected and advanced American honor.[59] The wars also witnessed the first, but far from the last, instance of regime change in a distant country. As in many of our "small wars," we took on an enemy that was comparatively weak, albeit elusive. And the wars indicate that America's assertions of power throughout the world are frequently guided by ideological as well as practical, defensive concerns. Americans viewed the Barbary Wars as battles against false religion, and as wars against tyranny. Americans used their growing power to push American liberty into the far corners of the world.

b. "Butcher and Bolt": Americans in the South Pacific

One of the more colorful veterans of the Barbary Wars was David Porter, whose exploits illustrate other dimensions of early American international embroilments. Porter was a volatile and strong-willed man. As a young sailor, he had killed a Baltimore tavernkeeper who asked him to leave his pub. In war, Porter was in his element. Promoted to lieutenant at the age of nineteen, he fought with distinction in the early years of the Barbary Wars. He was aboard the *Philadelphia* when the ship was captured, and he remained in captivity for eighteen months. He was deployed again during the War of 1812 as captain of the *Essex*, assigned to disrupt British commercial activity. His was the first American military ship to reach the Pacific, where he harassed British whalers around the Galapagos Islands. The strangest part of his career took place in the South Pacific.

In October 1813, the *Essex* arrived at Nukahiva, an island of the Marquesas chain. The ship needed servicing, and Porter was reluctant to sail close to South America for fear of encounters with the British. When they docked, Porter and his crew were greeted by the tribesmen and women of the cannibal Taaeh tribe, whose chief permitted Porter and his men to camp on the beach. In return for this hospitality, however, the chief asked that Porter help him in a war against another tribe, the Happahs. Porter agreed, and sent a message to the Happahs—an offer of peace backed by a threat of war. The Happahs ignored the offer and the threat, and were soon attacking the Taaehs again. Porter sent Lieutenant John Downes inland to teach the natives a lesson, but 3,000 to 4,000 Happahs waited for them in the mountains, and the Americans were beaten back. They were able to kill a few Happahs and capture several, which the Taaeh beat to death with clubs, using their bones for "necklaces and fan handles." Somehow the Happahs learned their lesson and made peace. In the safety of the truce, Porter's men built a small village, Madisonville, which was completed on November 19, 1813. During the celebration, Porter announced that the Taaehs had been adopted "into the great American family, whose pure republican policy approaches so near their own."[60]

Porter's wars were not over. The Typee tribe declared war on the Happahs and the Taaehs, both now allied with the United States. Porter sent thirty-five of his own men along with 5,000 natives to Typee, where they were initially repelled and forced back to Madisonville. Fearing for the safety of the American settlement, Porter led a larger force of Americans to attack Typee again; on November 30, 1813,

> the Americans, accompanied by Taaeh allies, made the almost vertical descent down a narrow path into the Typees' valley, a placid enclave nine miles long and three miles across, dotted with coconut and breadfruit trees. Before long, "the spears and stones were flying from the bush in every direction." The captain sent a message to the Typees that unless they ceased hostilities at once their villages would be burned. This message being ignored, the sailors marched the length of the valley, fighting every inch of the way, their progress marked by "a long line of smoking ruins." By day's end the battle was over. The Americans had won. Leaving behind "a scene of desolation and horror," Porter and his men returned to Madisonville.[61]

On December 9, 1813, Porter guided the *Essex* away from the island, leaving Lieutenant James Gamble in charge of Madisonville with a handful of Americans and some captured British sailors. Madison's State Department, despite the high honor of having the fort named for the president, did not respond to Porter's request to annex the island.

"Butcher and bolt"—that describes the conduct of Americans in many of their early encounters around the world: "Yankees arrive with the best of intentions, but soon find themselves sucked into the vortex of war. During the nineteenth century this pattern would repeat itself, from the Falklands to Formosa, from Sumatra to Samoa, from China to Chile. After killing some natives, the Americans seldom stayed long; nor did they usually involve themselves much in local politics.... Sometimes [they concluded] a trade treaty; at other times, [they achieved] simply the satisfaction of having instilled fear of the Stars and Stripes."[62] At times, American naval commanders acted without instructions from

Washington. Porter had no orders to build a fort or to get himself and his men into the middle of a tribal war. Officials at home renounced colonialism, but far from home and without oversight or guidance of elected civilians, ship captains could jolly well do what they pleased. Even when Washington gave the swashbuckling captains a disapproving look, they were aware of what the growing nation owed to the American navy: "Congress maintained only a small navy whose peacetime mission was to police the world, enforcing Western standards of behavior, protecting U.S. commerce, and serving as a general adjunct to U.S. diplomacy. No matter how tiny, the navy had little trouble overawing pirates and tribesmen with its vastly superior technology and training. With the navy's help, U.S. exports soared from $20 million in 1789 to $334 million in 1860. In short, naval captains were doing more or less the same job performed today by the World Trade Organization: integrating the world around the principle of free trade."[63] Freelance imperialism has been a recurring feature of American history.

c. Manifest Destiny: Conquest of a Continent

Today, our destiny to stretch from Atlantic to Pacific is so manifest that we take it very much for granted. It was not so when the idea of manifest destiny was first proposed in 1845 by John L. O'Sullivan in the *Democratic Review*. "The last order of civilization, which is democratic," O'Sullivan wrote, "received its first existence in this country." That was providential, for this is precisely the kind of country the world needs to establish a free society:

> A land separated from the influences of ancient arrangement, peculiar in its position, productions, and extent, wide enough to hold a numerous people, admitting, with facility, intercommunications and trade, vigorous and fresh from the hand of God, was requisite for the full and broad manifestation of the free spirit of the new-born democracy.
>
> The far-reaching and boundless future will be the era of American greatness. In its magnificent domain of space and time, the nation of many nations is destined to manifest to mankind the excellence of divine principles . . . her high example shall smite unto death the tyranny of kings, hierarchs, and oligarchs.[64]

Part II: Americanism

All of the tenants of Americanism are there, if subdued and with their biblical sources somewhat suppressed: America is the eschatological order of civilization; we are separated from everything old, a new Adamic people, an Eden, a Providential Israel in a new Canaan; given this identity and this future, America has a vocation to shine the light of our example to the world and to smite down by "high example" everything tyrannical. It is inaccurate to call this original declaration of manifest destiny a "secularization" of the Puritan vision, for the religious tonalities remain strong. It is not a "secularization" of a religious vision; it is an "Americanization" of a Christian one.[65] If the westward course of empire was an effort to escape from Calvin,[66] it was unsuccessful. You can take the American away from New England, remove him even from the little New Englands of the Midwest, but you cannot easily take the New England from the American. As we spread west, we remained devotees of Americanism.

It is very much in keeping with the American character that we expanded across the continent by purchase rather than by sheer conquest.[67] Between 1803 and 1898, the United States bought Louisiana, East Florida, the Pacific Northwest, Texas, California, New Mexico, Arizona, Alaska, and the Philippines. We got nearly two billion acres at a cost of $97 million.[68] We also purchased commercial outposts or harbor rights in many places around the world. Purchase and conquest, as we shall see, were not necessarily exclusive.

Seamen were not the only Americans to run ahead of official American policy. Even the expansion of Americans across the continental United States was less a guided policy from Washington than an expression of American impatience and restlessness:

> As one Mexican official observed, the process would begin with private Americans "introducing themselves into the territory they covet, upon pretense of commercial negotiations, or of the establishment of colonies, with or without the assent of the Government to which it belongs." The American-born population would grow until it outnumbered everyone else. Then the Americans would begin demanding their democratic "rights" from local authorities. When the authorities refused, as they had to, the Americans would start stirring up trouble, often with local Indian tribes. It was only a matter of time before the United States government stepped in, insisting its interests were affected by the trouble on its borders. Then began

the diplomatic negotiations, which invariably resulted in new territorial agreements favorable to the United States. Of course, sometimes [as in Florida] the United States skipped all these steps and simply invaded the territory.[69]

Even where private citizens ran ahead of federal oversight and control, the federal government eventually gave its imprimatur, whether because it was unable or because it was unwilling to curtail American restlessness.[70] In conflicts with Native Americans, the problem was usually one of ability. Washington's Secretary of War, Henry Knox, blamed white settlers for their problems with the Indians, and he predicted that American treatment of natives would cast a "black cloud of injustice and inhumanity . . . over our national character."[71] Knox believed that the "independent nations and tribes of the Indians ought to be considered as foreign nations, not as the subjects of any particular States."[72] For the first decades after independence, this viewpoint was official, assumed in numerous treaties with various tribes. Settlers violated treaties almost as soon as they were written,[73] but what could Knox do? "Either one or the other party must remove to a greater distance," Knox said, "or the Government must keep them both in awe by a strong hand, and compel them to be moderate and just."[74] The latter possibility was practically impossible, and as for the former: Knox knew as well as anyone that the "one that must move" would be the natives not the settlers.

In some important cases, expansion, and the consequent displacement of Indian tribes, was not only consistent with federal policy but directed from Washington, inspired by sentiments like those expressed by John Quincy Adams: "Shall [the Indian] doom an immense region of the globe to perpetual desolation, and to hear the howlings of the tiger and the wolf silence forever the voice of human gladness? Shall the fields and the vallies which a beneficent God has framed to teem with the life of innumerable multitudes, be condemned to everlasting barrenness?" Of course not: "Heaven has not been thus inconsistent in the works of its hands."[75] In exchange, the Indians would be given the great benefit of being introduced to Christianity and American civilization. Land for their everlasting souls—it seemed a bargain to most Americans, who did not worship mother earth and who had left the lands of their fathers' graves far behind.

In the most notorious case, the Cherokees had enthusiastically embraced American civilization. By an agreement of 1819, the Cherokee

Part II: Americanism

Nation occupied portions of what became Georgia, Alabama, Tennessee, and North Carolina. They settled and quickly took to agriculture. Trade flourished, and they established towns and adopted a written constitution in 1827. Cherokees intermarried with whites, and some even owned slaves. Sequoyah invented a written Cherokee language, and many converted to Christianity and were educated in missionary schools. But the more American the Cherokee became, the more settled they remained on their traditional lands, much to the displeasure of settlers and the governor of Georgia. In 1830, the Georgia legislature, without consulting the Cherokee, declared that Georgia's laws would extend to Cherokee territory. Over the following years, President Jackson, who considered negotiations with Indian tribes "an absurdity," pushed an Indian Removal Bill through Congress, ignoring a decision of Justice Marshall's Supreme Court in favor of the Cherokee.[76] Naked power and land hunger overwhelmed law and morality, and Christian Americans pushed Christian Cherokees down the Trail of Tears. When it was all over, 8,000 Cherokees had died, and with the forced migrations of other tribes, the eastern United States was left with only 1,200 Native Americans.[77] It was all according to divine plan, since according to Jackson the Indians "unwilling to submit to the laws and the States and mingle with their population" stood in the way of God's design for America.[78]

Many American Christians took the side of the Indians. Opponents of the removal bill organized through networks of Christian colleges and voluntary societies. In the Senate, Theodore Frelinghuysen opposed the bill, and in the House, Davy Crockett sacrificed his political future with his passionate opposition to Jackson's plan. Two heroic missionaries, Samuel Worcester and Elizur Butler, refused to leave Cherokee lands when the tribe was expelled, and were condemned by the Georgia government to four years of hard labor. Despite brutal treatment and a promise of pardon if they would acknowledge Georgia's jurisdiction over the Cherokee, the two held out and eventually appealed to the Supreme Court in *Worcester v. Georgia*.[79] Jackson's treatment of the Cherokees and other Indians exposes the reality behind Jacksonian democracy: "In the first place it was about the extension of white supremacy across the North American continent,"[80] a racially tinged modulation of the original Americanist eschatology and mission.

Jackson used the prospect of European nations allying with the Indians to stir up support for Indian removal, a tactic that instantly transformed a program of expansion into a program of anti-colonial defense. In fighting Indians, Americans were fighting the re-colonization of the American continent by the tyrannical powers of the old world.[81] It was not the first time that America's leaders had been (or pretended to be) fearful about European threats to the republic. Monroe's speech of 1823 arose from similar fears of the Holy Alliance's designs on America. "Russia might take California, Peru, Chili," John Quincy Adams wrote in his diary while serving as Monroe's Secretary of State. "France [might take] Mexico—where we know she has been intriguing to get a monarch under a prince of the House of Bourbon, as at Buenos Ayres. And Great Britain, as her last resort, if she could not resist this course of things, would take at least the island of Cuba for her share of the scramble. Then what would be our situation—England holding Cuba, France Mexico?"[82] It seemed that strengthening the federal government's ability to respond to threats was the only solution. That was undesirable, however, because it endangered the republic from another direction. But the dilemma was a false once, since the threats were wildly exaggerated. The Holy Alliance had no designs on Latin America, and the British and French were, as it turned out, no obstacle to American expansion across the continent. Europeans were preoccupied with European struggles, and increasingly with their own imperial schemes in the Middle East, Asia, and Africa. Recolonizing America was far from their minds.[83] Fear seems an odd motivation for aggressive expansion, but, as we saw in chapter 1, fear has always been a central motivation of Babelic imperialism.

James K. Polk resorted to a similar tactic to justify his war against Mexico in 1846, his seizure of California, and his purchase of the Oregon Territory from the British. He argued in an 1845 speech that the Europeans intended to set up European power bases in the hemisphere in order to establish the "doctrine" of a "balance of power." Polk and his allies cited a statement from French leader François Guizot, who had stated that it was not in France's interests for the American continent to be dominated by a single power to foment fears about European designs. "Balance of power" became the bogeyman of the house. Senator Lewis Cass declared that balance of power "is nothing more or less than a balance to maintain monarchical institutions under the guise of supporting a necessary equality."[84] Anti-Catholic animus was intertwined with the fear of European intervention. Despite a series of republican revolutions in Latin America, Protestant North America remained skeptical that Catholicism, with its "monarchical" church government and its division of loyalties, was consistent with free government on the Americanist model.

Texas had been independent from Mexico since the Texas revolt in 1836 ("Remember the Alamo!"). It was a classic case of American settlers running ahead of official American policy. The Mexican government offered favorable conditions to American settlers in Texas, and many moved there. Religion, culture, and the issue of slavery divided American settlers from the Mexicans, but, in something of a repeat of the American Revolution, the struggle came to a head over taxation, economic independence, and constitutional issues.[85] Once independent, Texas stood in an ambiguous position vis-à-vis the U.S. government and also carried on a border dispute with Mexico. Texans claimed that their territory reached to the Rio Grande, while Mexicans claimed territory north to the Arkansas and the Nueces Rivers.[86]

For a decade, Texas remained independent, but in 1845 Congress voted to annex the republic and make it the twenty-eighth state of the United States. Texas's border dispute with Mexico was now America's border dispute with Mexico, and Polk acted to provoke a decisive conflict. Mexico had already declared the annexation of Texas an "act of aggression," which made it easy for Polk to get something going. In April 1846, a Mexican force attacked a platoon of American soldiers under the command of Captain Seth Thorton, who were investigating reports that Mexicans had crossed the Rio Grande near where General Zachary Taylor's army was camped. Two weeks later, Taylor's report reached the White House, and Polk, already eager to declare war on Mexico, had his pretext to respond to what he called a Mexican invasion of "our territory" and Mexican wrong of "shedding American blood on American soil."[87] It was not an accident. Polk had dispatched Taylor in June 1845 to "approach as near the boundary line, the Rio Grande, as prudence will dictate."[88] It was the first example of a method of war that would be repeated regularly throughout American history: Pick a militarily weaker opponent, provoke the weaker party but wait for it to strike first, cry foul when the strike comes, and initiate a savage "defensive" war.[89] The venerable John Quincy Adams smelled a rat. He accused Polk of "unscrupulous suppression" of information and of manipulation of the public, actions that demonstrated to Adams "how utterly insufficient the reservation of power of declaring war to Congress is as a check upon the will of the President."[90] Mexico was partly to blame: They foolishly took the bait and war was on.

Polk wanted a quick and painless war, but he did not get it. Soon enough, American troops took Mexico City, but when the final casualty figures were in, 12,518 Americans were dead and the United States had spent $100 million.[91] Characteristically, America paid for the territory and gave sizable compensation to the Mexican government. Polk also hoped that the war would cause Americans to coalesce behind a great cause, but that too was a chimerical hope. Texas was in the Union, but was Texas a slave or free state? Sectional battles were not pacified by the annexation and conquest of Texas; they were exacerbated. Still, in seizing territory to the Rio Grande, Polk had fulfilled one of his stated aims as president.[92]

Polk's policies were guided by the vision of expansionist republicanism articulated by Madison and Monroe: "our system may be safely extended to the utmost bounds of our territorial limits," he said, and as it is extended "so far from being weakened, will be stronger."[93] But Polk did something new: He "was the first American president who could reasonably be called an expansionist by force of arms."[94]

Conclusion

In early American entanglements around the world, we acted neither more or less foolishly or wickedly than other nations have. Our treatment of American Indians remains a dark blot on our history, and it ill-prepared us for dealing with other forms of tribalism, such as Islam.[95] Our problem is not so much the history itself as the mythology or ideology of Americanism that blinds us to the real force of our history. The heresy of Americanism is a shield that allows us to act like Babel while convincing ourselves that we are fulfilling a divine mission on behalf of the human race. Such blindness became more dangerous as America assumed its preeminent place in the world.

Conclusion to Part II

The United States is one of the great Christian nations of the modern age, but it is a post-Christendom Christian nation, a nation founded after the metapolitical framework of Christendom had collapsed in Europe. When Christendom crumbled, so too did the theological, moral, and institutional constraints that it placed on medieval polities and rulers. Chief among these constraints was the church herself, God's empire, the bridal city that rules the kings of the earth. Beginning with the Puritans, and more insistently since, heretical Americanist typology has pushed the church to the political margins and replaced it with the American nation itself. America, and American Christians especially, have found no effective replacements for the checks built into the pluralistic system of Christendom. Checks and balances among the branches of the federal government are an inadequate guarantor of liberty. No American church is allowed to become independent or powerful enough to challenge American policy effectively; few try. Madison's scheme worked: Sects proliferate and proliferate, with the result that Christian witness to America is fragmented and diffused. Even Christian leaders in the United States are not in any real way accountable to the officers of God's *imperium*. Whatever their private convictions, public officials are not held publicly accountable to King Jesus. When was the last time an American politician was excommunicated? When was the last time an excommunication had any *effect* on American politics?

Christians do not try to check American power because American Christians are usually devotees of Americanism. Americanism rarely appears in pure form. It is usually mingled with traditional religious convictions and practices, but Americanism distorts even orthodox religious convictions because, in the absence of the metapolitics of

Conclusion to Part II

Christendom, Americanism is the *de facto* political theology for most American Christians. American churches cannot critique and confront American power because promotion of Americanism is what American churches stand for. Individual Christians do not have the virtues necessary to function as citizens of God's *imperium* because American churches have discipled them to function as citizens of the American *imperium* instead.

On the world stage, Americanism is an expansionist creed. Since America is the new Israel, America is the fulfillment of God's political purposes in the world, and since America is the harbinger of the world's future, America is an inherently expansionist project. Early in our history, we did not have the power to impose our will on the world. But as our power increased, Americanism was there, able to impel a Babelic form of imperialism.

PART III

Between Babel and Beast

CHAPTER 6

American Babel

Europe's secularization is its long retreat from Christendom, the disestablishment of the church, the decline of active Christianity, the migration of the holy from the church to the nation. Americanism is impervious to secularization of the European variety because America was never part of Christendom to begin with. America has no established church to disestablish, no throne to disentangle from altar, and no altar either. By the time America was founded, the holy had already well nigh migrated from table to church to nation. The heretical faith of Americanism is from the outset directed toward what is in the full Augustinian sense a "secular" reality, a reality of the *saeculum*, though one identified as a new departure in history, a *novum saeculum*. It cannot get any more secular than it began. Yet because it is thoroughly infused with the fervor and symbolism and rhetoric of biblical faith, Americanism is a wholly religious *saeculum*.

At the outset of the twentieth century and even at the outset of the twenty-first, Americans remain nearly as religious as they ever were, more or less smoothly combining progressivism in politics, technology, and culture with the most intense religious energy of any Western nation. As the United States entered the twentieth century, her sense of national purpose remained as thoroughly infused by American typology and American eschatology as it had been in 1620 or 1789 or 1840, though her international actions had become more overtly imperial.

Part III: Between Babel and Beast

Soon it would also have a chance to refresh itself by another massive sacrifice, this time on a global scale.

Expansion under New World-Conditions

At the turn of the twentieth century, the social gospel leader Josiah Strong opened his eyes to find that the world had changed. Since America's inception, he thought, she had been innocently isolated from the rest of the world, a maiden among the nations, but the time for luxurious irresponsibility had long past. New world conditions pertained, a new world order had emerged, and the United States needed to shoulder its share of the burden of supporting that order. Commerce had expanded everywhere, so that American interests were global, and it should be U.S. policy to protect and promote commerce. The nineteenth century had changed everything, developing new technologies, new ideas, a new civilization. America faced three choices: She could drift along without a plan or chart, "sail into this, to us, unknown sea recklessly and with a false chart," or boldly enter the world with a true chart. Strong's prescription was unambiguous: "the only wise course for us is frankly to recognize the changed conditions of the world and intelligently to adapt to them a new world policy."[1]

For Strong, this task was not primarily commercial, military, or political, but moral. The aim of the new world policy must be to advance "the noblest ministry to the new world life." He scoffed at Machiavellians who claimed that international politics had to be pursued amorally, and argued instead that the new world conditions require the development of a "new world conscience." It cannot be the case that "the Ten Commandments and the Sermon on the Mount have nothing to do with politics, either national or international." It was not possible that "a Christian statesman must needs be a Dr. Jekyll and Mr. Hyde; as if principles might bind men individually and yet not collectively; as if God might be the Ruler of nations, while yet nations are independent of His law; as if nations might be and must be selfish, while individuals are bound to be altruistic!"[2] Providence has prepared the way for a new, Christian public ethics, "a new political philosophy and ethics which will meet the new world conditions."[3] America need not deny her strength and energy, but on the contrary deploy that very strength for moral purposes, binding "ourselves with the law of right and justice, aye, and of benevolence too."[4] We would not be right to shirk our international obligations out of a desire to keep our hands clean of the dirty business of politics. The new world order requires a world police, and we should pay our share of the cost of watching the global neighborhood.

Moral action need not be nonviolent, Strong argued. Tolstoy and his followers sacrifice common sense to a theory of nonviolence, but logic and Christian morality make distinctions. He admitted that "the use of force may be selfish or benevolent." Force, too, is a last resort. But it is not necessarily selfish, and in fact "many instances might be given in which the use of force is not only not selfish, but is evidently benevolent." Nations as well as individuals must apply the Golden Rule, doing to other nations what we might wish them, had they the power, to do to us.[5] Among the "Anglo-Saxon peoples," armies are being transformed from instruments of destruction into a "reconstructive organization" that promotes "law, order, civilization." Britain's military fought famine and disease in India. Anglo-Saxon armies leave tax relief, railroad lines, open markets, and institutions of liberty in their wake. Strong did not believe Anglo-Saxon power was an end in itself. It served the interests of God's coming kingdom. But for Strong, as for many Americans, the spread of American institutions and the coming of the kingdom were difficult to distinguish.

Strong's exhibit #1 of the beneficial use of power was the American annexation of the Philippines.[6] The Filipinos lacked the necessary character and civilization to be free and self-governing, and "as part of a great world life, these people cannot be permitted a lawless independence." They are children, and the United States has fortunately taken a paternal interest in them, to bring them out of childhood into the family of free nations. Principles of Christianity and Anglo-Saxon civilization must govern the U.S. intervention in the Philippines: "It should in every particular aim at the well-being of the Filipinos. We must accept this new responsibility as a trust for civilization. We want no tribute-bearing colonies."[7] Unwise as it is to play the Don Quixote and tilt at every global windmill, we must accept the responsibility that God has placed upon us, since, as Emerson said, "Our whole history appears like a last effort of Divine Providence in behalf of the human race."[8] Strong argued that all the missionaries of his day agreed that the United States needed to take more leadership in the world, and in that missionary zeal the Wilsonian dream of a League of Nations and the elimination of war

Part III: Between Babel and Beast

was gestating.⁹ Strong could have sung Kipling's "White Man's Burden," without Kipling's irony. Strong was an apologist for American Babel, a world remade in America's image.

Americanism took its faith in the regenerating power of violent combat into the twentieth century, too. The Civil War had proven to some that a new nation could be born through blood, and the United States entered the Great War with similar dreams. Nearly everyone in America saw World War I in religious terms, and Theodore Roosevelt spoke for many when he summed up the war's aim as "righteousness." He proposed in 1914 an alliance "among all the civilized military powers" that would establish "a world league for the peace of righteousness." Though he envisioned a world at peace, Roosevelt had long urged Americans to be ready for war if they found that "the path which leads toward righteousness . . . also leads to war."¹⁰ Though a pacifist, Congregational minister Charles Jefferson of Broadway Tabernacle in Manhattan, believed that the war would bring in a "new era": "Through the smoke of battle I see a fairer world. Across the fields of blood there streams the light of a brighter day."¹¹ Others were more aggressive. On April 1, 1917, Randolph McKim preached a sermon titled "America Summoned to a Holy War," in which he proclaimed that "I have no hesitation . . . in saying that the voice of a just God summons us to this War and that it is in the highest sense of the word a Holy War." Great as the Crusades were, they "shrink into insignificance compared with the crusade to which we are summoned at the present moment."¹² At a New Jersey convention, Methodist ministers joined in singing "The Battle Hymn of the Republic," and a writer in the *Atlantic Monthly* expressed the hope that the Good Friday of the nation's war effort would eventually issue in an Easter when "the King of Glory may come in for the refreshment, the re-creation, the salvation of all humanity." Harry Emerson Fosdick agreed: Though Christ was now "crucified afresh by the sin of the world," he prayed that "after this Calvary" the Lord would "grant us . . . an Easter day and a triumphant Christ."¹³ The Great War was a virtual Armageddon, and a senator read a poem by that title into the record that included these lines:

> For from the beginning, 'twas decreed that God should lead
> Humanity e'er onward, upward, 'til beneath
> Blest Eden's tree of life all men shall brethren be
> In brotherhood of mutual love and trust and peace.

In this last apocalyptic battle, though, America stood in for the conquering Christ.

Soldierly martyrdom was to be the particular instrument for this world-redeeming atonement.[14] McKim pointed to Christian soldiers as the embodiment of the Christian virtue of self-sacrifice.[15] Above and beyond individual soldiers, though, there was the role of America herself, the "suffering servant" among the nations. For Frederick Lynch, America was the "Christ-Nation to the other nations of the world," and Charles Brown, the dean of Yale Divinity School, asked, "May we not believe that this country, strong and brave, generous and hopeful, is called by God to be in its own way a Messianic nation?"[16] For Lyman Abbot, the United States was the head-crushing deliverer promised by Genesis 3: "Now the head of the serpent is erect, it is running out its forked tongue, its eyes are red with wrath; its very breath is poison. We have a difficult time to get our heel on its head, but when we do, we will grind it to powder."[17] Presbyterian Joseph Odell argued in 1918 that America, and the American church, could herself be reborn through the war, redeemed to evaluate everything in the "pure white light of wisdom" and ready for "cosmic rehabilitation." Through the events of the war, "a manumitted mob has crossed the Red Sea and asks the nearest way to the Promised Land."[18] In the aftermath of the war, gripped with the same Americanist fervor, Woodrow Wilson, child of the manse, drew up a Fourteen Point plan to remake the world in our image, a constitution for all nations.[19]

Rules of Realism

Not all Americans of the twentieth century spoke in such highly wrought apocalyptic terms about our national mission, but the Americanist faith was so deeply entrenched in the American psyche that even realists aimed to ensure that the world played by American rules. One of the architects of twentieth-century American order was John Foster Dulles, secretary of state under Eisenhower. Like Strong, Dulles was a devout Christian, and his outlook on foreign affairs was rooted in his religious views and the philosophical training he received from Henri Bergson at the Sorbonne. He was a thoroughly establishment figure. His grandfather served as secretary of state under Harrison, and John Foster had accompanied him on various international excursions. After working for several years as an attorney, he turned his attention to international affairs. As he viewed things, peace and civilization would only survive if the United States not only took the lead but exercised dominance over the globe. He helped establish the Council on Foreign Relations, and wrote an article in the inaugural issue of the CFR's journal, *Foreign Affairs*, in 1922. During the twenties and thirties, he developed his theories about America's global reach, and in 1939 published *War, Peace, and Change*.

Dulles's sober and realist views, chastened by two world wars, differed significantly from the idealistic religious patriotism of Strong. According to Dulles, human beings are inherently and ineradicably selfish, and this selfishness means that human beings, individually and collectively, are plagued by constant dissatisfaction. Specifically, the "conflict of selfish desires assumed, in its simplest form, a struggle between those who primarily are satisfied and wish to retain that which they have and those who are dissatisfied and wish to acquire at the expense of others."[20] Globally, the haves and have-nots are constantly in tension, and this leads to what Dulles identified as the boundary-barrier situation. Some nations, known as the "group authority," have power to make rules, and these rules inevitably deny some of the wishes of those subjected to the rules. In responding to the demands of the have-nots, who do not make the rules, the group authority cannot accommodate to those demands because of the territorial, commercial, legal, and other boundaries that stand in the way. By Dulles's reckoning, the United States functioned in the mid-twentieth century as the group authority that would make the rules for everyone else. He hoped that the boundary of America's rules would be so expansive and impenetrable that no other nation, or realistic combination of nations, could effectively counter it.[21]

The proper aim of American policy was thus not to preserve or extend freedom or to end war, as fervid Wilsonians hoped. In place of freedom or the spread of civilization, Dulles argued that American policy should be guided above all by security, defined as "freedom from violent attack upon person and property."[22] Especially during the Cold War, when Dulles served as secretary of state, he argued that security demanded an expansion of America's sphere of influence. George Kennan's plan for containment would not be enough, and if America were going to expand the boundaries of its sovereignty, it would have to promote liberation of Soviet-controlled territories. With his brother

Allen, then director of the CIA, Dulles conceived the idea of using the intelligence agency to expand American rule-making. It was out of this matrix of ideas that the CIA conceived the plot to remove the prime minister of Iran, Mohammed Mossadegh, who was suspected of Soviet leanings, and to replace him with the pro-English General Fazlollah Zahedi.[23]

Dulles's realist foreign policy had very different motivations and aims than Strong's new world policy:

> Ironically given Dulles's religious background and his frequent references to spiritualism and the missionary impulse that had been historically integral to U.S. expansion, the compulsion to "uplift" less civilized peoples became a comparatively low priority. In this regard he differed from Eisenhower, who, again ironically, was more spiritual. But he agreed that the highest priority must be the security and defense of the American way of life. Toward this end Dulles had advocated expanding America's group authority. In light of his geopolitical zero-sum calculus, this meant diminishing that of the Soviets by enveloping within Washington's patrolled boundaries all peoples and territories within Moscow's. . . . The U.S. empire would grow at the expense of its allies'. That growth would strengthen the Free World's existing boundaries even as it extended them to the nonaligned periphery. America's long-standing anticolonialism would produce an innovative imperium. It may not have extended liberty, but it stymied a system that by definition was antiliberty.[24]

Radical as the differences between Wilson (and his Great War clerical chorus) and Dulles were, they converged at a crucial point: American policy must establish, ensure, and maintain the dominance of America. Whether the dominance was of American ideals or America as a great power dictating the terms of a world system made comparatively little difference: Either way, Americanism encouraged Americans of the twentieth century to play a Babelic role in the world.

America's current standing in the world is a fulfillment of Dulles's vision of an American rule-making hegemony. Inspired by Americanism, it fulfills the hope for an American Century, in which "Washington rules" become more and more the rules of the global system. Yet, in recent decades, the comparatively restrained security policy of Dulles has been reinfused with missionary fervor. On both sides of the establishment political spectrum are shared assumptions about American order and America's place among nations. America is the cutting edge of historical development, given a special mission to transform the world into its own image and to extend the range of its rule-making authority. We are the indispensable nation. This demand for America's "global leadership" requires a major military presence in every part of the world:

> The Pax Americana that Bush inherited from Bill Clinton derived from one very large but indisputable fact: over the previous century, the United States had achieved by force of arms a dominant position in four distinct regions of critical geopolitical and economic importance. Thanks to NATO, the United States remained in 2001 the leading power in Europe, even as the Cold War, the ostensible rationale for that alliance, faded into memory. With its commitment of 100,000 troops in East Asia—a commitment viewed as permanent despite a lapse of three decades since the last significant armed conflict there—the United States was also the leading power in the Pacific. With its various bases and garrisons established in and around the Persian Gulf subsequent to the war with Iraq, it was the guarantor of order and stability in that region as well. And that didn't even count America's sway over the Western Hemisphere, unquestioned for a century.[25]

The convergence of American foreign policy aims is neatly illustrated by a 2008 *Foreign Affairs* article in which former Secretary of State Condoleezza Rice sketched "a uniquely American realism" that implies that it is "America's job to change the world, and in its own image." Building democracies is not for visionaries anymore, but is "now an urgent component of our national interests" and one that "we will be engaged in . . . for years to come." Americans, after all, have never believed "we are powerless to change the world," and we have proven again and again that we are capable of achievements beyond "the boundaries of what most thought realistic at the time." She saw the democratization of Iraq as largely a success story, and one that will be repeated throughout the Middle East: "Our long-term partnerships with Afghanistan and Iraq, to which we must remain deeply committed, our new relationships with Central Asia, and our long-standing partnerships in the Persian Gulf provide a solid geo-strategic foundation for the generational work ahead of helping to bring about a better, more democratic, and more prosperous Middle East."²⁶ Realism and apocalypticism kiss each other, joined in the warm embrace of a muted (perhaps Episcopalian) version of the overarching Americanist faith.

Exporting Democracy?

Anyone who thinks that apocalyptic political rhetoric is a thing of the past, or who thinks that Americans have given up thinking of ourselves as a messianic nation, or who thinks that we have given up earlier childhood beliefs in the redemptive power of blood and missiles, or who thinks "we are all realists now" has not been listening carefully to the rhetoric of the war on terror.²⁷ George W. Bush did not invent the notion that America exists to "rid the world of evil" or to enact "infinite justice" using bombs and ground troops. He was speaking as a high priest of Americanism.²⁸ Yet Americanism frequently functions less as a practical guide for American policy and more as an ideological cover for policies with very different roots and goals. Americanism is a mythology that justifies American power and explains—and sometimes explains away—American action. Americanist rhetoric sometimes claims that the United States exercises its power cherubically, leaving other nations to themselves. Scratch Americanist rhetoric, and we find that the reality is often otherwise. Intellectually, Americanism is inconsistent with a deep commitment to self-determination for other nations. We believe everyone should be like us, and we believe that everyone *wants* to be. And we take steps to help them become like us, sometimes whether they want to or not. But beneath the rhetoric, are we doing anything more than promoting American interests? Over the past century, American policy has claimed, off and on, to be committed to the promotion of democracy and republican liberty. Scratch Americanist rhetoric, and the reality beneath the skin is often un-American and undemocratic. These inconsistencies are perhaps inherent in Babelic imperialism: Babels call the nations to a glorious vision of a single tower and city and speak with a single lip, but the aim is finally to promote Babel's interests and advance Babel's power.

Before and especially during the Cold War, the United States regularly intervened covertly or overtly to topple regimes that, for one reason or another, did not suit America's interests. Early in the twentieth century, after Congress decided against the construction of a canal through

Part III: Between Babel and Beast

Nicaragua, the United States began to view the nationalist President Jose Santos Zelaya as a threat to American interests. Zelaya regulated American businesses and received a 1.25 million pound loan from Europe to build a coast-to-coast railroad. Inspired by Theodore Roosevelt's codicil to the Monroe Doctrine, which threatened an "exercise of an international peace power" to any Latin American country engaged in "chronic wrongdoing," and with the assistance of business cronies, Taft's secretary of state, Philander Knox, plotted to overthrow Zelaya. After several unsuccessful attempts, he was able to stir up an American media campaign that denounced Zelaya's regime as a "reign of terror" and "the menace of Central America." Taft decided he could not "tolerate and deal with such a medieval despot." American businessmen in Nicaragua hired a provincial governor, General Juan Jose Estrada, to lead a coup. Two American adventurers, Lee Roy Cannon and Leonard Groce, assisted the rebels, were caught, and were executed for rebellion. Knox used the occasion to issue a letter to Zelaya: "It is notorious that President Zelaya has almost continually kept Central America in tension or turmoil," it began. And it concluded that "the government of the United States is convinced that the revolution represents the will of a majority of the Nicaraguan people more than does the government of President Zelaya." The letter was delivered on December 1, 1909. By December 16, Zelaya had resigned and gone into exile. It was "the first real American coup."[29]

It was not the last. The United States helped Ngo Dinh Diem take power in South Vietnam in 1955, but later gave at least tacit approval to his overthrow in 1963, which ended, to President Kennedy's horror, in Diem's brutal assassination. The American ambassador to Vietnam, Henry Cabot Lodge, helped organize the coup partly because Diem expressed his openness to a negotiated settlement with communist insurgents. In the 1970s, Nixon administration officials had decided to overthrow Salvador Allende Gossens from the presidency even before he took his seat as the democratically elected leader of Chile. Despite our long support of Manuel Noriega in Panama, the United States overthrew him when he was no longer useful. He was only one of a dozen brutes supported by the United States while they preyed on their people.

Democratic elections have not protected leaders from American subversion. Most infamously, the CIA led the 1953 overthrow of the elected prime minister of Iran, Mohammed Mossadegh, reinstalling the Shah and setting Iran up for an Islamic revolution whose consequences are clearly still with us. In Guatemala, the CIA orchestrated the overthrow of the democratically elected President Jacobo Arbenz Guzman in 1954.[30] For a decade and a half, the CIA repeatedly attempted to overthrow the government of Laos following its 1957 elections.[31] In 1961, we helped overthrow President Jose Velasco in Ecuador, and two years later, we overthrew the democratically elected government of Juan Bosch in the Dominican Republic.[32] In 1965, the CIA was involved in the overthrow of the democratically elected Sukarno in Indonesia, who was replaced by the aggressively anticommunist General Suharto.[33] Father Jean-Bertrand Aristide, elected in a landslide in Haiti's 1990 election and a sharp critic of U.S. policy in Haiti, was deposed within a year.[34] Like Babel, we claim to guarantee international order, but often spread confusion.

During the Cold War, most of those overthrown were tarred as "communist sympathizers." Though no doubt some in the various American administrations believed this to be true, it was frequently sheer propaganda woven from a few thin threads. More often, nationalist rulers became obstacles to the spread of Americanism in some form or another and had to be removed. Vietnamese nationalism, Iranian nationalism, Guatemalan nationalism: none could stand in the way of the triumphant nationalism of the ages, Americanism. Given the limitations of my knowledge, and given the inclinations of my expected audience, I do not wish to overstate the case. I am not suggesting that the United States invariably supports thugs and despots, that we are always an agent of unfreedom and tyranny. At least, the U.S. record of democracy promotion and the U.S. record of honoring the sovereignty of other nations is a decidedly mixed one. Sometimes we support democracy and political liberties. Other times we do not. The promotion of democracy can hardly be viewed as our overriding framework of international action, no matter what our Americanist mythology tells us. Americanist ideology gives sacred cover to our pursuit of national interest.

It is no accident that several of these coups and covert overthrows benefited large corporations. Mossadegh was overthrown when he nationalized British petroleum interests, and Guzman initiated a land reform campaign that included redistribution of large tracts of land belonging to the American company United Fruit. In the Barbary Wars, the U.S. Navy was deployed to open sea lanes to commerce, benefiting

Part III: Between Babel and Beast

American merchants and every other trader using the Mediterranean. Recent wars in the Gulf are about many things, but one of the big things they are about is oil—oil that will keep the American economy and the American way of life chugging along, oil that also fuels the developing economies of Africa and Asia.[35] One has to be willfully blind not to see how corporate interests have determined the use of American military power. At least in some cases, the United States has been willing to exert its power illegally and immorally for specific private benefit.

Yet the United States has never pursued a policy of global free trade. Early on, inspired by Hamiltonian aims, the United States protected domestic industry until it was strong enough to compete in the larger global marketplace. More recently, the United States has pursued mainly bilateral trade agreements rather than unilateral free market policies: "Rather than following the correct British policy of adopting unilateral free trade and then allowing its hegemony to spread the norm, the United States chose the extremely acrimonious route of multilateral and more recently bilateral negotiations to reduce trade barriers. This is due to the fact that, unlike the British who have correctly seen free trade as a non-zero sum game . . . the Americans have never accepted the classical liberal case for free trade. They have always looked upon trade as a zero-sum game."[36] Apart from "a brief period between 1846 and 1861," the United States has always had protectionist economic policies. In 1901, Theodore Roosevelt stated the guiding principle of American trade policy: "Reciprocity must be treated as the handmaiden of protection. Our first duty is to see that the protection granted by the tariff in every case where it is needed is maintained, and reciprocity be sought so far as it can be safely done without injury to our home industries."[37] This is counterproductive, argues economist Deepak Lal: "by perpetuating the myth that trade is a zero-sum game and that removing tariffs can only be done on the basis of reciprocity, the United States has ensured that issues of domestic policy will inevitably spill over into trade policy." He notes the ironic fact that "one of the largest unilateral movements to free trade has occurred in China since Deng Xiaoping adopted the Open Door policy."[38]

Protectionism is good for producers in protected industries, but it is bad policy for U.S. consumers forced to buy goods artificially inflated by tariffs. It is worse for international sellers who want to enter the American market. To be sure, U.S. tariffs are on average only 4 percent, "low by historic standards." But this openness to foreign goods is selective, and allied to a form of protectionism-by-subsidy: "the most protected U.S. sectors are those in which poorer countries specialize." In particular, "Agriculture is the most protected. U.S. farmers get direct subsidies and cheap insurance if they export."[39] Food aid also assists U.S. farmers in their competition with farmers in developing countries. Instead of sending cash aid, the United States sends its surplus food "at the expense of local farmers whose produce cannot compete with the subsidized U.S. exports." The United States gives particular assistance to agriculture and "lower-end industrial technologies like textiles, clothing, shoes, and increasingly (as poorer countries move into these areas) steel and autos." As a result, "Bangladesh pays more import tariffs in the U.S. than France does!"[40] While the United States sends $84 in aid to Bangladesh, the country returns $331 million in tariffs on its American imports. The United States is not alone in this tilt against competition from poor countries: Most of the developed world has "development programs . . . full of cant."[41]

Argentina is the world's largest producer of honey, and the world's leading exporter of honey as well, nearly half of it going to sweet-toothed Americans. When American honey producers complained that Argentine honey was being "dumped" on the U.S. market, the "U.S. Department of Commerce investigated and gave the Argentine beekeepers 30 days to answer a 150-page questionnaire in English. Few beekeepers responded. . . . The result? The U.S. slapped tariffs of up to 66 percent, causing $50 million in annual sales losses for Argentina." Argentine honey was competitively priced on the U.S. market, but not because of any unfair trade practices: "Their low prices came from cheap labor costs and efficient processing plants run by a nonprofit co-op." Argentina's Minister of Production said that the real issue is that the United States wants to protect its own producers, even at higher cost to American consumers, not to mention abuse of Argentine producers: "Whatever Argentina is capable of exporting, we know that the United States will administer its own trade in such a way as to be able to protect its own producers at our expense." Despite the neoliberal rhetoric, U.S. trade policy does not promote free trade: "It privileges American interests."[42] American farmers feed the world, yet our tariff policy hampers the efforts of Latin American farmers.

Part III: Between Babel and Beast

U.S. international aid is not typically charitable or spent for development purposes. Aid advances strategic ends. Most of it goes to a small number of countries in the Middle East: "A third goes to one of the 20 richest countries in the world—Israel. A fifth goes to Egypt, which is effectively being paid not to attack Israel. Tiny Jordan, also paid not to attack Israel, rivals massive India and Russia as the next largest recipient."[43] When we add the direct aid to Israel to the aid that prevents Muslims from attacking Israel, fully half of U.S. aid "goes to prop up the small state of Israel." Significant military aid also goes to countries needed for the current set of wars—including Pakistan, Yemen, Indonesia, Qatar, and several of the former Soviet "stans."[44]

We are the richest country on earth, and simply by virtue of being the most productive and the most consumptive of nations, our behavior has a huge impact on the world economy. In addition, though, we affect the world economy—and especially the economies of smaller and developing nations—through the key position we occupy in three key international economic institutions—the International Monetary Fund, the World Bank, and the World Trade Organization. The first two were established in 1944, the IMF "to lend money to countries in balance of payments crises so that they could reduce their balance of payments deficits without having to resort to deflation," and the World Bank "to help the reconstruction of war-torn countries in Europe and the economic development of post-colonial societies."[45] After 1982's Third World debt crisis, the IMF and World Back changed their aims: "They started to exert a much stronger policy influence on developing countries" by requiring structural adjustments to their economies as conditions for loans. The adjustments could be wide-ranging, including "democracy, government decentralization, central independence and corporate governance." In 1997, the IMF put limits on "the amount of debt that *private sector* companies could have" in Korea.[46] Many of the policies imposed as conditions for loans "have little to do with fixing [the borrowing country's] economy" but instead "serve the interests of the rich countries lending the money." The conditions laid on Korea's loans in 1997 would, one commentator noted, reduce trade barriers to Japanese products, open "capital markets so that foreign investors can have majority ownership of Korean firms," and "expand direct [foreign] participation in banking and other financial services." The impetus behind the IMF and World Bank policies is a one-size-fits-all neoliberal framework, which is "considered to be universally valid by the rich countries" but which ignores local and regional variations.[47]

According to Korean economist Ha-Joon Chang, the wealthy countries are "Bad Samaritans" when they insist that developing countries adopt liberal policies. Advanced countries are also hypocritical since they "used protection and subsidies, while discriminating against foreign investors" during their rise to economic might.[48] Britain and America both have "kicked away the ladder" of protectionism and domestic subsidies that helped them reach their heights. But now they want lesser economies to rise without the ladder at all. IMF and World Bank policies, in short, help open markets for American and European goods. They do not necessarily serve the interests of economic development elsewhere.[49] Rhetorically, we demand that everyone conform to "our" model, but the reality is that we do not even conform to "our" model. Our economic policies are not guided by the pursuit of free markets but by national interest; we use our power to make sure the rules for weaker nations work to our advantage.[50]

Killings Civilians

America and especially the American military take pride in its humaneness, and this is not entirely a myth. As I finished work on this book, the media reported on two American Coast Guard rescues of Iranian seamen near the Persian Gulf, and this at a time of heightened tensions between the United States and Iran over Iranian muscle-flexing in the Strait of Hormuz and Iran's nuclear program.[51] The U.S. military has been deployed in humanitarian actions and spends enormous resources building rather than breaking things. The U.S. military regularly reviews tactics and improves technologies in an effort to minimize "collateral damage."[52] Yet American power has often been the opposite of benign.

In 1923, a conference at The Hague issued "Rules of Aerial Warfare," which proscribed "aerial bombardment for the purpose of terrorizing or damaging private property not of a military character, or of injuring non-combatants," and the United States conformed to that rule. At the beginning of World War II, President Roosevelt urged the combatants "under no circumstances [to] undertake the bombardment from the air of civilian populations or of unfortified cities."[53] The Hague conference's prohibition of targeting noncombatants was consistent with centuries-old standards of just war theory. For a war to be just, both the cause and the conduct of war have to be just. According to Grotius' influential formula, combatants should take "the greatest precaution . . . against involving the innocent in danger, except in cases of extreme urgency and utility." Citing classical and biblical authorities, he argued that women and children should be spared, and even men "whose modes of life are entirely removed from the use of arms."[54] This has been one of the principal standards of the Christian notion of *jus in bello* since the theory was first formulated.

At first, Britain, France, and Germany agreed to limit their bombs to military targets. In May 1940, the RAF began bombing civilian targets, including oil plants, factories, and railway yards near the cities of Berlin, Hamburg, and Bremen. In the same month, German bombs destroyed the center of Rotterdam. Germany did not begin bombing England until August 1940, and for a time they were strictly prohibited from bombing cities. The first German bombing of London in mid-August was accidental, but in September Hitler gave the order to begin bombing civilian targets, retaliating for Allied bombing of Berlin. During Operation Blitz, which lasted for nine months in 1940–41, Germany unrelentingly attacked London, Coventry, Birmingham, and Manchester, slaughtering 60,000 English civilians and demolishing some 2 million homes.[55] In the Pacific theater, the Japanese bombed Shanghai, Nanjing, Wuhan, and other cities. In Chongqing alone, they killed nearly 12,000 residents. After the beginning of 1942, Britain intensified the attacks, bombing Essen, Kiel, Stuttgart, Mannheim, and Rostock. British planes dropped 7,000 tons of bombs on Hamburg and killed around 45,000 people.[56] By the end of the war, Churchill and Arthur Harris, the British commander in charge of aerial bombing, devoted (in the words of Max Hastings) "all available forces for the progressive, systematic destruction of the urban areas of the Reich, city block by city block, factory by factory, until the enemy became a nation of troglodytes, scratching in the ruins."[57]

Even after Pearl Harbor, the United States refused to target civilians—for a time. By 1943 they had agreed to turn a blind eye to Britain's bombing of cities while the United States kept its principles intact by focusing on military targets. As the war dragged on and on, the United States changed course. Armed with newly invented napalm and guided on night raids by perfected radars, U.S. planes joined in attacks on European cities. In some circumstances, combatants and noncombatants are difficult to distinguish. A young woman with no uniform might have a bomb strapped under her dress. But that was not the situation that produced America's policy change in the mid-1940s. America joined its allies in trying to break the will of the Axis powers by killing civilians. It was classic Girardian mimesis: We mimic our rivals and soon enough become all but indistinguishable.

On February 14–15, 1945, British and American bombers decimated Dresden, killing tens of thousands. Kurt Vonnegut, a POW in Dresden during the bombing, never got over some of the haunting sights: "When we went into them, a typical shelter, an ordinary basement usually, looked like a streetcar full of people who'd simultaneously had heart failure. Just people sitting there in their chairs, all dead."[58] On March 9–10, the United States dropped firebombs on an area of Tokyo that was almost entirely residential. Hurricane force winds spread the flames. Estimates of the dead range from 85,000 to 125,000. Fifteen square miles of the city were destroyed, leaving more than a million homeless. Between December 6, 1944, and August 13, 1945, the United States launched sixty-five raids on Tokyo, killing nearly 150,000. Bombings were extended to Nagoya, Osaka, and Kobe. According to Mark Selden's summary, during the first half of 1945, Americans demolished 40 percent of the 66 cities targeted, "destroyed 180 square miles of sixty-seven [Japanese] cities, killed more than 300,000 people, and injured an additional 400,000." The U.S. campaign slaughtered "civilian populations on a scale that had no parallel in the history of bombing,"[59] and these numbers do not include the atomic bombings of Hiroshima and Nagasaki.

The bombing of Dresden provoked protests in the United States and especially in Britain. In response to press criticism, Secretary of State Henry Stimson defended the administration's war making by saying that "our policy never has been to inflict terror bombing on civilian populations," and Stimson claimed that Dresden was a legitimate military target because it was a transportation hub.[60] It was an evasion, but an effective one. Virtually no one protested the U.S. bombing of Japanese civilians or indiscriminate devastation of Japanese cities. Dead civilians were collateral damage. We in the United States convinced ourselves, and have convinced ourselves since, that we never attack civilians. Americanist churches remained silent or cheered on the bombings. No

Part III: Between Babel and Beast

more than in the Civil War was any effective moral voice raised to challenge the sacrifices of our nationalist religion.

Since World War II, aerial bombing, including bombing of noncombatant civilians, has been a centerpiece of the American way of war. Air strikes have obvious practical advantages: Attackers are relatively safe, and are even more so today when we can deploy unmanned drones. Aerial attacks have psychological advantages too: Bombers do not grapple with their victims, never see them light up like matchsticks, never smell the piles of rotting and burning corpses they leave behind. The practice is defended by the claim that attacking civilian targets effectively breaks the will of the enemy and therefore actually saves lives. But the tallies are numbing:

- "In the last five months of World War II, American bombing killed more than 900,000 Japanese civilians, not counting the casualties from the atomic strikes against Hiroshima and Nagasaki. This is more than twice the total number of combat deaths (441,513) the United States has suffered in all its foreign wars combined."[61]

- The nuclear attacks killed over 127,000 Japanese, nearly 30 percent of the total number of Americans killed in over two centuries of war.[62]

- American bombs killed 83,793 Japanese on March 9–10, 1945, more "than the 80,942 combat fatalities the United States sustained in the Korean and Vietnam wars combined."[63]

- "More German civilians died in the three-night-long Anglo-American firebombing of Dresden than American soldiers died in World War I." One historian says that "at the time the Dresden raids constituted the largest slaughter of civilians by military forces in one place at one time since the campaigns of Genghis Khan."[64]

- "Out of a prewar population of 9.49 million, an estimated 1 million (North) Korean civilians are believed to have died as a result of the actions of American forces during the 1950–53 conflict there."[65] Gen. Curtis LeMay recalled that the Pentagon refused to grant permission to "burn down five of the biggest towns in North Korea," but observed that "over a period of three years or so . . . we burned down every town in North Korea and South Korea too." ⁶⁶ The ratio was 30:1: "Almost 34,000 American soldiers were killed during [the Korean War], meaning that U.S. forces killed approximately 30 North Korean civilians for every American soldier who died." ⁶⁷

- Casualties in Vietnam are even more difficult to estimate than in other conflicts, but "some 365,000 Vietnamese civilians are believed to have died as a result of the war during the period of American involvement." Again, the ratio is remarkable: "Eight Vietnamese civilian deaths for every American killed in the war."⁶⁸ Nearly four million acres of arable land in Vietnam were ruined by American defoliation chemicals.⁶⁹

- In December 1970, Nixon ordered massive bombing of Cambodia, which had already been subjected to U.S. bombing for several years. Overall, "between October 4, 1965, to August 15, 1973, the United States dropped . . . 2,756,941 tons [on Cambodia], dropped in 230,516 sorties on 113,716 sites." One study concluded that "civilian casualties in Cambodia drove an enraged populace into the arms of an insurgency that had enjoyed relatively little support until the bombing began, setting in motion the expansion of the Vietnam War deeper into Cambodia, a coup d'etat in 1970, the rapid rise of the Khmer Rouge, and ultimately the Cambodian genocide."⁷⁰

And we keep it up. Applying the theory of Harlan Ullman, senior fellow at the Center for Strategic and International Studies, the United States bombed Baghdad in the opening days of the Iraq War with the aim of "destroying everything that makes life in Baghdad livable."⁷¹ Bombing sorties did not end after the initial invasion. Largely unreported, the Americans made over 300 air strikes in 2004, and dropped 26 tons on Fallujah during the battle for the city in November 2004. 2007 saw another fivefold increase in air strikes, and it was reported that during the battle of Arab Jabour, the United States dropped 40,000 pounds of bombs in ten minutes. Drone bombs target militants in Pakistan, but occasionally strike civilians. Even when they do not, the intrusion on Pakistani sovereignty is blatant: "For the United States to unleash a salvo of missiles at a Pakistani village thought to house an al-Qaeda chieftain is the equivalent of the Mexican government bombing a southern California condo complex suspected of harboring a drug kingpin."[72]

Conclusion

In economic policy as well as in our political and military dealings with lesser powers, we do not consistently promote democracy or free trade. For all the genuine care of the American military, we have been vicious more than we like to admit. The most consistent policy aim has been the promotion of American interests. That is hardly exceptional; it is what great powers do. The scale of our violence is rare, and not merely due to technical advances in the destructiveness of weapons. Americanism and the expansion of American power require sacrifices, both of our own and of others. Still, many ruthless powers throughout the ages have killed civilians to achieve their political and strategic goals. In this we are not exceptional.

What makes us exceptional is not our self-interest or the fact that we fight wars or the fact that we fight to win. We are exceptional in our blindness to our use of power. Americanism fools us into thinking that we are acting for high-minded ideals rather than for grubby national advantage. Worse, Americanism mythologizes and sanctifies our not uncommon big-country-on-the-planet bullying and hypocrisy. We protect our favored industries yet demand open doors into small, developing Asian economies. We sing the praises of democracy while sending CIA operatives to overthrow elected rulers. We meddle in other nations' business in ways that we would not tolerate for a moment if we were on the receiving end. We pile up burning corpses and tell ourselves we are regenerating the world. We can get away with all this because Americanism persuades us that we are invariably, no matter what the cause or how we behave, the global good guy.

Babel-like, we believe we have brought history effectively to its conclusion: American democracy is everyone's tomorrow.[73] Babel-like, we want everyone everywhere to confess with one lip our American creed of liberty, democracy, and free markets. Babel-like, we are anxious until everyone looks like us—with a McDonald's in every major city, and a Walmart to boot—or until we can force most everyone to play by our rules. American power in the world might be entirely nonviolent and benign were it not for the third plank of the Americanist creed, the sacrificial consecration of war and violence. Vast and complex as it is, the United States does act consistently in terms of its Americanist convictions, but it is no aberration when it does. When we violently impose our will on the world, we are acting against the better angels of our nature. But we are not betraying our true selves. We are being as Americanist as apple pie.

Chapter 7

Among Beasts

Persecution of the saints is the mark of a bestial polity, and also the sign of the doom of the beast. America is not a beast. Neither domestically nor internationally do we directly and deliberately suppress Christian faith or Christian churches. In fact, alone among the major powers, the United States officially integrated promotion of religious freedom into our foreign policy with the adoption of the 1998 International Religious Freedom Act, which established an Office of International Religious Freedom at the State Department.[1] Is there another nation that gives any support or recognition to Voice of the Martyrs?[2] What other country would intervene to save an Afghan convert to Christianity who faced death for apostasy?[3] Officially, it is not uncommon for us to exert our superpower to defend martyrs rather than to slaughter them. In this instance, we use our power the way power is supposed to be used—to protect and empower the powerless (see Psalm 72). This is a substantial good.

But the good is tarnished, if not undermined by evils. There is, as always, a complicated story of bureaucratic sabotage and interdepartmental conflict behind the advances at the State Department. Even when we take action, it often has little effect on the conduct of religiously repressive states. According to the 1998 legislation, the executive branch can label nations Countries of Particular Concern (CPCs), which lays the legal groundwork for more aggressive efforts to confront religious repression. In practice, CPC designation has little effect, and in practice the State Department applies the criteria selectively to let our favorite, or the most lucrative, oppressors off the hook.[4] More fundamentally, the State Department generally operates on "secularist" assumptions that foolishly marginalize religion as a factor in international relations.[5] "Secularist" is not quite the right word here. It never is when we are talking about America. Rather, the same heretical Americanist suspicion of public religion that shapes domestic culture and politics also shapes American foreign policy.[6] What drives American foreign policy is not solicitation for Christians or other religious minorities around the world. What drives American foreign policy is national interest, dressed up as divine mission by Americanist rhetoric and the fervor of our nationalism.

Empires are not static. Babels can turn bestial, and so can cherubic Cyrian empires, as Rome did. America is not a beast, but Americanism could adapt itself to bestial ideology. Though we are not a beast, we enjoy the company of beasts; we send them money, train their soldiers, and have even permitted beasts to write constitutions that leave them free to be beasts.[7] If we are at times a tamer of beasts, we spend considerable money and effort to keep their feeding troughs, and their arsenals, well stocked.

Funding Persecution

In August 2011, the Pew Research Center released a report on global restrictions on religion.[8] The Pew analysis divided restrictions on religious liberty into two categories. The analysis analyzes governmental efforts to control religious groups, prevent conversion, limit preaching and proselytizing, as well as laws prohibiting blasphemy, apostasy, and defamation of religion (Government Restriction Index, GRI). The Pew survey also estimates unofficial social hostility promoted by individuals, private organizations, and groups (Social Hostility Index, SHI), which is manifested in mob violence, religiously motivated crimes, physical conflict about conversions, harassment for wearing distinctive religious clothing, terrorist acts, and war. Both measures are based on a survey of various types of religious restrictions, and are summed up on a 1–10 scale. Overall, 21 percent of the surveyed countries had a high (4.7–7.1) or very high (7.2–8.3) rating in government restrictions on religion, but given the large populations of many of these countries, about 59 percent of the world's population lives under highly or very highly restrictive conditions. Twenty-two percent of the world's nations have high or very high ratings in the SHI, and that includes 48 percent of the world's population.

What is remarkable is the number of U.S. "allies" that appear on the Pew Forum's list of nations that place very high or high restrictions on religion. In the former category are Egypt, Uzbekistan, Indonesia, and Saudi Arabia. The highly restrictive nations include U.S. aid recipients Pakistan, Russia, India, Turkey, Kuwait, Yemen, Jordan, and America's number one aid recipient, Israel. Though the Pew Forum study found that Muslims are persecuted in 117 countries, most of the nations that receive U.S. military aid are not restricting the religious freedom of Muslims. Many suppress Jews, and nearly all of them restrict the freedom of Christians of one variety or another, sometimes of every variety. The following chart correlates American expenditures of military aid with Pew statistics about religious repression:

Country	Military Expenditure (in millions)[9]			Pew Rating (2009; cmp 2008)	
	2005	2007	2008	Govt. restricts	Social Hostilities
Afghanistan	2,252	5,813	8,892	5.9 (+.6)	8.2 (+.1)
Iraq	9,482	7,959	7,506	5.3 (+.2)	9.0 (-.4)
Egypt	1,563	1,972	1,492	8.3 (+.7)	7.2 (+.7)
Israel	2,714	2,510	2,425	4.7 (+.2)	7.2 (no change)
West Bank	350	165	575	3.4 (+.1)	6.5 (+.2)
Sudan	1,043	1,180	1,416	5.5 (-.2)	6.2 (-.6)
Russia	1,585	1,593	1,261	6.5 (+.5)	4.9 (+.8)
Pakistan	758	975	963	7.1 (+.6)	8.8 (+.4)
Jordan	683	542	879	5.4 (+.1)	5.0 (+.7)
Indonesia	195	236	208	7.2 (+.4)	7.8 (no change)

Many of these U.S.-supported regimes are in the Middle East. The increased U.S. presence in the region has not resulted in greater religious freedom or in relief from persecution of Christians. On the contrary,

Among Beasts

over the past decade, the region has rapidly de-Christianized, often in countries that depend on massive infusions of U.S. support.

a. Egypt[10]

As I drafted this chapter (October 2011), the news media were abuzz with reports about the Cairo riots in which at least twenty-five Coptic Christians were killed and nearly two hundred, mostly Christians, were injured. The clash in Cairo had its roots in late September 2011. Muslims in the village of Aswan complained about the Coptic church's renovations and objected to Christian symbols visible on the outside of the church. Even though the Christians agreed to remove crosses and bells from the church, the mob returned a week later, demanding that the church remove its domes. When the Copts refused, a Muslim mob of 3,000 attacked and looted the church before burning it to the ground. Several Christian-owned homes and businesses were also burned. A villager reported that imams from more than twenty mosques encouraged the attack. Though the attack was carried out by a "private" mob, Christians claimed that the government colluded by refusing to enforce laws against vandalism and "thuggery."[11]

The September attack was the culmination of months of assaults. On New Year's Day, 2011, Alexandria's Two Saints Church was bombed, killing twenty-three people. From January to September 2011, three churches had been burned and many others looted. So in early October, several hundred Coptic Christians staged what they insisted was a peaceful protest in Cairo. As the march approached the state television headquarters, gunfire broke out. According to the protesters, the army fired on the peaceful marchers, and there were reports of military vehicles running down protesters. Others claimed that the gunfire first came from within the Coptic crowd. Non-military Muslims appeared carrying sticks and dragged Copts, including women, into back alleys. Vehicles with a crucifix dangling from the mirror were firebombed. Riots spread to Tahrir Square, scene of protests against Hosni Mubarak only a few months before, and the hospitals that treated the wounded were also attacked. Activist Hossam Bahgat said, "What happened today is unprecedented. Seventeen corpses were crushed by military trucks."[12] The Coptic Pope, Shenouda III, issued a statement after consulting with bishops. He blamed "strangers" who "got in the middle of our sons and committed mistakes to be blamed on our sons," but also accused the government of failing to protect Christians: "The Copts feel that problems are repeated and the perpetrators go unpunished."[13]

Suppression of the minority Coptic population is not new. In November 2010, while Mubarak still held power, the U.S. State Department reported that respect for religious freedom in Egypt "remained poor," and elaborated:

> The government also sometimes arrested, detained, and harassed Muslims such as Shi'a, Ahmadiyas, Quranists, converts from Islam to Christianity, and members of other religious groups whose beliefs and/or practices it deemed to deviate from mainstream Islamic beliefs and whose activities it alleged to jeopardize communal harmony. Government authorities often refused to provide converts with new identity documents indicating their chosen faith. The government failed to prosecute perpetrators of violence against Coptic Christians in a number of cases, including in Baghoura, Farshout, and Marsa Matruh. . . . The government again failed to redress laws—particularly laws relating to church construction and renovation—and governmental practices, especially government hiring, that discriminate against Christians, effectively allowing their discriminatory effects and their modeling effect on society to become further entrenched. The government continued to sponsor informal reconciliation sessions following sectarian attacks. This practice generally prevented the criminal prosecution of perpetrators of crimes against Copts, precluded their recourse to the judicial system for restitution, and contributed to a climate of impunity that encouraged further assaults.[14]

The State Department "raised concerns" and protested. Meanwhile, hundreds of millions of dollars continued to flow into Egypt to support its military. When the State Department issued its 2011 report on religious freedom, Egypt was not listed as a Country of Particular Concern.

If we are not a beast, why are we consorting with one?

b. Pakistan

The United States began sending aid to Pakistan in 1948, though through the mid-1950s the aid was exclusively economic. Beginning in 1955, the

United States began sending military aid, which by 2010 totaled $2.5 billion. Since 1948, the United States has given more than $30 billion in direct aid, almost half of it military aid.[15] Whether the strategic investment is worth the money is debatable. Whether it has helped liberalize Pakistan is not. It remains one of the most repressive regimes in the world, and has become our favorite frenemy. Frenemy status does not, apparently, interrupt the flow of military assistance.

Social hostility to Christians in Pakistan is intense. Eighteen Protestants were killed in the Punjab in 2001 by a mob of motorcycle gunmen, probably associated with an Islamicist group. Five people were killed in an assault on a church in Islamabad in 2002. In August 2002, gunmen stormed a missionary school, killing six, and in the same month three nurses were killed in a Christian hospital by a grenade attack. On October 25, 2002, two terrorists executed seven Christians who worked with the Peace and Justice Institute of Karachi. Three Christian girls were killed in a church in late 2002 by a grenade. When Christian Yousaf Masih allegedly blasphemed in 2005, 3,000 Muslims attacked Christians and destroyed Roman Catholic, Salvation Army, and Presbyterian churches in Sangla Hill. Christian Nasir Ashraf was beaten in June 2006 by Muslims who accused him of "polluting" a glass he had used for a drink of water. In August 2009, six Christians were burned alive in a church in Gojra. On March 2, 2011, the only Christian minister in Pakistan's government was gunned down for his opposition to Islam's blasphemy laws.[16] In August 2011, armed Muslims kidnapped a fourteen-year-old Christian girl from her home. One of the kidnappers said his intent was to convert her to Islam to become the kidnapper's mistress. A Catholic spokesman observed that such events are common in Pakistan, and added that "because the law favors [Muslims]," Christians can do little to stop it.[17]

According to Section 295-C of Pakistan's penal code, "Whoever . . . defiles the sacred name of the Holy Prophet Muhammad (peace be upon him) shall be punished with death, or imprisonment for life, and shall also be liable to fine." The blasphemy law had been on the books for a long time, but in 1986 blasphemy was made a capital crime. Since then, 962 cases of blasphemy have been prosecuted, most against Ahmadi Muslims but over 100 against Christians. The most celebrated case is that of Asia Noreen Bibi. This Christian woman was a farm worker in the village of Ittan Wali. While working in the field in June 2009,

Part III: Between Babel and Beast

she fetched water for a group of coworkers, but some of them refused to drink because she had touched the water and "defiled" it. A woman insulted Bibi, who insulted her back. Some of her coworkers told a local Muslim cleric that she had insulted the Prophet Muhammad. A mob attacked her house, and beat her and other members of her family before the police intervened. When the police investigated, they arrested her and charged her with blasphemy. In November 2010, she was sentenced to death by hanging. Bibi's husband appealed to the Lahore High Court, which ruled that the Pakistani president may not pardon her while the case is before the court. One cleric has offered a $6,000 reward to anyone who kills Bibi. Two officials who spoke in behalf of Bibi—Minister of Religious Minorities Shahbaz Bhatti and Salmon Taseer, Muslim governor of Punjab—were assassinated.[18]

Still, huge amounts of money flow from the United States to Pakistan's military. Pakistan punishes anyone who speaks against the Prophet of Islam, and the United States gives Pakistan the military support it needs to maintain its religious repression. The United States does not have blasphemy laws, nor does it approve of Pakistan's laws; but it can hardly be seen as a force for Christian civilization in Pakistan. Indeed, when the United States does have the opportunity to act forcefully against Pakistan, it flinches. In September 2011, the State Department issued its annual report on religious freedom. Eight Countries of Particular Concern were listed, since these had "engaged in or tolerated particularly severe violations of religious freedom." While the report criticized Pakistani discrimination and social abuses, it did not list Pakistan as a CPC.[19]

If we are not a beast, why do we keep sending money to feed and arm one?

c. Saudi Arabia

Oil-rich Saudi Arabia receives little direct military aid from the United States, but it receives aid in many other forms. Since 1951, the United States has had a Military Training Mission in Saudi Arabia that provides training and other security services to the Saudi army. Military installations have been built with the aid of the U.S. Army Corps of Engineers. In 2007 Saudi Arabia received a military package worth $13 billion, part of a $60 billion package to Middle Eastern countries. The U.S. ambassador to the United Nations explained that the Saudis were getting aid because they "are not doing all they can to help us in Iraq."[20] It is, in short, a very expensive bribe.

It is a bribe to keep the oil flowing, a bribe to the Bush family's "good friends," the Royal House of Saud.[21] It is a large bribe to a Wahhabist regime that officially prohibits the practice of Christianity. There are somewhere between 500,000 and 1 million Catholics in Saudi Arabia, mostly Filipino and other Asian immigrants who take menial jobs that Saudis disdain.[22] Orthodox believers and Protestants are also residents. It is illegal for Christians to have Bibles and crucifixes, to build churches, wear religious symbols, or even hang Christian images in private homes, and Christians are arrested and beaten for violations.[23] During 2010–2011, a number of incidents occurred:

- In October 2010, twelve Filipino migrant workers were arrested at a Mass and charged with proselytizing.[24]
- In March, two Indian Christians were beaten, arrested, and sentenced to 45-day prison terms for attending a private prayer meeting.[25] They were finally released after six months.[26]
- In July, a Christian refugee from Eritrea, Mussie Eyob, was expelled from Saudi Arabia after being arrested for proselytizing. Initially, he faced a death penalty.[27] He may well be killed when he returns to Eritrea.

These isolated incidents are part of a larger pattern of suppression and intimidation. Saudi Arabia's laws permit private worship by non-Muslims, but ban public worship, supposedly in conformity with the Prophet's dying wishes. In practice, services "must remain small and inconspicuous. They must not occur regularly at a particular location, lest a church or other non-Muslim place of worship de facto be established." "Religious police," or *Mutawwa'in*, infiltrate church groups, whose services are "vulnerable to raids." Few priests are allowed into the kingdom.[28]

The U.S. State Department is well aware of Saudi abuses,[29] yet Saudi Arabia is still regarded as an "indispensable ally." The United States rarely intervenes in defense of religious minorities, lest we lose what we view as a crucial friendly power in a critical region of the world. When Thomas Farr proposed to Saudi officials that they purchase buildings to

Part III: Between Babel and Beast

rent to non-Muslim religious groups, condemn or criminalize the activities of the *Mutawwa'in*, and permit more priests to enter the country, U.S. officials showed "distinct discomfort" and the Saudi officials found themselves "called away to some other emergency."[30]

Clearly, promotion of Christianity, or of religious freedom, does not determine our Saudi policy. Unsurprisingly, intertwined economic and strategic goals are paramount. We are a great power, and we act like one. Worse, we pay deference to monsters. Saudi Arabia is a beast, but on whose back does Saudi Arabia ride?

d. Iraq

In Egypt, Pakistan, and Saudi Arabia, U.S. power is exercised indirectly. Between 2003 and 2011, the United States occupied Iraq. Treatment of religious minorities, including Christians, depended largely on the United States. The current Iraqi constitution attempts to combine adherence to Islamic law with adherence to democratic principles, and explicitly recognizes freedom of religion for both Muslims and non-Muslims. Further, the Iraqi government has been quick to speak on behalf of Christians and to protect other religious minorities.[31]

Still, U.S. occupation has not been good for the Christians of Iraq. The Statement Department claims that the Christian population has declined from 1.4 milllion/800,000 to 400,000/600,000, but some have estimated that the number of Christians has fallen from 800,000 to 150,000 between 2001–2011.[32] No one knows for sure. The exodus of Iraqi Christians sped up after an October 2010 attack on Our Lady of Salvation Church in Baghdad, called by *The New York Times* the "worst massacre of Iraqi Christians since the war began here in 2003." Fifty-eight hostages were killed, another seventy injured, as were at least fifteen security force members who stormed the church to free to hostages.[33] The State Department reports:

> Spurred by the October 31 attack against the Sayidat al-Najat Church, the rate of Christian displacement was greater than in the previous reporting period. Between November 1 and December 7, over 800 families fled violence against Christians in Baghdad and Mosul; approximately 175 families fled to Erbil; and over 400 families fled to the Ninewa Plains. On December 9 the Ministry of Displacement and Migration announced

that it had distributed aid to 138 Christian families, and on December 7 the Directorate of Migration and Displacement in Dohuk Province reported 84 Christian families displaced from Baghdad and Ninewa had relocated to the province. Due to attacks and threats against Christians in Baghdad, Mosul, and other cities, approximately 1,400 Christian families relocated to the KRG and Ninewa Plains by year's end. The number of Christians displaced may be higher since many displaced Christians stayed with family, relatives, and friends in those areas. Some Christian families sought refuge in Kirkuk province. Additional press reports noted that Christians also fled to Jordan and Turkey, hoping to ultimately emigrate to Europe or North America.[34]

The attack on the church was only one incident of dozens. Sixty-six churches, besides convents, a monastery, and an orphanage, have been attacked.[35] In a March 2011 press release, Catholic Archbishop Bashar Warda of Erbil detailed other attacks on Christians:

> Since the occupation of Iraq in 2003 over 500 Christians have been killed in religious and politically motivated conflicts. Forty percent of the killings took place in northern Iraq, 58% in the Baghdad region and 2% in the south.
>
> Killings of Christians began in earnest in 2003 when the first translator was killed in Baghdad. In 2006, targeted killings of Christian leaders escalated when an Orthodox Christian priest, Boulos Iskander, was kidnapped, beheaded and dismembered despite payment of a ransom.
>
> Between 2006 and 2010, 17 Iraqi priests and 2 Iraqi Bishops were kidnapped in Baghdad, Mosul and Kirkuk. Many were held for days; some for weeks. All were beaten or tortured by their kidnappers. Most were released, but one bishop, four priests and three sub-deacons were killed. In most cases, those responsible for the crimes stated they wanted Christians out of Iraq.
>
> These kidnappings and murders have left their mark on the minds and bodies of the Iraqi churches. Not only have our religious leaders been murdered, but also simple families, shop keepers, children, teachers, the elderly, mothers and their babies, and members of all elements of Christian society.[36]

Part III: Between Babel and Beast

Despite improved security in Iraq, Christians and other minorities have continued to flee, as the central government proves incapable of protecting them from jihadists.

The rage against Christians in Iraq came unexpectedly to the U.S. government. It was not what the United States wanted.[37] Not that the United States has done much to stop it. In September 2007, then-Senator Barack Obama wrote to Secretary of State Condoleezza Rice about the fate of Christians and other minorities in Iraq, pointing out the refugee crisis that was resulting.[38] In November 2010, now-President Obama received a similar letter from John Eibner, CEO of Christian Solidarity International. Eibner wrote in response to the attack on Our Lady of Salvation and warned that a group known as the "Islamic State of Iraq" had vowed to exterminate Iraqi Christians. He concluded with this plea: "The American and Iraqi governments have succeeded in guaranteeing security for Iraq's once vulnerable oil installations. Please, Mr. President, spare no effort to ensure that Iraq's Christian community receives at least the same level of protection."[39] Neither the Bush nor the Obama administrations responded in any decisive fashion. As Walter Russell Mead has said, "Officials seemed to feel that making an issue of widespread persecution of religious minorities would be either a propaganda victory for opponents of the Iraq War or, by making the U.S. appear to be an advocate for Iraqi Christians, confirm Muslim suspicions about an alleged anti-Islamic or 'crusader' U.S. agenda." The U.S. government has not even done the minimum for Iraqi Christians that they have done for refugees for the last half century: "In a truly grotesque dereliction of duty, neither administration made allowances for minority refugees to resettle in America, something we have done in past conflicts and that has benefited asylum-seekers from South Vietnam to Somalia. Historically tight-knit, these communities are now dispersed across Jordan, Syria, Iran, and elsewhere and will probably disappear in time."[40]

In 2004, Iraq was removed from the list of CPCs.[41]

e. Israel

Two things keep us embroiled in the Middle East—oil and Israel. Were our economy not dependent on oil, we could downsize our presence in the region without losing much besides our dignity. Little can be done about oil. It is where it is, and for the foreseeable future, we will need a lot of it. The solution probably lies far down the road, in some economically feasible alternative source of energy or some extraordinary self-restraint on the part of us Americans, not known for our self-restraint. For the time being, oil is an ideal symbol of our indulgence of "imperialism as a way of life." Were we not allied in a special relationship with Israel, the intensity of Arab hatred for the United States would significantly diminish, and we would not be embroiled in every conflict in the region. As it is, Israel receives more U.S. aid than any country, other than the ones we have occupied during the past decade.

Israel's treatment of religious minorities is founded on the earlier British model. Unlike most Islamic countries, Israeli law officially endorses religious freedom and gives official recognition to a number of Christian groups, though some that have applied for official standing have been left in limbo for years. Still, Israel is not a welcome place for Christians. Proselytizing is also officially legal, but the State Department reports that "the government has taken a number of steps that encouraged the perception that proselytizing is against government policy." For example, it "has detained individuals suspected of being 'missionaries,' and required of such persons bail and a pledge to abstain from missionary activity, in addition to refusing them entry into the country. It maintained denunciations of such activity from anti-missionary groups like Yad L'Achim in its border control databases.... [It] has also cited proselytism as a reason to deny student, work, and religious visa extensions, as well as to deny permanent residency petitions." Government policy apart, "society's attitudes toward missionary activities and conversion generally were negative. Most Jews opposed missionary activity directed at Jews, and some were hostile to Jewish converts to Christianity. While proselytism is officially legal, missionaries continued to face harassment and discrimination by some Jewish activists and organizations. The Messianic Jewish and Jehovah's Witnesses communities, among others, accused groups such as Yad L'Achim and Lev L'Achim, Jewish religious organizations opposed to missionary activity, of harassing and occasionally assaulting their members."[42]

When Israeli mistreatment of Christians is brought up, Christian advocates of religious freedom often avert their eyes: "In a June 2006 hearing by the House Subcommittee on Africa, Global Human Rights and International Opeations, Chair Chris Smith sought to raise the plight of Palestinian Christians affected by Israel's separation wall. He called on Nina Shea, vice chair of the U.S. Commission on International Religious Freedom, to report his concerns about the negative impact of the wall and the unrealistic level of compensation paid for the loss of Palestinian land." A courageous crusader of religious freedom in the Muslim world, Shea initially ignored Smith's request, and when she did report her concerns, she changed "the subject to Christian persecution at the hands of Muslims in Iraq."[43]

More can be done about our policy toward Israel than about oil, but here a peculiar twist on Americanist faith gets in the way. Particularly during recent Republican administrations, Christian Zionists established a significant base of power in Washington. Driven by dispensationalist theology that views modern Israel as a chosen vessel, they have resisted any dispassionate review of American policy toward Israel.[44] On grounds of sheer national interest, we do not need a special relationship with Israel.[45] Were U.S. foreign policy worked out in the metapolitical framework of Christendom, we would not be committed to open-ended support for an Israeli state, and we would be more sensitive to the claims of Palestinians, especially the minority Christian population.

f. Lesser Beasts

Yemen's dictator, Ali Abdullah Saleh, has long been propped up by U.S. military aid, training, and weapons, with the occasional air strike thrown in. Military aid doubled in 2010, and the U.S. Senate called on Obama to "use all appropriate measures" to keep him in power. The U.S.-trained forces have spent the past year cracking down on activists who want the Arab Spring to spread, killing protesters and putting dissenting army officers under arrest.[46] Meanwhile, the Yemeni Constitution proclaims Yemen an Islamic state whose laws are derived from sharia. Conversion to Christianity is illegal, and converts from Islam might face capital punishment. It is illegal in Yemen to proselytize Muslims.[47]

Indonesia received over $200 million in military aid in past years. Yet attacks on Christians have become common. Two house churches in Riau were burned in August 2011, culminating a series of attacks on religious minorities. A police spokesman said that the homes burned because they were so cheap—"only made of board"—and another police spokesman said that they "easily burned because they were made of planks, thus flammable." Christian persecution watchdogs claim that lenient sentences in earlier attacks have encouraged extremists.[48] In Bogor, members of a church began praying on the sidewalk when their church was closed down by authorities. In October 2011, local authorities forced them to leave because they were "holding prayers on public premises without permission."[49]

Several former Soviet states have become important U.S. allies as bases for the war in Afghanistan. Aid to Turkmenistan jumped from only $150,000 in 2009 to $2 million in 2010. Uzbekistan's share of U.S. military support declined after a 2005 massacre of protesters, but more recently the Obama administration has made efforts to repair the relationship so that Uzbekistan can continue to serve as a conduit of supplies into Afghanistan.[50] Though Turkmenistan's constitution guarantees religious freedom, in practice the government restricts it. According to a State Department report, "The activities of unregistered religious groups remained illegal, with violators subject to fines under the administrative code. Individuals suspected of unauthorized religious activity may be subjected to search, detention, confiscation of religious materials, verbal abuse, and pressure to confess to holding an illegal meeting."[51] In Uzbekistan there are even sharper contradictions. The constitution guarantees religious liberty, but other laws restrict religion and these restrictions are enforced. The State Department reports that "the law restricts the religious freedom of unregistered groups and prohibits many activities, such as proselytizing; many members of minority religious groups faced heavy fines and short jail terms for violations of these laws." The government maintains surveillance of religious groups, and authorities have raided Christian worship services, both of registered and unregistered Christian groups. Many Christian churches have been unable to register. Christian literature has been confiscated, fines have been imposed for possession of Christian literature, and the government has blocked access to Christian websites. Ethnic Uzbeks who convert to Christianity are harassed and face discrimination of various kinds.[52]

As a result of harassment, persecution, and discrimination, the Middle East is being emptied of Christians. Yet, the United States continues to dole out millions in military aid, and does little when the threats to Christians are brought to their attention. On a visit to Paris, for instance, the Maronite Catholic Patriarch Bechara Rai of Lebanon warned President Sarkozy that the fall of Assad in Syria might give extremist Muslims an opening to act against Christians. The French Foreign Ministry responded with "surprise and disappointment" to Rai's warning. Because of his comments in Paris, Rai was blackballed on a subsequent visit to the United States. Initially, President Obama was scheduled to meet with Rai, but after his abrasive comments in Paris, all meetings with the Obama administration were cancelled.[53] These are not the actions of a country that acknowledges that its end is the end of the church, which is the kingdom of God.

Conclusion

For much of the last century, the United States has forged alliances with repressive despots. During the Cold War, we thought we needed the brutes to stave off the Red Menace. Now, as we wage the war on terror, we say we need friendly beasts to help us deal with the less friendly ones. It sounds reasonable; it is the very model of realist foreign policy. Such realism is unrealistic, shortsighted, and counterproductive. Spreading Islamic propaganda seemed reasonable when the jihadists were fighting the Soviets, but thirty years on, it resembles a child playing with a nuke. Stationing our troops in Saudi Arabia seemed necessary and natural after the first Gulf War—until bin Laden slammed two planes into the Twin Towers to purge our defilement of the land of the Prophet. Supporting Middle Eastern tyrants seems to be good policy, but it has actually "helped spawn Islamist transnational terrorism."[54]

Realism of this type is not only foolish, but it puts us on the path to doing great evil, and doing it hypocritically: We pay killers, and we reassure ourselves because we are not doing the killing. We buy the booze, even if we are still teetotalers who refrain from drinking the blood of saints. We are not a beast, but we spend a lot of our wealth to keep some of the world's most ferocious beasts in business. We play with beasts, and our Americanist lenses do not allow us to see the danger. We fund our favorite beasts, then turn a blind eye when they devour the saints. It is a dangerous position, not only for the Christians who suffer at the hands of our allies but also for the United States. Those who consort with beasts might become bestial, and beasts do not long survive.

Conclusion

William Appleman Williams once wrote that "American policy is guided by three conceptions":

> One is the warm, generous, humanitarian impulse to help other people solve their problems. A second is the principle of self-determination applied at the international level, which asserts the right of every society to establish its own goals or objectives, and to realize them internally through the means that are appropriate.¹

As Williams said, these two goals are complementary. And they express the bright side of America and the American character, for we are a Christian nation that, for all our faults, has at times acted (and still acts) with something that bears a family resemblance to Christian charity.

But there are *three* conceptions: "the third idea entertained by many Americans is one which insists that other people cannot *really* solve their problems and improve their lives unless they go about it in the same way as the United States."² This third plank is the crucial one, for it is the heresy that perturbs the compatibility of the first two. It is the Americanist confidence that we are God's new Israel, the political harbinger for all future ages, the redeemer nation that performs periodic regenerating sacrifices for the world. Americanism fools us into thinking that we always act charitably, in the best interests of everyone, when in fact we are simply acting in our own self-interest.

As far as Christians are concerned, the only appropriate response is to repent of being Americanists. American churches need to remove the flags from their podiums—and stop treating July 4 as a high holy day. American churches need to teach and preach from a de-Americanized Bible, one that understands that the *imperium* of the church, not American hegemony, fulfills the hopes of Israel. American churches need to commemorate the final sacrifice of Jesus in regular eucharistic celebrations, and they need to work out the practicalities of a eucharistic politics—the end of sacred warfare, the formation of an international ecclesial *imperium* that includes *all* Christians, the cultivation of the virtues of martyrs, the forging of bonds of brotherhood that would inhibit Christians from shedding Christian blood. Churches should not teach Christians to hate America, or to hate American power; but we must train disciples to hate injustice and violence even when perpetrated by our fellow citizens. Churches do not necessarily need to discourage Christians from participation in American government, or even the American military, though the churches should reserve the right to judge the justice of America's wars and to forbid Christians from participating in unjust wars or supporting oppressive policies.[3] Churches should instead encourage Christians to discover ways to turn American power toward justice, peace, and charity.

The required repentance is profoundly painful. Americanism is so ingrained in our character, institutions, symbols, and practices that renouncing it will feel like repenting of being American. But the stakes for America's future, and the near-term future of the world, could not be higher. Unless Americans renounce this heresy, we will remain a Babel, demanding uniformity and leaving chaos in our wake. Unless Americans renounce this heresy, we will never see ourselves accurately. Unless Americans renounce this heresy, the United States likely will not remain between Babel and Beast. Empires do not stay still, and Babels easily slip or rush into bestiality.

Throughout Scripture, the only power that can overcome the seemingly invincible omnipotence of a Babel or a Beast is the power of martyrdom, the power of witness to King Jesus to the point of loss and death. American Christianity has not done a good job of producing martyrs, and that is because we have done such an outstanding job of nurturing Americanists who regret that they have only one life to give for their country. Americanists cannot break Babelic or bestial power because they cannot distinguish heretical Americanism from Christian orthodoxy. Until we do, America will lurch along the path that leads from Babel to beast. If America is to be put in its place—put right—Christians must risk martyrdom and force Babel to the crux where it has to decide either to acknowledge Jesus as *imperator* and the church as God's *imperium* or to begin drinking holy blood.

Endnotes

Chapter 1

1. The Bible has no word that corresponds to our Latin-derived "empire" or "imperial." The NASB uses the word "empire" only once (Dan 11:2) to translate מַלְכוּת, which means kingdom, royal dominion, realm (cf. Num 24:7; 1 Sam 20:31; 1 Kgs 2:12; etc.). Emperors are called "kings" (cf. 2 Kgs 24:1; John 19:15; Acts 17:7), empires are "kingdoms" (cf. 2 Chron 36:20; Dan 2:40; 7:23; 8:22). Terminologically, the Bible blurs distinctions that we make among political orders. The Bible commonly eschews general categories entirely and speaks instead of specific political orders—Babel, Egypt, Moab, Babylon, Persia, the οἰκουμηνη of Greco-Rome. These historical political entities contribute to political theology not because they are instances of the genus *empire*, but as *types*. Though a historical political project in its own right, "Babel" becomes a trope for a particular configuration of political power (e.g., Zech 2:7; 1 Pet 5:13; Revelation 17–18), as do "Sodom" (Deut 29:23; Isa 1:9–10; Ezek 16:46–56) and "Egypt" (Rev 11:8).

The absence of the terminology of empire does not necessarily mean that the Bible says nothing about empires, but it should at least make us cautious about imposing our own categories on the biblical material. When we reshuffle the Bible into our own (ultimately Aristotelian) schemes for analyzing political life, we neutralize the Bible's distinctive contribution to our politics and we run the risk of sacralizing our own political predilections. Terminology illumines, but it can also blind. Perhaps the most obvious illustration of the problem in recent theology is the near-universal use of the singular "empire," which bewitches scholars into thinking that there are no theologically nor morally relevant distinctions between Babel, Persia, and Rome, or between Nimrod, Cyrus, and Nero. I assume that the terminological incommensurability between Scripture and modern political theory indicates substantive differences between the biblical understanding of political life and our own, and where they conflict I have attempted to shed or modify my own prejudices in order to think as fully as possible within the biblical framework. Throughout this book, I attempt to follow Oliver O'Donovan's lead in constructing the basic categories of political analysis from Scripture rather than bringing preexisting categories *to* Scripture (*The Desire of Nations: Recovering the Roots of Political Theology* [Cambridge: Cambridge University Press, 1999]).

Theologians are far more confident they know what "empire" means than political scientists or historians, and the sheer lack of consensus about definition should give

Endnotes

theologians more pause than it does. Every historian who thinks seriously about the matter highlights the variety of "empires" and "imperialisms." (For a splendid, concise historical treatment that highlights the point, see Anthony Pagden, *Peoples and Empires: A Short History of European Migration* [New York: Random House, 2003]; see also, for instance, Charles S. Maier, *Among Empires: American Ascendancy and Its Predecessors* [Cambridge: Harvard University Press, 2006]). The point is glaringly obvious on briefest reflection: After all, empires have been around for most of human history, and only an insistent attachment to essentializing would make one think these are all instances of a single reality. In their recent survey, Jane Burbank and Frederick Cooper note that more peoples in history have lived in tribes, city-states, or under empires than in nation-states (*Empires in World History: Power and the Politics of Difference* [Princeton: Princeton University Press, 2010] 8–9).

Stephen Howe warns that "Ideas about empire have . . . seemed to spread and multiply beyond all limit or control. 'Imperialism,' as a word has gone imperial; 'colonialism' has colonized our languages. . . . They have come to be used, at the extreme, to describe anyone's, any group's, or anything's supposed superiority, or domination, or even just influence, over any other person, or group, or thing. Some of these uses are clearly metaphorical; others seem to be intended literally" (*Empire: A Very Short Introduction* [Oxford: Oxford University Press, 2002] 10). The colonization of our political imagination by "empire" is most evident in Michael Hardt and Antonio Negri's *Empire* (Cambridge: Harvard University Press, 2001), which claims that the age of imperialism has been succeeded by the age of all-pervasive, uncentered "Empire." (For a lively critique, see J. Alexander Motyl, "Is Everything Empire? Is Empire Everything?" *Comparative Politics* 38:2 [2006] 229–49). Hardt and Negri have been popular among theological critics of empire, partly I think because their broadly conceived "Empire" is something of a Marxist riff on Augustine's notion of "the city of man."

Political scientists try to define imperialism more rigorously. Most offer political definitions: An empire is a particular distribution of international political power. David Abernethy, for instance, defines empire as "a relationship of domination and subordination between one polity (called the metropole) and one or more territories (called colonies) that lie outside the metropole's boundaries yet are claimed as its lawful possessions." Other sorts of control will be included, but the political control is central. Abernethy offers a series of clarifying standards. There is empire when "the dominant state claims the right to make authoritative decisions affecting the weaker territory's domestic affairs and external relations"; when "the weaker territory is not recognized as a sovereign state by major actors in the interstate system"; when "the dominant state establishes and staffs administrative structures that extract resources, allocate resources, and enforce regulations within some economically or strategically significant portion of the weaker territory." On the other hand, "empire" does not include unequal relations between nations in which the dominant state makes no claim to control the weaker states affairs, when the weaker territory is recognized as a sovereign state. Even when the stronger state's institutions exert marked influence on the weaker state, and even when the stronger state exploits the weaker, it is not an empire-colony relation. Abernethy thus finds that the notion of "informal imperialism" covers too much ground, since any sort of influence can be described as "informal imperialism" (*The Dynamics of Global Dominance: European Overseas Empires, 1415–1980* [New Haven: Yale University Press, 2002] 20). Stephen Howe defines an empire as "a large, composite, multi-ethnic or multinational political unit, usually created by conquest, and divided between a dominant centre and subordinate, sometimes far distant, peripheries." Imperialism includes the "actions and attitudes" that produce empires, but can also refer to "less obvious and direct kinds of control or domination by one people or country over others." Thus it is possible to have "cultural or economic" imperialism without having an empire. Colonialism, as he defines it, is "more specific and strictly political: systems of rule by one group over another, where the first claims a right (a 'right' again usually established by conquest) to exercise exclusive sovereignty over the second and to shape its destiny." Colonization is the process of population movements from the center to the colonies. On these definitions, Soviet control over Poland and U.S. control over the Philippines can be described as "imperialism," but it is "not colonialism, since Poland and the Philippines retained formal political sovereignty." And there was no "colonization," since Russians didn't move into Poland, nor Americans into the Philippines (Howe, *Empire*, 30–31). Charles Maier (*Among Empires*, 1–15) emphasizes the ethnic hierarchicalization of imperial polities, and throughout his book highlights the irony that successful empires tend to subvert themselves by undermining ethnic divisions between conqueror and conquered. Useful as such definitions and distinctions are, I have, as noted, attempted to stay close to the biblical categories and types.

Empires have become empires in a variety of ways. Some achieve dominance of other nations through military superiority and sheer conquest. Commonly, though, smaller nations attach themselves in quasi-feudal fashion to larger and more powerful empires for protection from their own enemies. For some Roman historians, this was the source of Roman expansion. See the classic treatment in Tenney Frank, *Roman Imperialism* (New York: Macmillan, 1914). Britain established a beachhead in India through the East India Company, which originally was a private, though royally chartered, monopoly. The East India Company hired its own mercenaries and administered areas of India until the British government took over in the mid nineteenth century. Recognizing this variety is crucial for any fair assessment of American power today. Our military presence in Europe, for instance, is at least partly a result of the not uncommon phenomenon of "empire by invitation" (Geir Lundstad, "Empire by Invitation? The United States and Western Europe, 1945–1962," *Journal of Peace Research* 23:3 [1986] 263–77). We might describe the infiltration of McDonald's and Starbucks throughout Asia as a kind of imperialism, but we would be foolish to simply conflate this sort of commercial imperialism with the rubber plantations of King Leopold's Congo.

Inevitably, I use the words "empire" and "imperial" throughout this book, and for me the terms refer loosely to certain formal political structures in which one people, kingdom, or nation exercises dominance over or otherwise leads and guides and shapes another nation or people. Sometimes, the "imperial" nation forces another nation or nations to do its bidding by violence, threats of violence, economic manipulations, or other tools of domination. Yet, I also use the terms "empire" and "imperial" to describe situations where one nation voluntarily submits itself to the leadership and protection of another nation and where the imperial nation does not "dominate" the subordinate nation. Some peoples joined the Roman empire voluntarily, and in the Bible the human future is envisioned as an "imperial" one, though the nations voluntarily, joyfully ascend the mountain to worship Zion's king.

2. Elisabeth Schüssler Fiorenza finds anti-imperial interpreters like Richard Horsley far too conservative. Writers like Horsley "have highlighted the interplay of religion and politics in the emperor cult, identified the imperial cross-cultural patronage system, and elaborated Paul's counterimperial gospel, which is regarded as being patterned after but

Endnotes

totally different from the gospel of Caesar." But these works fail to acknowledge the postcolonial insight that "even resistance literature will re-inscribe the structures of domination against which it seeks to argue." For feminist postcolonial critics, "the anti-imperial approach, like the 'new perspective,' still remains within the traditional Protestant paradigm, which uncritically accepts Paul's rhetorical self-construction and continues to celebrate Paul as an heroic individual and great the*logian, but now no longer constructs him over and against Judaism but over and against the political domination and religious paganism of the Roman Empire." Schüssler Fiorenza chides anti-imperial readers of Paul for trying "to eliminate all Pauline statements to the contrary," all the statements in Paul's letters that seem to support rather than subvert empire: "anti-imperial biblical scholarship cannot grasp the imperial ideology at work in early Christian writings, such as in Paul's letters or the book of Revelation" (Schüssler Fiorenza, *The Power of the Word: Scripture and the Rhetoric of Empire* [Minneapolis: Fortress, 2007] 2–7). Steven D. Moore (*Empire and Apocalypse: Postcolonialism and the New Testament* [Sheffield: Sheffield Phoenix, 2006] 119) likewise claims that the contest of Revelation is "empire v. empire," and worries over the "reinscription" of empire into the Bible, which, he fears, can only fuel violence, exploitation, and homophobia (99). Schüssler Fiorenza explicitly takes "radical democracy" as her standard, and looks for biblical support for her program. She searches for "traces of a scriptural rhetoric that can inspire the resistance to empire." We cannot assume that Scripture is anti-imperial, but instead have to "identify the languages of empire and its death-dealing ideologies inscribed in scriptures" and also "identify biblical visions and values that would contribute to a radical democratic understanding of society and religion" (9–10).

3. According to some scholars, the history in between is a history of Israel's more or less "faithful resistance" to imperial projects. (The phrase is taken from the subtitle of Richard A. Horsley, ed., *In the Shadow of Empire: Reclaiming the Bible as a History of Faithful Resistance* [Louisville: Westminster John Knox, 2008]). Richard Horsley, the dean of Bible-and-empire studies, observes that Israel "originated in reaction against oppressive imperial regimes." Not only did Moses lead Israel out from Egypt, the largest imperial power of its day, but the Sinai Covenant "was in effect a declaration of independence from imperial kings and their forced labor." The Mosaic laws ordered "social-economic relations among Israelites so that no one would gain power to become an imperial-style king." The anti-imperial thrust of Judaism and Christianity is evident in the major holidays of each: "Passover commemorates the exodus from hard bondage under the pharaoh in Egypt. Hanukkah celebrates God's deliverance of the Judeans struggling to resist the first attempt by a Western empire to suppress the Israelite-Judean traditional covenantal way of life. Christmas celebrates the birth of a peasant child as the true 'Savior' of a people who had been conquered and laid under tribute (the census) by Caesar, whom the whole world had already acclaimed as the 'Savior' who had brought 'Peace and Security' to the world. It also commemorates the Roman client king's dispatch of counterinsurgency forces to massacre the innocents in order to check the deliverance movement before it got started. Good Friday and Easter remember Jesus' arrest and crucifixion by the Roman imperial rulers followed by his vindication by God as the true Lord and Savior, as opposed to the imperials 'lord' and 'savior'" (Horsley, "Introduction: The Bible and Empires," in *Shadow of Empire*, 7). At the same time, Horsley admits that "biblical books are not unanimously and unambiguously anti-imperial or pro-imperial. They speak with different and sometimes ambivalent voices" (7). Jack Nelson-Pallmeyer

also acknowledges that there is both a pro- and an anti-imperial thread in the Bible (*Saving Christianity from Empire* [New York: Continuum, 2005]).

Other biblical scholars have acknowledged the same ambivalence, but clearly favor the notes of resistance. In an informative summary of the Persian period, Jon Berquist notes that the rebuilding of the temple gave the Jews in the Persian colony of Yehud an identity over against the empire, as did the cultivation of practices of Sabbath keeping and prayer. Among "later scribes" who wrote the first six chapters of Daniel, he finds a dual effort to remain "loyal to their imperial patrons" while also "firm adherents of a local religion" (Berquist "Resistance and Accommodation in the Persian Empire," in *Shadow of Empire*, 56). He adds, "Daniel and the other heroes in these tales serve in the imperial court. But when they are put in positions of being asked or forced to violate the covenantal laws of their God, they refuse and suffer the consequences. They always stand firm in their knowledge that the God of heaven, the Most High God, is the ultimate king and sovereign, who gives imperial sovereignty to a king for a time, and can take it away. In these tales the faithful scribal heroes are at the end vindicated by God, sometimes even by the imperial king who has suddenly recognized the ultimately kingship of the God of Daniel" (56). Stories about Daniel "helped prepare the way for outright resistance by later generations." After 175 BC, as Hellenistic culture was spreading into Judea, scribes "were torn between their loyalty to and economic dependence on their aristocratic patrons and their loyalty to the Judean laws and traditions." These were probably responsible for Daniel 7–8, 10–12, with its visions that "represent the succession of empires that ruled Judea as horribly destructive beasts of prey." These forms of resistance "led to the Maccabean revolt against the empire," in which "large numbers of villagers, led by ordinary priests in villages and towns, chose to fight and even to die rather than to abandon their traditional way of life" (56–57). Though Berquist notes tensions and struggles regarding empire, it is clear both from the content of his article and from its rhetoric that he favors the anti-imperial features of the text. Jews who find their way into imperial courts are "accommodating" while those who resist militarily during the Maccabean period are martyrs dying for their "traditional way of life."

By contrast, Norman K. Gottwald argues that the exodus and Sinai traditions of "early Israel" left a straightforward and consistent "anti-imperial legacy" to later Israel, a legacy abandoned during the monarchy. Gottwald, "Early Israel as an Anti-Imperial Community," in *Shadow of Empire*, 9–24.

I do not think "ambivalence" or "ambiguity" accurately characterizes the biblical treatment of empire, largely because the Bible acknowledges a plurality of kinds of imperial power. Favoring Cyrus, who sends Jews from exile and supports their temple project, and hating Nero, who lit Christians as living lanterns, betrays no "ambivalence" or "ambiguity" toward some essence called "empire." Differing evaluations are a simple matter of recognizing moral differences.

4. For all his mellowed wisdom, Richard Neuhaus's generic use of "Babylon" or "Babel" to describe the "city of man" is oversimplified and distorts the more varied biblical picture (*American Babylon: Notes of a Christian Exile* [New York: Basic Books, 2009]). Ironically, it is the same oversimplification that distorts the political theology of some of Neuhaus's opponents.

5. We have only to pair Eusebius and Augustine to realize that the complexity of the biblical account of empire has been evident in the Christian tradition. See the range of views in Kwok Pui-lan, et al., eds., *Empire & the Christian Tradition: New Readings of Classical Theologians* (Minneapolis: Fortress, 2007).

Endnotes

6. Note, for instance, the elements of court ceremony that are paralleled in Christian liturgy, a process that is already evident in the heavenly worship of Revelation 4–5. See David E. Aune, "The Influence of Roman Imperial Court Ceremonial on the Apocalypse of John," *Biblical Research* 18 (1983) 5–26. The implication of Revelation is that the imperial ceremony is an infernal counterfeit of the heavenly worship of the Lamb, the world's true Lord.

7. James B. Jordan, "Babylon and the Babel Project," Biblical Horizons Occasional Paper #39 (Niceville, FL: Biblical Horizons, 2011) 16.

8. This theme has been taken up in recent years by scholars in various disciplines. Rene Girard is the best known of the sacrificial theorists of culture and has written on the subject in numerous books. Legal scholar and political theorist Paul W. Kahn examines this theme in *Sacred Violence: Torture, Terror, and Sovereignty* (Ann Arbor: University of Michigan Press, 2008) and *Putting Liberalism in Its Place* (Princeton: Princeton University Press, 2005). From a historical perspective, see Ivan Strenski, *Contesting Sacrifice: Religion, Nationalism, and Social Thought in France* (Chicago: University of Chicago Press, 2002) and *Why Politics Can't Be Freed from Religion* (London: Wiley-Blackwell, 2010).

9. Though English distinguishes "Babel" from "Babylon," Hebrew does not. Both English words translate the same Hebrew term, בָּבֶל.

10. See James B. Jordan, "Babel Project."

11. In European history, the distinction between "empire" and "nation-state" is blurry. On the one side, nations gestated in the womb of empire. Rome set up administrative districts that later became the nations and principalities that succeeded the empire. Anthony Pagden writes, "Spain, Britain, and Gaul were all in various ways creations of Rome. So too was Italy itself. The modern states of eastern and central Europe took shape under the aegis of the Holy Roman Empire. Spanish viceregal divisions lie behind the modern frontiers of the republics of Spanish America. Much of the present distribution of peoples in eastern and central Europe is the creation of the Austro-Hungarian Empire, or the empire of the tsars, or the Soviet Union" (*Peoples and Empires*, 160). On the other side, the nation-states that emerged in the early modern period took the shape they did through internal conquests. The big story of early modern political history was the centralization of the state, and this took place as some rulers of principalities expanded their territories at the expense of others. The nation-states that have emerged since decolonization in the middle of the twentieth century have also been forged by imperial experience, though in a different way. European colonial powers were able to take control of vast stretches of Africa during the nineteenth century because of their superior military technology and wealth, and also because they had a unified political will. They confronted a ragtag collection of tribes who had no consciousness of being a single nation or people. Resistance to colonization became severe when the colonized began to take on the consciousness of the colonizers. They had to develop some sort of national consciousness, ironically becoming more European as they fought off European hegemony. Pagden writes, "Resistance to any kind of rule requires organization and courage. In the case of resistance to colonial rule, however, it also requires some vision of a better future in some postcolonial world. It requires an ideology capable of mobilizing those who might otherwise be prepared to continue to accept the status quo as merely inevitable. Ironically, this ideology was provided by the same refashioning of society that had been the driving force behind most modern imperialism, namely nationalism. Of all of Lord Macaulay's 'European Institutions,' the only one that most colonial peoples in

the twentieth century have ever consistently demanded is the independent nation-state" (Pagden, *Peoples and Empires*, 158).

12. Eber is עֵבֶר, and a few chapters later Abram is described as an "Eberite" or "Hebrew" (עִבְרִי). Abram's genealogy confirms that he is a descendent of Eber (Gen 11:16–26). This is the obvious meaning of "Hebrew" in Genesis. Speculative connections with the *hapiru* are unnecessary and misleading.

13. Commentators commonly ignore the variation of terms or take it as poetic parallelism, emphasizing the linguistic unity of early humanity. See U. Cassuto, *A Commentary on the Book of Genesis, Part II: From Noah to Abraham*, trans. Israel Abrahams (Jerusalem: Magnes, 1964) 239.

14. I am dependent here on the arguments of James B. Jordan, "Babylon and the Babel Project."

15. Amy Chua argues that all enduring empires ("hyperpowers") have been characterized by toleration, and sounds warnings about the revival of American nativism (*Day of Empire: How Hyperpowers Rise to Global Dominance—and Why They Fall* [New York: Anchor, 2007]). In biblical terms, her warning is directed to Babelic empires.

16. Jordan, "Babel Project," 1, 6. Religious motivations have been semi-secularized in the modern world and carry on this religious aim under the heading of "civilizing." See Brett Bowden, *Empire of Civilization: The Evolution of an Imperial Idea* (Chicago: University of Chicago Press, 2009).

17. *City of God*, 1.30.

18. For a summary of Augustine's analysis of the role of fear in Roman imperialism, see Robert Dodaro, *Christ and the Just Society in the Thought of Augustine* (Cambridge: Cambridge University Press, 2004) 41–43.

19. As we will see in chapter 2, this is not characteristic of every biblical empire.

20. Jordan, "Babel Project," 9.

21. Ibid., 9–10.

22. The fall of each renewed "Babel" is accompanied by a similar confusion and scattering (ibid., 2). The fall of neo-Babylon to the Persians comes on the heels of the "handwriting on the wall" episode (Daniel 6), and the impending doom of Israel-in-Empire is marked by the gift of tongues at Pentecost (Acts 2), which inverts the confusion of tongues and lips at Babel.

23. The reference to Nimrod as the founder of Babel (Gen 10:9–10) suggests that this centralization may have gone even further, concentrating power not only in a single capital but in a single emperor.

24. The first sentences of this paragraph sketch some elements of a "theory of imperialism" that, if filled out in sufficient detail, would be more satisfying and complete than many of the theories constructed in the past century. Empires cannot, I think, be explained adequately in terms of purely political or economic pressures or interests. Though these pragmatic interests may explain much imperial behavior, imperial actors will rarely make the necessary sacrifices if they are not convinced that they serve something more than interest. To succeed, imperialism requires an eschatologically excited ideology or mythology.

For an introduction to the theoretical discussion, see Wolfgang J. Mommsen, *Theories of Imperialism*, trans. P. S. Falla (Chicago: University of Chicago Press, 1982); Alejandro Colas, *Empire* (Cambridge: Polity, 2007); and Herrfried Munkler, *Empires: The Logic of World Domination from Ancient Rome to the United States*, trans. Patrick Camiller (Cambridge: Polity, 2007). The most historically influential theory is that of Lenin, who

Endnotes

considered imperialism the highest stage of capitalism (*Imperialism: The Highest Stage of Capitalism* [Chippendale, Australia: Resistance, 1999]). Much of Lenin's data was drawn from J. A. Hobson's *Imperialism: A Study* (London: J. Pott, 1902). Recent decades have seen an explosion of cultural analyses of imperialism, especially in postcolonial theory, which, unlike earlier politically focused studies, give detailed attention to the religious aspects of imperialism. See Edward W. Said, *Culture and Imperialism* (New York: Vintage, 1993) and the early classic, Frantz Fanon, *The Wretched of the Earth*, trans. Richard Philcox (New York: Grove, 2004). Studies of globalization, especially those inspired by the Frankfurt School, have likewise focused on cultural power.

25. The sequence has repeated itself at various times: Rome collapses, but even before it collapses monks are establishing outposts of Christian community on the frontiers. What might have been waiting in the chrysalis of the Soviet bloc or Maoist China during years of horrific repression? What Abraham might be called out when American hegemony vanishes? See Liao Yiwu, *God Is Red: The Secret Story of How Christianity Survived and Flourished in Communist China* (San Francisco: HarperOne, 2011).

26. This point is made by Jack Nelson-Pallmeyer, *Saving Christianity from Empire*, 111, describing Abraham as "the father of empire." Many scholars complain that the Bible "reinscribes" imperial aims and agendas into its own categories and expectations. "Reinscription" is a poorly chosen term, since it implies that Israel was originally purified from all imperial taint but was later defiled. My argument is that imperial hopes and aspirations are embedded in God's original program for Israel. Empire is inscribed, not *re*inscribed. Deleting "reinscription" entails deleting most of Israel's history.

27. Jordan, "Babel Project," 11.

28. Ibid., 3.

29. According to Matthew's schematic summary, the call of Abraham and the exile are two of the key seams in Israel's history. Abraham begins Israel's history with a call out of an empire; Israel's history is broken again when they are sent into Babylon and when, even after their release, they continue under the dominion of ancient empires.

30. Van Leeuwen, *Christianity in World History: The Meaning of the Faiths of East and West*, trans. H. H. Hoskins (New York: Scribner's, 1964) 97–98.

31. Ibid., 98.

32. Ibid., 111.

33. Ibid., 110.

34. Ibid., 100.

35. Oliver O'Donovan, *Ways of Judgment* (Grand Rapids: Eerdmans, 2005) 211. O'Donovan points to Psalm 87 to show that Israel's hopes were to have the nations look to Zion as "mother."

36. Later, Chaldea becomes a synonym for Babel (cf. 2 Kgs 24:2; 25:4–5, 10; Isa 13:19; 23:13; etc.). Even before the exodus from Egypt, Israel's story is one of detachment from the Babel project.

37. Abram's departure from Ur anticipated Israel's later departure from Egypt. Haran, Abram's brother, died in Ur, a sign that Ur, like Egypt later, is a place of death (Gen 11:28). On the way to the land that the Lord shows, Abram's father Terah dies at Haran, as the Exodus generation later will die on the way to the promised land (Gen 11:32). When Abram enters the land, he sets up altars throughout, often at the very places where Israel will later fight major battles. He builds altars in the land in a proto-conquest of Canaan (Genesis 12–13). See Jordan, "Babel Project," 19.

Endnotes

CHAPTER 2

1. The prophets make the same point. Ezekiel 16 depicts in grotesque detail harlot Judah's erotic obsession with the idols of Egypt, Assyria, and Chaldea.
2. On Egyptian political theology, Henri Frankfort, *Kingship and the Gods: A Study of Ancient Near Eastern Religion as the Integration of Society and Nature* (Chicago: University of Chicago Press, 1978) remains a classic.
3. A number of verbal echoes link the opening chapter of Exodus with the story of Babel in Genesis 11. The men of Babel make the tower and city with bricks and mortar, and the Israelites in Egypt are enlisted to work on Pharaoh's storage cities with the same materials (Exod 1:14). Earlier, descendants of Eber worked willingly with Nimrod to establish Babel, but now they are forced to participate. At Babel, Yahweh confused the "lip" of the nations, and in Egypt too He befuddles the gods of the Egyptians and triumphs over them (Exod 12:12). James B. Jordan, "Babylon and the Babel Project," Biblical Horizons Occasional Paper #39 (Niceville, FL: Biblical Horizons, 2011) 21.
4. This entire paragraph is dependent on Jordan, "Babel Project," 21–22.
5. Thanks to my colleague Chris Schlect for this detail about Assyrian civic architecture.
6. Walter Brueggemann, "Faith in the Empire," in Richard Horsley, ed., *In the Shadow of Empire: Reclaiming the Bible as a History of Faithful Resistance* (Louisville: Westminster John Knox, 2008) 32.
7. The phrase עַם עֶבְרָתִי ("people of my wrath") puns on the verb for "pass over" (עָבַר; cf. Exod 12:12, 23; 13:12; 15:16).
8. The combination of "rod" and "staff" occurs only in Psalm 23:4; Isaiah 9:4; Isaiah 10:5, 24. Babylon too is Yahweh's instrument, though pictured not as a "rod" but as a "cup of wrath" that is poured out on the nations (Jer 25; 51:7ff.).
9. Similarly, Yahweh later makes war on Jerusalem through Nebuchadnezzar (Jer 21:1–7). Isaiah makes the same point in his description of Assyria's triumphal procession at the end of the chapter. Assyria marches south, relentlessly scattering towns, leaving lamentation, fear, and destruction in their wake. When they get to Nob, they have to stop and can go no further. All they can do is shake their fist in impotent fury at the Lord's house on Zion and Jerusalem. This seems to be specifically a prophecy of the Assyrian invasion and siege that is described later in the book of Isaiah. See J. Alec Motyer, *The Prophecy of Isaiah: An Introduction and Commentary* (Downers Grove, IL: InterVarsity, 1993).
10. This is the first time that Yahweh pronounces a woe against a Gentile nation, and it is very rare in Scripture, but it sets the pattern for Yahweh's dealings with future empires, empires that He uses for His purposes and then judges.
11. As Augustine saw, the problem with the city of man is not its lack of an overriding aim, but its misdirected love. Like Rome, the Assyrian emperor had a single focused purpose, self-promotion. See O'Donovan in *Bonds of Imperfection: Christian Politics, Past and Present* (Grand Rapids: Eerdmans, 2004) 58.
12. Later, Yahweh throws down Babylon for similar reasons. They gloat over Israel (Jer 50:11ff.) and devour her (Jer 50:17; 51:34–40), in arrogance (Jer 50:29f.) mistreating the Abrahamic people (Jer 50:33f.), thus bringing on themselves a curse. Yahweh punishes them for their idolatry (Jer 50:38). As with Assyria, Israel becomes an agent for shattering the empire (Jer 51:19ff.), and thus Babylon's fall is the vindication of the people of God (Jer 51:11).

Endnotes

13. The "thorns and briers" might be Assyria. The low and unproductive among the Assyrians are tinder for the flame. Assyria comes against Judah and against Yahweh who dwells in consuming fire, but they are a bunch of briers and thorns, a bramble bush, ready for the fire. And Yahweh is going to consume them. Or, the briers and thorns might, as they have elsewhere in Isaiah, refer to the useless plants in the land of Judah. In that case, Assyria comes to devour Judah, and they start the fire that consumes the wicked in Judah, the useless members of the people of God. But that only ends up burning up Assyria too.

14. Brueggemann, "Faith in the Empire," in *Shadow of Empire*, 35. As I note in my *1-2 Kings* (Grand Rapids: Brazos, 2006), Hezekiah is the only king in 1-2 Kings who uses the temple as it was designed to be used—for prayer rather than plunder.

15. Brueggemann, "Faith in the Empire," in *Shadow of Empire*, 37.

16. Jordan, "Babel Project," 27.

17. The verb פוץ is used for the Babel (Gen 11:4), and for Israel in exile (Jer 9:16; 30:11).

18. Van Leeuwen, *Christianity in World History: The Meaning of the Faiths of East and West*, trans. H. H. Hoskins (New York: Scribner's, 1964) 101. Van Leeuwen points out that Yahweh achieves His purposes through remnants that function as parts for the whole; in this sense, Israel herself is a remnant nation.

19. The AV translates the clause "unto whom it seemed meet unto me," but the NASB translation provided above is preferable. יָשַׁר refers not to the fitness of Yahweh's decision but the fitness of the person to whom Yahweh gives the earth. The word means "straight," "right" or "pleasing" (cf. Judg 14:3, 7; 1 Chron 13:4; Ps 119:128; Prov 15:21; Isa 40:3). Yahweh gives to the one who is found "straight" in His judgment, His eyes. The gift of the nations is Yahweh's reward to Nebuchadnezzar for some virtue of character, as the dominion of Rome was the fitting though limited reward, according to Augustine, for limited though genuine Roman virtue. Jeremiah's description of Nebuchadnezzar is consistent with historical neo-Babylon, which was seen as a liberator from Assyrian cruelty by many of the peoples who became part of the empire. Thanks to my colleague Chris Schlect for this comment.

20. The claim that Yahweh has given everything "into the hand" of the king of Babylon is repeated in Ezra 5:12; Jer 20:4; 32:4.

21. Consistent with this, the "good figs" of Jeremiah's vision are not the Jews who remain in the land but those who are harvested and carried to the storehouse of Babylon.

22. I don't agree with all the conclusions John Howard Yoder draws from this point, but the basic point is exactly right: From the exile to the time of Jesus, Israel was called to a Jeremian practice. See *The Jewish-Christian Schism Revisited* (Grand Rapids: Eerdmans, 2003).

23. See James B. Jordan, *The Handwriting on the Wall: A Commentary on the Book of Daniel* (Atlanta: American Vision, 2007).

24. Cf. Nebuchadnezzar's treatment of the prophet Jeremiah (Jeremiah 39).

25. The final chapters of Kings are arranged in three similar cycles that record three stages of Judah's exile. The first cycle recounts the events leading to the exile of Jehoichin, followed by the exile of Zedekiah, which is then followed by the tragic governorship of Gedeliah who is assassinated by Ishmael. The first two narratives are told in almost exact parallel, and the last has a number of resemblances to the first two.

The story of Jehoiachin begins with his father Jehoiakim. His predecessor, Jehoahaz, was carted off to Egypt by Pharaoh Neco (23:34), who placed Eliakim on the throne and changed his name to Jehoiakim (23:34). He did evil in Yahweh's sight (23:37), and as a result Yahweh subjects him to Nebuchadnezzar of Babylon, whom he serves for three years (24:1). After Jehoiakim rebels against Babylon (24:1), Yahweh sends bands of Chaldeans, Arameans, Moabites, and Ammonites against Judah to destroy it, just as He had warned through the prophets (24:2). After a quick summary of Judah's sins (24:3-4: the sins of Manasseh, and innocent blood), Jehoiakim is dispatched from the story and Jehoiachin his son takes his place (24:5-9). Meanwhile, Nebuchadnezzar has been marching from Babylon to Jerusalem to avenge Jehoikim's rebellion, but finds the son on the throne in place of his father (24:10-11). Jehoiachin "goes out" to the king of Babylon, along with the queen mother and his chief servants (24:12); Nebuchadnezzar takes Jehoiachin prisoner and removes him, his mother and servants, and "all Jerusalem" to Babylon (24:12), leaving only the poorest in the land (24:14-16). Nestled between the two references to exiles, the text lists the gold treasures that Nebuchadnezzar removes from the temple (24:13).

At this point, the narrative resets and begins the very similar account of Zedekiah's exile. Jehoiachin goes off into exile just like Jehoahaz, though to Babylon rather than Egypt. Like Neco in the previous chapter, Nebuchadnezzar places a puppet king on the throne, Jehoiachin's uncle Mattaniah (24:17) and like Neco, Nebuchadnezzar changes his name, with pointed irony, to Zedekiah—"Yah is righteous!" (24:17). Zedekiah is evil like Jehoiakim, and like Jehoiakim he rebels against Nebuchadnezzar (24:18-20). In response, Nebuchadnezzar comes back to Jerusalem once again (25:1). Instead of going out to the king of Babylon, Zedekiah flees (25:4-5), ineffectively as it turns out, since he is rapidly caught and taken to Nebuchadnezzar who slaughters his sons before his eyes before blinding him and taking him to Babylon (25:6-7) along with the citizens of Jerusalem (25:11), once again leaving the poorest of the land (25:12). In addition to slaughtering Zedekiah's sons, Nebuzaradan brings sixty of the chief men of the land at Riblah, where they are struck down on Nebuchadnezzar's orders (25:18-21). As in the first cycle, a description of temple plunder is nestled between two paragraphs that describe the slaughter of officials (25:13-17; cf. vv. 6-7, 18-21).

With Zedekiah and his officials out of the way, the story resets again. The third cycle is more compressed than the first two, but has a similar overall shape. Nebuchadnezzar again sets up a puppet ruler, Gedeliah, on the throne in Jerusalem (25:22). Gedeliah's policy is the same as Jehoiachin's: Live in the land and serve the king of Babylon, and it will be well with you (25:24). Ishmael ben Nethaniah is the rebel in this cycle. He assassinates Gedeliah (25:25), and then flees to Egypt with "all the people" to escape Nebuchadnezzar's inevitable retaliation. The three cycles end where they began, with references to Egypt, which becomes the Omega of Israel's history as it was the Alpha (cf. 23:34 and 25:26). Like Zedekiah, Ishmael simply disappears from the story.

The similarities between the three narrative cycles of course invite comparison among the principal events and characters. Babylon is far more destructive in the second cycle than in the first. When Nebuchadnezzar takes Jehoiachin into exile, he leaves the city and temple intact, though the latter is emptied of its most valuable implements and furnishings. In retaliation for Zedekiah's rebellion, however, he burns the temple, the palace, and every great house in the city, then breaks the walls of Jerusalem (25:10-12). Though Zedekiah survives to be taken to Babylon, he disappears from the text. The change in the materials of the temple implements matches this intensification of violence and the concomitant tarnishing of Judah. 2 Kings 24:13 mentions "vessels of gold" cut and shipped to Babylon, but most of the temple furnishings listed in 2 Kings 25:13-17 are bronze.

Endnotes

Gold to bronze; which, being translated, means "Ichabod." The glory is departing, not only the most glorious glory of gold but the lesser glory of bronze, as it began to depart long before in the proto-exile when Pharaoh Shishak captured Solomon's gold shields and Rehoboam replaced them with bronze (1 Kgs 14:25–27).

26. This means that Christopher Begg's claim ("The Significance of Jehoiachin's Release: A New Proposal," *Journal for the Study of the Old Testament* 36 [1986] 51) that Jehoiachin is an impenitent "bad king" is overstated. Jehoiachin is characterized as an evildoer (24:9), but he follows Jeremiah's instructions in surrendering to Babylon, an act of faith rewarded by the compassion that Babylon shows.

27. James Jordan pointed out the chronology to me years ago: Daniel enters Babylon early in Nebuchadnezzar's reign in the third year of Jehoiakim (Dan 1:1–7), and is installed as a wise man in Nebuchadnezzar's second year (Dan 2:1). Nebuchadnezzar besieges Jerusalem in the ninth year of Zedekiah and again in the nineteenth year of Nebuchadnezzar's reign (2 Kgs 25:1, 8). By the time Jeremiah urges Judah to surrender, Daniel is well ensconced in the Babylonian court.

28. Commentators are divided about what Jehoiachin's rehabilitation means. Pessimists (led by Martin Noth) say it is a dismal conclusion to a tragic story of failure and destruction. Optimists (led by Gerhard von Rad) have taken it as a sign that, despite Judah's sins, Yahweh remains faithful to His promise to give David an eternal dynasty. Forced to choose, I would side with the optimists, partly for the structural reasons that I have already described, but the pessimists have a point. Donald Murray provides both a summary of the debate, and an important contribution in "Of All the Years the Hopes—or Fears? Jehoiachin in Babylon (2 Kgs 25:27–30)," *Journal of Biblical Literature* 120:2 (2001) 245–65. See also Jon D. Levenson, "The Last Four Verses of Kings," *Journal of Biblical Literature* 103:3 (1984) 353–61, esp. 353–54.

29. Better a throne than a cell, better a robe than a striped jumpsuit, better the king's portion than prison fare, but Jehoiachin is still a client of Babylon, and we cannot tell whether or not his favored status will last. There is no reference to sons, much less sons who share his privileges, and 2 Kgs 25:27 might imply that Evil-merodach ruled only a year. What happened after? We are not told. If 1–2 Kings ends with hope, it seems at best a sober and modest hope. Murray ("Of all the Years," 262) expresses the point through phrases like "dying glimmers" and "flickering light . . . through the deep gloom" and "a mocking phantasm of YHWH's solemn undertaking to David."

30. Murray ("Of all the Years," 253–56) argues that all of these expressions of favor are ambiguous, but at a number of points his arguments are overly subtle.

31. See Jeremy Schipper, "'Significant Resonances' with Mephibosheth in 2 Kings 25:27–30: A Response to Donald F. Murray," *Journal of Biblical Literature* 124:3 (2005) 521–29.

32. Kari Latvus, "Decolonizing Yahweh: A Postcolonial Reading of 2 Kings 24–25," in R. S. Sugirtharajah, ed., *The Postcolonial Biblical Reader* (London: Blackwell, 2006) 189. Latvus notes these connections, but draws very different conclusions from them than I have done. Latvus and Begg ("Significance," 54) are both correct that 2 Kings is a pro-Babylonian text. Levenson ("Last Four," 358–59) points to the sharp contrast between the attitude of 2 Kings toward Jehoiachin's alliance with Evil-merodach and Isaiah's scathing assault on Ahaz's early alliance with Tiglath-pileser.

33. Levenson, "Last Four," 361.

Endnotes

34. Though the wording of the two passages is not identical (7:47: לֹא נֶחְקַר מִשְׁקַל הַנְּחֹשֶׁת; 25:26: לֹא הָיָה מִשְׁקָל), both use מִשְׁקָל, which is used only one other time in Kings (1 Kgs 10:14).

35. The two pillars, Jachin and Boaz, represented vertically and visibly what the temple was horizontally and secretly. The capitals correspond to the דְּבִיר (Most Holy Place), the collar border at the base of the capital to the הֵיכָל (the nave or Holy Place) and the bronze trunk to the porch, the אוּלָם. Chains around the base of the capital correspond to the chains that separated the inner sanctuary from the הֵיכָל (1 Kgs 6:21), and the lily design of the capital (1 Kgs 7:19) architecturally echoes the flowers carved on the walls of the inner and outer sanctuary (1 Kgs 6:29, 32). At the same time, the pillars are humaniform. The capitals are "heads" of the pillars (רֹאשׁ), and the pillar as a whole is a monumental human guardian at the doorway of the temple. The names of the two pillars point to more specific associations. The name Jachin ("he will establish") appears in priestly lists (1 Chron 9:20; 24:17), while Boaz was a well-known ancestor in the Davidic line (Ruth 4). I am depending here on unpublished work of my former student, Lisa Beyeler, who in turn is dependent on the studies of James B. Jordan. See also Carol Meyers, "Jachin and Boaz in Religious and Political Perspective," *Catholic Biblical Quarterly* 45:2 (1983) 167–78.

36. Wes Howard-Brook (*"Come Out, My People!": God's Call out of Empire in the Bible and Beyond* [Maryknoll, NY: Orbis, 2010] 236–37) skims rapidly over these titles for Cyrus.

37. Bruce Lincoln, *Religion, Empire & Torture: The Case of Achaemenian Persia, with a Postscript on Abu Ghraib* (Chicago: University of Chicago Press, 2007) 40–43.

38. This characterization is strengthened if Begg and Levenson are correct that Evil-merodach enters into a "vassal treaty" with Jehoiachin (Begg, "Significance," 52; Levenson, "Last Four," 357).

39. Isaiah 49 states much the same. In the AV's happy translation, the prophet promises that Yahweh will make kings "nursing fathers" to Israel, and queens "nursing mothers." The allusion here is not to David, but reaches further, to the exodus and to Moses' complaint that Yahweh had made him "nurse" to an unwieldy son (Numbers 12). Gentile kings take up the Mosaic task of delivering Israel from exile. Scattered throughout the nations, it is not surprising that Israel would embrace Cyrus so enthusiastically. For a powerless subject people, a sympathetic emperor is a national savior. The analogies with Constantine are worth remarking.

40. Jordan ("Babel Project," 32) distinguishes between the uniformity of Babylon and the multiculturalism of the Persian empire. Berquist (*Shadow of Empire*, 45, 47, 56) agrees that the Persians allowed a significant degree of local autonomy, arranged for the resettlement of lands, and did not impose religious or cultural norms on their subject peoples. Berquist, however, sees the temple as a compromised gift from empire (50), and argues that Jews had to develop tactics of resistance to empire during this period, including new genres of writing, prayer, and Sabbath keeping (54–55). This point was confirmed to me in conversation with my colleague, Chris Schlect.

41. It is widely recognized that the Aramaic portion of Daniel (chs. 2–7) is arranged chiastically in such a way that Nebuchadnezzar's dream and Daniel's vision are parallel. See Dorsey, *Literary Structure of the Old Testament: A Commentary on Genesis-Malachi* (Grand Rapids: Baker, 2004) ch. 26.

42. Jordan, *Handwriting on the Wall.*

Endnotes

43. For discussion of the universalist thrust of Christianity in comparison to empire, and the argument that globalization is the secularized product of Christian eschatology, see Graham Ward, *The Politics of Discipleship: Becoming Postmaterial Citizens* (Grand Rapids: Baker, 2009) 79–98.

Chapter 3

1. Andrew Perriman convincingly argues that οικουμηνη in the New Testament does not refer to the world as a whole, but to the Greco-Roman world (*The Future of the People of God: Reading Romans Before and After Western Christendom* [Eugene, OR: Cascade Books, 2010] 54–55). More precisely, I believe it refers not just to the political configuration of the Gentile world, but to the Israel-in-Empire system established during and after Israel's Babylonian exile.

2. Richard Horsley (in Richard A. Horsley, ed., *In the Shadow of Empire: Reclaiming the Bible as a History of Faithful Resistance* [Louisville: Westminster John Knox, 2008] 95) claims that Jesus' ministry was "primarily" opposed to Rome. Opposition to Rome is found, by Horsley's lights, in the birth narratives, Jesus' exorcisms, his proclamation of the kingdom, and the condemnation of the priests. N. T. Wright's claim (*Jesus and the Victory of God* [Minneapolis: Fortress, 1997] 451, 466, 564, 605) that Jesus battles the "enemy behind the enemy," the Satanic forces that drive Roman oppression, is more accurate, but even Wright fails to reckon with the development of Rome and Judaism. The New Testament does not depict them as statically satanic entities. For more on Roman political theology, see John Dominic Crossan, "Roman Imperial Theology," in *Shadow of Empire*, 59–74; Horsley, "Jesus and Empire," in *Shadow of Empire*, 77–83. A number of scholars have emphasized the cultural and ideological dimensions of Roman power—Roman "soft power": S. R. F. Price, "Rituals and power," in Richard A. Horsley, ed., *Paul and Empire: Religion and Power in Roman Imperial Society* (Harrisburg, PA: Trinity, 1997) 47–71; Paul Zanker, "The Power of Images," in *Paul and Empire*, 72–86. See also the brief summary in Joerg Rieger, *Christ & Empire: From Paul to Postcolonial Times* (Minneapolis: Fortress, 2007) 26–30.

3. See the brief summary of the political situation of first-century Palestine in Richard Horsley, "Jesus and Empire," in *Shadow of Empire*, 77–83. At more length, see N. T. Wright, *The New Testament and the People of God* (Minneapolis: Fortress, 1992) chs. 6–7. Horsley employs the theories of James Scott in examining the forms of peasant resistance to Rome in *Jesus in Context: Power, People, & Performance* (Minneapolis: Fortress, 2008) chs. 8–9.

4. Βασιλεια was the Greek term for the Roman "empire." See Tatha Wiley, *Encountering Paul: Understanding Paul and his Message* (Lanham, MD: Rowman & Littlefield, 2009) 27; Don H. Compier and Joerg Rieger, eds., *Empire and the Christian Tradition: New Readings of Classical Theologians* (Minneapolis: Fortress, 2007) 49.

5. Even His ministry of exorcism and healing is viewed by some as part of His response to the effects of imperial domination (Horsley, "Jesus and Empire," 85–86). If that sounds odd, it is worth reminding ourselves that Jesus did expel a coterie of demons that gave him/themselves the very Roman name "Legion." That neither Jesus nor the disciples engaged in actions that we would recognize as "political" is not surprising. By the first century, Roman politics had become an elite undertaking, and citizens like the apostles had virtually no role in Roman government (Rieger, *Christ & Empire*, 30.).

Endnotes

6. The importance of this point has been forcefully made by Neil Elliott in, among other places, "The Anti-Imperial Message of the Cross," in *Paul and Empire*, 167–83.

7. James B. Jordan, "Babylon and the Babel Project," Biblical Horizons Occasional Paper #39 (Niceville, FL: Biblical Horizons, 2011) 4.

8. See Samuel Wells, *Improvisation: The Drama of Christian Ethics* (Grand Rapids: Brazos, 2004) for a discussion of how the categories of improv are relevant to Christian ethics.

9. See James Scott, *Weapons of the Weak: Everyday Forms of Peasant Resistance* (New Haven: Yale University Press, 1987); *Domination and the Arts of Resistance: Hidden Transcripts* (New Haven: Yale University Press, 1992).

10. Arend Th. van Leeuwen, *Christianity in World History: The Meeting of East and West*, trans. H. H. Hoskins (New York: Scribner's, 1964) 116.

11. I have discussed the echoes of Cyrus's decree in the Great Commission in "Jesus as Israel: The Typological Structure of Matthew's Gospel," available online at http://www.leithart.com/downloads/.

12. Perriman, *Future*, 56. Perriman's characterization of Constantine's regime—"adoption of Christianity as the religion of the empire"—is inaccurate. Constantine certainly favored the church and placed restrictions on paganism, but he did not officially establish Christianity as the religion of the empire. For a treatment of Constantine's policy of "concord," see Elizabeth Digeser, *The Making of a Christian Empire: Lactantius and Rome* (Ithaca: Cornell University Press, 1999). My own treatment of the issue is heavily dependent on Digeser; see *Defending Constantine: The Twilight of an Empire and the Dawn of Christendom* (Downers Grove, IL: InterVarsity, 2010) ch. 5.

13. See Horsley's summary in *Paul and Empire*, 140–47.

14. I do not find arguments against Pauline authorship of the pastorals convincing.

15. Perriman, *Future*, 21.

16. According to Neil Elliott, Paul taught his assemblies to expect the Lord's imminent arrival, his Parousia, when "sudden destruction" would fall on those who proclaim "peace and security." That is, Paul hoped for Jesus to arrive to dislodge Claudius and take the throne. Unfortunately, Paul misread the signs of the times: "He was wrong about the imminent arrival (Parousia) of the Lord, the messiah; wrong about the 'passing away' of 'the present form of the world'; wrong about the subjugation of hostile authorities; wrong about the coming unification of the nations in the worship of Israel's God" (Elliott, "Paul and Empire" in *Shadow of Empire*, 114).

17. See below, and Andrew Perriman, *Future*. For detailed interpretation of Jesus' expectations concerning the end of the temple and the collapse of Jerusalem's elites, see N. T. Wright, *Jesus and the Victory of God*.

18. Elliott, "Romans 13:1–7 in the Context of Imperial Propaganda" in *Paul and Empire*, 196, 201. Some recent writers have argued that Jesus' assault on the temple authorities was also a denunciation of Roman imperial power because the temple authorities were merely instruments of Rome. Wes Howard-Brook, for instance, argues that in John's gospel the word Ιουδαιοι refers not to a "religion" nor even in the end to an ethnic group in distinction from Gentiles but to "anyone—whether among the elite or the lowly, whether ethnically/religiously 'Jew' or 'Greek'—who upholds the imperial status quo embodied by the Jerusalem temple" (Howard-Brook, *"Come Out, My People!": God's Call out of Empire in the Bible and Beyond* [Maryknoll, NY: Orbis, 2010] 437). Paul's conversion, thus, is "not from 'Jew' to 'Christian' but from defender of the establishment status quo to defender of the Way of Jesus" (433). Howard-Brook is not entirely mistaken here, but his

Endnotes

portrait of first-century Palestine flattens out a complex reality. After all, Jesus frequently clashed with Pharisees who were certainly part of the Jewish "establishment" but just as certainly deeply hostile to the Roman occupiers. N. T. Wright wisely notes the danger of imposing fashionable twenty-first-century anti-imperialism on Paul ("Paul's Gospel and Caesar's Empire," in *Paul and Politics*, 164).

It is not at all clear what practical direction the anti-imperial interpretation provides. "Come out, My people" is, Howard-Brook says, God's call to early Christians and to us. But what does it mean to *come out* of empire? What, in particular, does it mean if Hardt and Negri are correct in their claim that empire is everything and everywhere? Does it mean a literal move out of Washington, DC or Seattle into the hinterland? Are believers who remain in DC, or believers who remain in the U.S. military, or believers who serve as agents for the Internal Revenue Service, compromised by the fact that they remain in those posts? Does "come out" mean cutting oneself off from the Internet, which is, after all, a global and imperial technology? Does it mean that I stop using imperial coinage, that I drop out of the imperial economy in favor of . . . what? A barter economy in my local church?

These questions are not *reductios* or mockery. If Jesus demands that we stop using imperial coins and driving on imperial roadways in order to be His disciples, then so be it. My objection is not that these demands are too radical or too difficult. My objection is that the New Testament does not impose such demands on Christians. Howard-Brook is correct to point out that John the Baptist's instructions to tax collectors and Roman soldiers do not necessarily constitute *carte blanche* "support" for the Roman empire, and he may even be correct that, if his instructions were followed, tax collectors and Roman soldiers would soon find themselves unable to support themselves in their vocations (421). Still, John does not tell tax collectors or soldiers to "come out" of the imperial system. Nor does Paul ever encourage any of the Roman officials before whom he appears to step down from their positions in a Satanic empire. If "come out" means adopting a new way of life *within* empire, resisting the lures and values of Greco-Roman culture in order to build a Christian way of life from within the empire, then the anti-imperial interpretation of the New Testament begins to sound much less radical than it appears to want to sound. That Howard-Brook endorses this more moderate viewpoint is supported by his favorable citation of Dorothy Day's comment that the Christian aim is to "build a new civilization within the shell of the old" (433).

As in chapter 1, my complaints against the anti-imperial scholarship are twofold. First, much of this scholarship is simplistic because ahistorical. Empire is empire is empire. There is no discrimination between better and worse empires or emperors, no sense that the empire might be more or less favorable, or more or less hostile, to the church, or that the church might be able to be more or less cooperative with empire. Church and empire are locked in a timeless, changeless struggle. That is a far more static and monologic picture of empire and church than the New Testament itself presents. Second, it is true that the New Testament employs imperial language in its own teaching and proclamation, but I do not believe this is accidental or a sign of the corruption of a pure anti-imperial gospel. See Stephen D. Moore, *Empire and Apocalypse: Postcolonialism and the New Testament* (Sheffield: Sheffield Phoenix, 2006), who uses Homi Bhabha's theory about parody turning to mimicry to explore how the New Testament, Revelation in particular, ends up with a "conception of the divine sphere as . . . empire writ large" (121). That seems to be another variation on the old liberal paradigm that sees the first century of the church's history as slippage toward compromise. Older liberals told the story as

Endnotes

a decline from low-church Protestant toward Catholic; political exegetes see a decline from the purely peasant anti-imperialism of Jesus toward the compromises of Paul and pseudo-Pauls. The stories have the same form, and neither is convincing. As in the Old Testament, so in the New: "Ambiguity" or complexity marks the Bible's assessment of empires throughout.

19. Blumenfeld, *The Political Paul: Justice, Democracy and Kingship in a Hellenistic Framework*, JSOT Supplement 210 (New York: Continuum, 2001) 368–413. John Milbank draws similar conclusions in "Paul against Biopolitics," in Milbank et al., *Paul's New Moment: Continental Philosophy and the Future of Christian Theology* (Grand Rapids: Brazos, 2010) 71–72.

20. Van Leeuwen, *Christianity in World History*, 125.

21. Ibid., 126–27. Van Leeuwen connects this with Paul's claim in Romans 2 that the Gentiles have a law on their heart. He does not see this as a reference to a general, permanent substructure of natural law; rather, it is a new conscience among the Roman Gentiles that fulfills the hopes of Jeremiah 31 and is a product of the cross and resurrection of Jesus.

22. To her credit, Brigitte Kahl recognizes that Acts gives a fairly sympathetic portrait of Rome (Kahl, "Acts of the Apostles: Pro(to)-Imperial Script," in *Shadow of Empire*, 137–56). In the various episodes where Paul is suspected of subverting the empire, "Acts makes every effort to draw as favorable a picture as possible," not only of Paul's ministry but of Roman officials: "Many times Roman officials testify that Paul is no threat to Roman rule." It is not to her credit, though, that Kahl then attempts to show that Luke reinvented the story of Paul in the aftermath of the destruction of the temple as a way of providing security for Christians who might be under suspicion: "we should understand him to be rewriting the history of the early Jesus movement and of Paul within the parameters of the post-70 Roman imperial context of special concern about security, particularly with regard to movements deeply rooted in Judean history and heritage. In some ways he is not unlike his contemporary Flavius Josephus, who surrendered to the Romans during their reconquest of Galilee and Judea and subsequently rewrote the history of the Judean people and of their tragic revolt against Rome from a Flavian perspective." Luke bends facts "in a pro-imperial direction," an example of "re-presenting and redrafting the past under the censorship of the now-dominant order," creating a "pro(to)-imperial script of the events preceding and following the death of Jesus of Nazareth" (143–48). Kahl's Luke is at war with himself, subversive in spite of his intentions. He lists the peoples who receive the Spirit in a kind of parody of imperial conquest lists; he depicts Jesus' apotheosis into heaven, an assault and a blasphemy against the imperial theology; in his recorded speeches, Paul never praises the *pax Romana* in his appearances before Roman officials, as advocates were expected to do. Yet, Luke omits and adds to his portrayal of Paul in his zeal to make Paul appear "safe" and thus contributes, like the Pastorals, to a "canonical betrayal" of Paul (156; the phrase is Neil Elliott's). Some of Kahl's Luke v. Luke is intriguing, but it is gratuitous that, faced with an account that has both pro- and anti-Roman features, she decides that the latter is the genuine evangel and the former an accommodation to circumstance. The technique is familiar: Paul's genuine theology of gender comes at the end of Galatians 3, but he is betrayed by his conservative imitators in Ephesians and the Pastorals. Familiar, but hardly conducive to arriving at a fair summary of the New Testament portrait of the relation of church and empire.

23. Howard-Brook, *"Come Out, My People!,"* 429.

24. James Jordan made this observation in personal conversation.

Endnotes

25. I am currently at work on an extended commentary on Revelation that will defend this reading in detail. For now, see James B. Jordan, *A Brief Reader's Guide to Revelation*. For other treatments of Revelation and empire, see Moore, *Empire and Apocalypse*; Wes Howard-Brook and Anthony Gwyther, *Unveiling Empire: Reading Revelation Then and Now* (Maryknoll, NY: Orbis, 2000); Leonard Thompson, *The Book of Revelation: Apocalypse and Empire* (New York: Oxford University Press, 1990). Thompson's study has convinced many that the period in which Revelation was written was not one of intense persecution or of inflated imperial claims. Thompson's arguments about Domitian's reign are convincing, but I think they are irrelevant to the interpretation of Revelation since I take the view that Revelation was written in the 1960s, decades before Domitian.

26. The fact that she "reigns over the kings of the earth" (17:18) is consistent with the identification of the city as Jerusalem, since from a biblical perspective Zion had long been the center of the world.

27. Jordan, "Babel Project," 23.

28. *Empire and Apocalypse*, 114: Stephen Moore writes, "More than any other early Christian text, Revelation is replete with the language of war, conquest, and empire—so much so, indeed, as to beggar description. Note in particular, however, that the promised reward for faithful Christian discipleship in Revelation is joint rulership of the Empire of empires soon destined to succeed Rome (3.21; 5.10; 20.4-6; 22.5), a messianic Empire established by means of mass-slaughter on a surreal scale . . . calculated to make the combined military campaigns of Julius Caesar, Augustus, and all their successors pale to insignificance by comparison. All this suggests that Revelation's overt resistance to and expressed revulsion toward Roman imperial ideology is surreptitiously compromised and undercut by covert compliance and attraction." Moore sees Revelation's vision fulfilled in "Constantinian Christianity," since Revelation "counters empire with empire" (119). Moore is mostly correct on his fundamental claim: Revelation does "reinscribe" the discourse of empire. He is mistaken, however, to see this as somehow a betrayal of the gospel or an accommodation. On the contrary, the transfer of imperial authority from kings to martyrs is an essential dimension of the good news, fulfilling, as I argued in chapter 1, the Abrahamic program of empire.

29. E. Michael Rusten, "The Structure of the Book of Revelation," unpublished paper presented at Evangelical Theological Society annual meeting, Atlanta, 2010.

30. The lampstands of the tabernacle are described as almond trees (Exod 25:33-34; 37:19-20).

31. For simplicity's sake, I call the male speaker "Solomon" or "the Lover" and the female "the bride" or "the beloved." I leave the question of authorship to the side.

32. I have explored the Solomonic imagery at length in "Imperial Lover: John's Vision of Jesus in Revelation 1," *Modern Theology* (forthcoming).

33. The conclusion of the seven letters to the churches confirms that the Song of Songs has contributed to the initial unveiling of Jesus. After a sharp rebuke of Laodicean complacency and lukewarmness, Jesus says He stands and knocks at the door of the church seeking entry: "Behold, I stand at the door and knock; if anyone hears My voice and opens the door, I will come in to Him, and will dine with him, and he with Me" (Rev 3:20; Gr. ιδου εστηκα επι την θυραν και κρουω). The promise to dine with the receptive members of the Laodicean church anticipates the marriage supper of the Lamb at the end of Revelation (19:9), and the Eucharistic overtones are clear. The scene strongly recalls Song of Songs 5:2, where the bride awakes to the sound of her lover's knocking on her door (LXX, κρουει επι την θυραν) and the sound of his voice (LXX, φωνη). In

the Song, the lover wants to make love, and the immediately preceding verse describes the lovemaking as a feast: "I have eaten my honeycomb and my honey; I have drunk my wine and my milk. Eat friends; drink and imbibe deeply, O lovers" (5:1). The lover seeks entry to make a feast of his beloved, and the allusion to this scene in Rev 3:20 lends an erotic overtone to Jesus' invitation to the Laodiceans. Jesus seeks entry to enjoy a feast of love with the few remaining in the Laodicean church who are still passionate members of His Bride. John works through the Song in reverse order. He begins the vision with a *wasf* (like that of Song of Songs 5:10-16) and moves back to the opening verses of Song of Songs 5, the lover's knocking (5:2), and finally to the feast (5:1).

34. For simplicity's sake, I leave out the iron-and-clay feet.

35. This is a commonplace observation among commentators. See David Aune, *Revelation 1-5*, Word Biblical Commentary (Waco, TX: Word, 1997) 95, 99.

36. That Jesus is revealed as the heir of the glory and authority of ancient empires provides another lens through which to read the "letters" that make up the bulk of the Patmos section of Revelation (see Aune, "The Form and Function of the Proclamations to the Seven Churches (Revelation 2-3)," *New Testament Studies* 36 [1990] 182-204). The messages to the churches resemble imperial edicts in various details, and "the author's use of the royal/imperial edict form is part of his strategy to polarize God/Jesus and the Roman emperor" (Aune, *Revelation 1-5*, 126-29).

37. I take αγγελος as a reference to human messengers or leaders in the church, essentially the presiding bishop of the church in each city of Asia. The simplest argument for this interpretation is the commonsensical one offered by James Jordan: If Jesus addressed spiritual angels, why would He write through a human amanuensis?

38. Horsley (*Paul and Politics*, 98) sees a pattern of martyrdom, vindication, renewal, and judgment on imperial rulers in Paul, and that same sequence is evident in Revelation. Horsley underplays, however, the transfer of imperial authority to the saints that is found in both Paul and Revelation.

39. This point is much emphasized, with some distortions, by R. A. Markus, *Saeculum: History and Society in the Theology of St. Augustine* (Cambridge: Cambridge University Press, 1970).

CHAPTER 4

1. I am drawing here on Eugen Rosenstock-Huessy's ideas about the "resurrection of the body": "A new soul, a fresh originality of the human heart, thereby survives the man or nation in which it came to birth and incarnates itself in a spiritual succession of typical representatives through the ages. For there are definite new phases of human existent never lived before . . . and, if they are genuine, they force themselves upon man's plasticity with such impressiveness that they don the bodies of later men and women in turn, and shame them into the same time" (*The Christian Future* [New York: Scribner's, 1946] 222).

2. See Kevin Phillips, *The Cousins' War: Religion, Politics, & the Triumph of Anglo-America* (New York: Basic Books, 1999).

3. Stanley Hauuerwas, *War and the American Difference: Theological Reflections on Violence and National Destiny* (Grand Rapids: Baker Academic, 2011) 15.

4. Between 2001 and 2005, in the heyday of Bush's faith-based initiatives, USAID gave over $374 million to World Vision, another $49 million to Food for the Hungry, and $31 million to Samaritan's Purse. This does not include, of course, the millions that

Endnotes

Americans donate privately. Numbers from Lee Marsden, *For God's Sake: The Christian Right and US Foreign Policy* (London: Zed, 2008) 130.

5. Gelernter, *Americanism: The Fourth Great Western Religion* (New York: Doubleday, 2007). Gelernter's thesis is a particularly arresting form of the notion of "civil religion," on which see Sidney Mead, *The Nation with the Soul of a Church* (New York: Harper & Row, 1975); Russell E. Richey and Donald G. Jones, eds., *American Civil Religion* (New York: Harper & Row, 1974).

6. Robert T. Handy, "The American Messianic Consciousness: The Concept of the Chosen People and Manifest Destiny," *Review and Expositor* 73:1 (1976) 47–58.

7. For a brief introduction to Wolin's contributions to the history of political thought, see C. C. Pecknold, *Christianity and Politics: A Brief Guide to the History*, Cascade Companions (Eugene, OR: Cascade Books, 2010) xiv–xxii.

8. *Politics and Vision: Continuity and Innovation in Western Political Thought*, exp. ed. (Princeton: Princeton University Press, 2006) 86.

9. Ibid., 87.

10. Ibid., 92. The independent status of the church in Western Christendom is a key theme in John Neville Figgis, *Studies of Political Thought from Gerson to Grotius, 1414–1625* (Cambridge: Cambridge University Press, 2011). See also Figgis, *Churches in the Modern State* (Ithaca: Cornell University Library, 2009).

11. Wolin, *Politics and Vision*, 119.

12. Pecknold, *Christianity and Politics*, 23–24. Kahn describes the early church as "a sort of inverse image of the state" (*Putting Liberalism in Its Place* [Princeton: Princeton University Press, 2008] 81).

13. See my *Defending Constantine* (Downers Grove, IL: InterVarsity, 2010) esp. ch. 14.

14. John Strayer, *On the Medieval Origins of the Modern State*, 2nd ed. (Princeton: Princeton University Press, 2005) 3.

15. Kahn, *Putting Liberalism in Its Place*, 81–84. Kahn observes that Christian resistance "has been generalized as a fundamental tenet of the Western—and particularly American—understandings of the relationship of the individual to the state," producing that unique form of political life, the "conscientious objector." Because martyrdom gets generalized, "politics and morality can never merge completely" in Western politics: "Conscientious objection remains a moral possibility that stands outside of every political value. The conscientious objectors bears witness; he does not organize a political party." Thus, "The Western state actually exists . . . under the very real threat of Christian martyrdom: a threat to expose the state and its claim to power as nothing at all. In the end, sacrifice is always stronger than murder. The martyr wields a power to defeat his murderer, which cannot be answered on the field of battle." Kahn insists that martyrdom is not a thing of the past: "think of the continuing place for the politics of human rights or the nonviolent resistance of the civil rights movement." This is the original source of Western fears of religious infiltration of politics. It is not originally a fear of theocracy. It is instead a fear that Christianity would expose the impotence of the state: "Separation of church and state enters the Western imagination not as an expression of a philosophically justified, secular politics, but as an aspect of religious belief. It includes not simply an idea that the state poses a danger to religion, but equally the opposite idea that religion poses a threat to the state because it reveals the insubstantiality of the concerns of the state and the limits of the state's power over the individual. The state's power is ultimately

Endnotes

the power to threaten life, but Christianity begins with a sacrificial act that undermines that threat by announcing life to be death, and true life to be beyond death" (83).

16. Kahn, *Putting Liberalism in Its Place*, 81–84.

17. See Anna Wilson, "Biographical Models: The Constantinian Period and Beyond," in *Constantine: History, Historiography and Legend*, ed. Samuel Lieu and Dominic Montserrat (London: Routledge, 1998) 107–35. Eusebius sometimes interpreted prophecy in a way that highlighted the church's role in bringing peace and pacifying the wild beasts that ruled the nations. See Michael J. Hollerich, "Religion and Politics in the Writings of Eusebius: Reassessing the First 'Court Theologian,'" *Church History* 59 (1990).

18. See R. A. Markus, *Saeculum: History and Society in the Theology of Augustine*, rev. ed. (Cambridge: Cambridge University Press, 2007) chs. 1–2.

19. Schmemann, *Church, World, Kingdom: Reflections on Orthodoxy and the West* (Crestwood, NY: St. Vladimir's Seminary Press, 1979).

20. Meyendorff, *Imperial Unity and Christian Divisions* (Crestwood, NY: St. Vladimir's Seminary Press, 1989) 30.

21. Pecknold, *Christianity and Politics*, 45. On the need for grace in the development of political virtue, see Robert Dodaro, *Christ and the Just Society in the Thought of Augustine* (Cambridge: Cambridge University Press, 2008).

22. For summaries of the shifts in general, see Pecknold, *Christianity and Politics*, 61–68; Figgis, *Political Thought*, Lecture II, who emphasizes the epochal struggle between Conciliarists and Papalists; Louis Dumont, *Essays on Individualism: Modern Ideology in Anthropological Perspective* (Chicago: University of Chicago Press, 1992) 44–103.

23. Henri de Lubac, *Corpus Mysticum: The Eucharist and the Church in the Middle Ages*, trans. Gemma Simmonds (Notre Dame: University of Notre Dame Press, 2007).

24. Wolin, *Politics and Vision*, 120–21. The final quotation is from Joseph Mazzini, *The Duties of Man and Other Essays*.

25. The term is from John Bossy, recently used by William Cavanaugh, *Migrations of the Holy* (Grand Rapids: Eerdmans, 2011).

26. *Contra Faustum*, XXII. See Daniel J. Castellano, "The First Crusade and the Medieval Concept of Holy War," 4–6, available at http://www.arcaneknowledge.org/histschol/firstcrusade.htm.

27. James A. Brundage, "Holy War and the Medieval Lawyers," in Thomas Patrick Murphy, ed., *The Holy War* (Columbus: Ohio State University Press, 1976) 104–5.

28. On state-building in the late medieval and early modern period, see Charles Tilly, "War Making and State Building as Organized Crime," available at http://www.jesusradicals.com/wp-content/uploads/warmaking.pdf; Tilly, *Coercion, Capital and European States: AD 990–1992*, rev. ed. (London: Wiley-Blackwell, 1992); Tilly, ed., *The Formation of National States in Western Europe* (Princeton: Princeton University Press, 1975). Tilly's theories and studies form part of the basis for Victor Lee Burke's *The Clash of Civilizations: War-Making and State Formation in Europe* (Cambridge: Polity, 1997). William Cavanaugh has also relied on Tilly's work in various books. See also Anthony Giddens, *The Nation-State and Violence* (Berkeley: University of California Press, 1987) and Richard Bean, "War and the Birth of the Nation State," *Journal of Economic History* 33 (1973) 203–21. In both England and France, the state taxed the clergy over the protests of the Pope, and everyone accepted the decision. In France the state asserted its right to try high clergy for treason. Though the French clergy were not favorable to the king, they did not stand up for Papal authority either, perhaps on the assumption that "it was better to preserve harmony and unity in France than to defend the reputation of

Endnotes

the pope." In any case, this change "produced no martyrs" and the clergy "did not even criticize royal policy" (Strayer, *Medieval Origins*, 45–47, 54–55).

29. Strayer, *Medieval Origins*, 56–57.

30. See Adrian Hastings, *The Construction of Nationhood: Ethnicity, Religion and Nationalism* (Cambridge: Cambridge University Press, 1997) 196–97. Hastings makes the arresting argument that the Bible was the key source in the development of national identity in the West; the relatively rare use of the Latin *natio* in the Vulgate and the frequent use of the English "nation" in English Bibles offered Israel to English readers and hearers as a worked-out model of nationhood (14–27, 55–58).

31. See Anthony W. Marx, *Faith in Nation: Exclusionary Origins of Nationalism* (Oxford: Oxford University Press, 2003).

32. I find William Cavanaugh's arguments against the notion of "religious war" utterly compelling. See especially *The Myth of Religious Violence* (Oxford: Oxford University Press, 2009) ch. 3.

33. On "totalitarian" society, see Bernd Wannenwetsch, *Political Worship* (Oxford: Oxford University Press, 2004) 207–18; on the medieval notion of "the whole" as a congeries of societies, see Dumont, *Individualism*, 74–75.

34. Kahn, *Putting Liberalism in Its Place*, 86: The modern state is "to maintain the historical presence of an experience of ultimate meaning," an ultimate meaning that comes to expression in sacrificial death on behalf of the nation.

35. By "an-ecclesial," I intend something stronger than "non-ecclesial." I want to say that the American typology has no place for a church independent of the nation.

36. My friend Kelly Kerr has worked out the typology in some detail (personal communication, December 16, 2011): As Israel left Egypt through the sea, so Americans crossed the sea to leave the oppression of Europe; the Sinai covenant is replicated in the Mayflower Compact and the covenant-commitments of Massachusetts Bay; the Indians fill the role of Canaanites, sins filled up and ready for expulsion. Kelly points also to the fact that America, like Israel, split into Northern and Southern "kingdoms."

37. The well-known phrase is, of course, Perry Miller's.

38. Adam in Eden has also loomed large in the American imagination. See David Noble, *The Eternal Adam and the New World Garden: The Central Myth of the American Novel since 1830* (New York: Braziller, 1968).

39. Before the America's were settled, English Christians had developed a theology of national election, fueled in large measure by the work of John Foxe, whose *Book of Martyrs* was one of the most widely and deeply read books in early modern England. In that history, Foxe combined English chronicle with spiritual biography, creating a unique blend of national and redemptive history. As Sacvan Bercovitch describes it, Foxe's conflation "became the staple of the entire literature of national election" which "asserted the confluence, in Britain alone, of the national union and the covenant of grace" (Bercovitch, *The Puritan Origins of the American Self* [New Haven: Yale University Press, 1975] 78). Despite this conflation, Foxe's book was marked by an ecclesiological ambiguity since Foxe recognized that "Church is *not* nation . . . nor the country religion, nor God English" (78). Hastings also emphasizes the role of Foxe in the formation of British national identity (*Construction of Nationhood*, 55–59).

40. Practically, New England churches remained distinct from the state. Four colonies—Rhode Island, New Jersey, Pennsylvania, and Delaware—had no established church. Even in the majority of colonies that had established churches, the churches were institutionally and functionally distinct from the civil order. Pastors were not to

Endnotes

perform the duties of magistrates, nor were magistrates to meddle in church affairs. The two institutions were closely entwined. Following European Reformed precedent, the Cambridge Platform of 1648 stated that it was the "Duty of the Magistrate to take care of matters of Religion, and to improve his Civil Authority." Religious sins bore civil penalties: "Idolatry, Blasphemy, Heresie, venting corrupt and pernicious Opinions, that destroy the Foundation, open contempt of the Word preached, Profanation of the Lords Day, disturbing the peaceable Administration and Exercise of the Worship and holy things of God, and the like, are to be restrained and punished by Civil Authority." Quoted in Robert T. Handy, *A Christian America: Protestant Hopes and Historical Realities* (New York: Oxford University Press, 1971) 12–13.

41. "A Modell of Christian Charity," in Cherry, ed., *God's New Israel*, 40.

42. The conflation of New England and Israel is evident, for instance, in the eighteenth-century debate between Increase Mather and Solomon Stoddard concerning admission to the Lord's table. According to Stoddard, "the entire nation comprised the church, because the entire nation, saints and sinners alike, enjoyed a special covenant with God" (Robert Middlekauf, *The Mathers*, quoted in Conor Cruise O'Brien, *God Land: Reflections on Religion and Nationalism* [Cambridge: Harvard University Press, 1988] 30). Mather insisted that New England churches must function differently from the churches of the old world. Yet Mather's rhetoric indicated that he shared with Stoddard the view that the entire colony constituted the people of God. Stoddard's program of open communion robbed "New England of the type . . . Beautiful as Tirzah, Comely as Jerusalem, Terrible as an Amy With Banners . . . on which hangs all the glory of the house of Israel . . . of its glory at the end of history." Mather's statement is studded with phrases from the Song of Songs, which historically had been applied to the Church. He resorted frequently to the Son to express his rapture over the beauties of his country: "Awake, Awake, put on thy strength, O New-England Zion, and put on thy Beautiful Garments, O American Jerusalem. . . Put on thy Beautiful Garments, O America, the holy city" (quoted in Bercovitch, *Puritan Origins*, 107). Other traditional ecclesial images were also applied to the American colonies: Preachers often spoke this invocation, "Christ may bestow upon America . . . that salutation, 'O my dove!'" (Song 2:14). Philip Freneau borrowed the related bridal imagery of the Apocalypse: America is "a new Jerusalem sent down from heaven . . . a pattern for the world beside" (quoted in Russel Nye, *This Almost Chosen People: Essays in the History of American Ideas* [East Lansing: Michigan State University Press, 1966] 169).

The dove type linked with other biblical incidents and also with earlier American history. As Bercovitch says, "The colonial clergy applied the image [of the dove] punning on Columbus/*columbina* (Latin for 'dove'), specifically, 'peculiarly,' to their redemptive journey toward a new heaven and new earth—the new Age of the Holy Spirit in the New World. [Cotton] Mather frequently draws out this application: in his biography of Francis Higginson, for example, the 'American Noah,' and, at the start of the *Magnalia*, in his description of the transatlantic crossing as the voyage of a second, greater 'family of Noah,' which changed geography into 'Christiano-graphy.' 'The Old World,' he explains, referring to Noah's time as a type of Israel's degeneracy, 'was destroyed, because the grant Prophecy of our SAVIOUR was forgotten in it, and a New World was brought on for the Revival of that Prophecy'" (Bercovitch, *Puritan Origins*, 98–99). England's condition was part of the flood typology. Winthrop was convinced that "God will bring some heavy Affliction upon this land and that speedily," and America showed itself God's "means to

Endnotes

save out of this generall callamitie," as the ark was Noah's salvation from a corrupt world (quoted in Bercovitch, *Puritan Origins*, 102).

43. Quoted in Bercovitch, *Puritan Origins*, 103-4.
44. Ibid., 110.
45. Ibid., 100.
46. See William R. Hutchison, *Errand to the World: American Protestant Thought and Foreign Missions* (Chicago: University of Chicago Press, 1987) 1-42.
47. The nationalist direction of American typology is an episode in the narrative that Milbank tells concerning the Hobbes cooption of the Bible by the state. *Theology and Social Theory: Beyond Secular Reason* (London: Wiley-Blackwell, 2006).
48. Street, "The American States Acting Over the Part of the Children of Israel in the Wilderness and Thereby Impeding Their Entrance into Canaan's Rest," in Conrad Cherry, ed., *God's New Israel: Religious Interpretations of American Destiny*, rev. ed. (Chapel Hill: University of North Carolina Press, 1998) 69.
49. Street, "American States Acting," 69, 75: "When we are favoured with a little success, we are apt to be elated in our minds like the children of Israel after the overthrow of the Egyptians in the red sea, and then with them to rejoice and to encourage ourselves in the cause in which we are engaged; then we can trust, as we imagine, in God, and hope for his salvation and deliverance.... we are acting over the like sins with the children of Israel in the wilderness.... We are apt to think that our cause is so righteous with regard to Great-Britain, that I fear we are ready to forget our unrighteousness towards God. And while we are endeavouring to get rid of the unreasonable commands of an earthly sovereign, I fear we forget to obey the most reasonable commands of the rightful Sovereign of the Universe. Let us look upon the ground on which we stand; consider our guilt and danger, and be humble for our sins, and under all the tokens of God's displeasure against us on the account of our sins, repent and reform whatever is amiss in the midst of us."
50. Quoted in Bruce Feiler, *America's Prophet: Moses and the American Story* (New York: William Morrow, 2009) 4.
51. Quoted in Feiler, *America's Prophet*, 64.
52. Young, "Discourses," in Cherry, ed., *God's New Israel*, 131. Harold Bloom correctly argues that Mormonism is the most distinctively American of American religions, the perfect specimen of the Gnostic American religion. *The American Religion: The Emergence of the Post-Christian Nation* (New York: Simon & Schuster, 1993).
53. Beecher, "The Battle Set in Array," in Cherry, ed., *God's New Israel*, 171-72.
54. Quoted in Stephen H. Webb, *American Providence: A Nation With a Mission* (New York: Continuum, 2004) 37. The quotation is from *White Jacket* (1850).
55. In his study of the use of Moses in American political life, Bruce Feiler summarizes: "Columbus comparing himself to Moses when he sailed in 1492. George Whitfield quoting Moses as he traveled the colonies in the 1730s forging the Great Awakening. Thomas Paine, in *Common Sense*, comparing King George to the pharaoh. Benjamin Franklin, Thomas Jefferson, and John Adams, in the summer of 1776, proposing that Moses be on the seal of the United States. And the references didn't stop. Harriet Tubman adopting Moses' name on the Underground Railroad. Abraham Lincoln being eulogized as Moses' incarnation. The Statue of Liberty being molded in Moses' honor. Woodrow Wilson, Franklin Roosevelt, and Lyndon Johnson tapping into Moses during wartime. Cecil B. DeMille recasting Moses as a hero for the Cold War. Martin Luther King, Jr., likening himself to Moses on the night before he was killed" (*America's Prophet*, 4).

Endnotes

56 See George McKenna, *The Puritan Origins of American Patriotism* (New Haven: Yale University Press, 2007). The political results of typology are perhaps most evident in the visceral reaction of American Protestants to Roman Catholicism. Religion was perfectly welcome in public. Christianity in fact was perfectly welcome, so long as it was a group of competing sects. But "Catholicism *was* a church," and for many Americans this meant that Catholics were inherently suspect, divided in loyalty between a church society and American society, anti-American and anti-freedom (McKenna, *Puritan Origins*, 101–3). Protestantism could be tolerated and even celebrated. It was essential to the whole system. But it was welcomed only insofar as it was ecclesially defanged, only insofar as it had ceased to act in public like a church, only insofar as it had been absorbed into America as a component of the larger reality of God's New Israel, only insofar as it renounced any strong claims to be itself that new Israel. Protestantism was celebrated in the American system only insofar as Protestantism abandoned the most original, and most potent, political claim of the church—that it was a separate polity founded and ruled by Jesus and His Spirit. Protestantism could be lionized when it lent its support to the real American faith, Americanism.

57. Quoted in Stephen B. Chapman, "Imperial Exegesis: When Caesar Interprets Scripture," in Wes Avram, ed., *Anxious About Empire: Theological Essays on the New Global Realities* (Grand Rapids: Brazos, 2004) 91.

58. Dispensationalists reject nationalist readings, but their alternative is equally heretical. Instead of finding types of the Abrahamic imperium of the church in Israel's history, they find types of modern Israel. Richard Land puts it bluntly: America is not God's chosen people because "God established one chosen nation and people: the Jews" (*The Divided States of America* [Nashville: Thomas Nelson, 2011] 192). This theology has had a profound influence on U.S. policy in the Middle East, but the effects on American theological metapolitics are even more profoundly disturbing.

59. Richard Neuhaus returns again and again to the political consequences of anemic ecclesiology in his last book, *American Babylon: Notes of a Christian Exile* (New York: Basic Books, 2009).

The late founding of America's first colonies also lends a particular cast to American economic life. Though there are doubtless feudal elements in early American life, America was founded after the transformation of medieval economic life and thought was an accomplished fact. The medieval elements are stressed by Rousas J. Rushdoony, *This Independent Republic; The Nature of the American System*. We have a verbal indicator of this in the fact that most American states are divided into counties. On the development of early modern economies, see See Karl Polanyi, *The Great Transformation: The Political and Economic Origins of Our Time*, 2nd ed. (Boston: Beacon, 2001) 33–76. On the construction of new ways of imagining economic life in the seventeenth century, see Joyce Oldham Appleby, *Economic Thought and Ideology in Seventeenth-Century England* (Los Angeles: Figueroa, [1978] 2004). The United States has pursued quasi-mercantilist policies throughout its history, but it has no inheritance of feudal privilege and never had a peasantry. Puritans rapidly abandoned their experiment with common lands; there was no pitched battle over enclosure as in England. The American colonies were founded as the modern economic system was taking form, as both the "industrial" and the "industrious" revolutions were picking up steam (The latter phrase comes from Jan de Vries, *The Industrious Revolution: Consumer Behavior and the Household Economy, 1650 to the Present* [Cambridge: Cambridge University Press, 2008]). If America was the

Endnotes

first country to be created on the basis of the "myth" of wars of religion, it is also the first country to be created as an emerging modern capitalist system.

In addition to the lack of institutional and historical obstacles to the formation of a modern economic system, America's colonizers were heirs of the Reformed branch of the Reformation that Weber famously saw as the source of a new "spirit of capitalism." Weber's thesis has been challenged from many angles, and I think Weber quite wrong in what he says about both Calvin and his heirs, but that there is *some* sort of connection between Puritanism is hard to gainsay. Dutch Calvinism was conducive to the development of "the first modern economy" because Dutch Calvinist preachers and moralists were willing to leave economic conduct to entrepreneurs, merchants, and manufacturers. Issues of finance and trade on which the medieval church might legislate were left untouched: "In such questions as overseas expansion, missionary activities, monetary policy, the toleration of monopolies, lending and usury, the clerical writers sought to avoid crossing an invisible line that would land them in the sphere of the secular authority" (De Vries and van der Woude, *The First Modern Economy: Success, Failure, and Perseverance of the Dutch Economy, 1500–1815* [Cambridge: Cambridge University Press, 1997]). In America, as in the Netherlands, religious toleration eventually became established Constitutional principle, ensuring that the unity of Americans would not be rooted in common sacramental participation but in common exchanges and purchases. There was, moreover, the simple fact that Protestant America never had a monastic network with extensive land holdings. Henry VIII had ensured that all productive land in the English colonies of American could be put to productive uses. De Vries and van der Woude note the transfer of church property to cities and provinces in the Netherlands: In pre-Reformation Utrecht, "some 31 percent of all land within the city walls had been in the hands of churches, monasteries, brotherhoods, immunities, and the like." Transfer of this land to the city and private owners enabled the city to expand its population without expanding the city walls (*First Modern Economy*, 169).

C. B. MacPherson's description of "possessive individualism" sounds like nothing more than an economic riff on American Protestantism. According to this theory, a man is free insofar as he is not dependent on the will of others and is the "proprietor of his own person and capacities," society is viewed as a "series of market relations" established by contract and founded for the protection of the individual's property in person and goods (MacPherson, *The Political Theory of Possessive Individualism: Hobbes to Locke* [Oxford: Oxford University Press, (1962) 2011] 263–64). On the other hand, see Barry Alan Shain, *The Myth of American Individualism: The Protestant Origins of American Political Thought* (Princeton: Princeton University Press, 1994), who finds America's founding ideology to be rooted in a Reformed Protestant communal republicanism. Shain's powerful argument against certain claims about American individualism does not refute my more specifically theological arguments In sum, the an-ecclesial instincts of American typology lent metapolitical support to the development of a particular kind of economic system.

60. Berger, *The Heretical Imperative: Contemporary Possibilities of Religious Affirmation* (Garden City, NY: Doubleday, 1980).

61. Ecclesiological and sociological "heresy" converge in the church-state settlement of the First Amendment. The Founders of the Revolutionary period suppressed the role of a public church for pragmatic political reasons. Though there is little evidence that the Founders subscribed wholesale to what William Cavanaugh has called the "myth of religious violence," they did worry about the alliance of the church, and especially

Endnotes

the clergy, with political power that had, in their minds, plagued Europe for centuries. In *Federalist* #51, Publius pointed out that a republic needed to protect society not only from oppression by rulers but from oppression of one portion of society by another. The danger can be averted either by the creation of a power in the community separate from the majority—a hereditary caste of rulers—or, on the other hand, by "comprehending in the society so many separate descriptions of citizens as will render an unjust combination of a majority of the whole very improbable, if not impracticable."

The second path has been taken by the American Republic, and this method applied to religious sects as well as to other parties whose minority interests might tyrannize others: "Whilst all authority in it will be derived from and dependent on the society, the society itself will be broken into so many parts, interests, and classes of citizens, that the rights of individuals, or of the minority, will be in little danger from interested combinations of the majority. In a free government the security for civil rights must be the same as that for religious rights. It consists in the one case in the multiplicity of interests, and in the other in the multiplicity of sects. The degree of security in both cases will depend on the number of interests and sects; and this may be presumed to depend on the extent of country and number of people comprehended under the same government. This view of the subject must particularly recommend a proper federal system to all the sincere and considerate friends of republican government, since it shows that in exact proportion as the territory of the Union may be formed into more circumscribed Confederacies, or States oppressive combinations of a majority will be facilitated: the best security, under the republican forms, for the rights of every class of citizens, will be diminished: and consequently the stability and independence of some member of the government, the only other security, must be proportionately increased." Available online at http://www.constitution.org/fed/federa51.htm

Recent Supreme Court decisions attribute the myth to the Founders. In his majority opinion in *Everson v. Board of Education* (1947), Hugo Black wrote, "The centuries immediately before and contemporaneous with the colonization of America had been filled with turmoil, civil strife, persecutions, generated in large part by established sects determined to maintain their absolute political and religious supremacy. With the power of government supporting them, at various times and places, Catholics had persecuted Protestants, Protestants had persecuted Catholics, Protestant sects had persecuted other Protestant sects, Catholics of one shade of belief had persecuted Catholics of another shade of belief, and all of these had from time to time persecuted Jews.... [The] words of the First Amendment reflected in the midst of early Americans a vivid mental picture of conditions and practices which they fervently wished to stamp out in order to preserve liberty for themselves and for their prosperity" (quoted in Cavanaugh, *Myth*, 185–86).

The legal scholars I have consulted have been unable to tell me if Black is correct in his historical analysis. On this point, see Philip Hamburger, *Separation of Church and State* (Cambridge: Harvard University Press, 2004) 111–89, who describes a convergence between Baptist worries about the purity of the church and Jefferson's anticlericalism. Also, Richard W. Garnett, "Introduction: Religion, Division, and the Constitution," *William & Mary Bill of Rights Journal* 15:1 (2006), 1–6; Garnett, "Religion, Division, and the First Amendment," *Georgetown Law Journal* 94 (2005–2006) 1667–1724. Thanks too to my son, Woelke, for several conversations about his continuing research on this topic.

The most explicit use of the myth comes from Madison. Madison was one of the strongest advocates of disestablishment. In his 1795 "Memorial and Remonstrance" against state funding of religious education, Madison warned that the measure would

Endnotes

destroy the "moderation and harmony" that America's determination to avoid meddling with religion had brought and might spark new religious wars: "Torrents of blood have been split in the old world, by vain attempts of the secular arm, to extinguish Religious disscord, by proscribing all difference in Religious opinion. Time has at length revealed the true remedy. Every relaxation of narrow and rigorous policy, wherever it has been tried, has been found to assuage the disease. The American Theatre has exhibited proofs that equal and compleat liberty, if it does not wholly eradicate it, sufficiently destroys its malignant influence on the health and prosperity of the State. If with the salutary effects of this system under our own eyes, we begin to contract the bounds of Religious freedom, we know no name that will too severely reproach our folly. At least let warning be taken at the first fruits of the threatened innovation. The very appearance of the Bill has transformed 'that Christian forbearance, love and charity,' which of late mutually prevailed, into animosities and jealousies, which may not soon be appeased. What mischiefs may not be dreaded, should this enemy to the public quiet be armed with the force of a law?" (Available online at http://religiousfreedom.lib.virginia.edu/sacred/madison_m&r_1785.html.) Along similar lines, Jefferson remarked in his first inaugural address that Americans had "banished from our land that religious intolerance under which mankind so long bled and suffered" (Jefferson, "First Inaugural Address," in Cherry, ed., *God's New Israel*, 107).

The result will be to encourage sects in the direction of justice and the common good: "In the extended republic of the United States, and among the great variety of interests, parties, and sects which it embraces, a coalition of a majority of the whole society could seldom take place on any other principles than those of justice and the general good." *Federalist* #10 made the same point: "A religious sect may degenerate into a political faction in a part of the Confederacy; but the variety of sects dispersed over the entire face of it must secure the national councils against any danger from that source." The Founders attempted to divert the strength of religious passion by diffusing that passion in a thousand different directions. For a bracing but overly cynical treatment of this point, see Kenneth Craycraft, *The American Myth of Religious Freedom* (Dallas: Spence, 1999). Vigorous competition has kept American churches sharp and lively. Vigorous competition among sects, consciously encouraged by the U.S. Constitution, has not promoted catholicity.

62. These distinctions are helpfully laid out by O'Brien, *God Land*, 41–42. O'Brien suggests (in 1988) that the "needle of holy nationalism in the United States seems to have been hovering somewhere between 'holy nation' and 'deified nation'" (69).

63. Nye, *Almost Chosen*, 55–58. The claim that the Great Awakening encouraged patriotism is controversial, but it seems undeniable that it had at least an indirect impact on the development of American nationalism, insofar as it chipped away the remnants of churchly consciousness that the Puritans had retained and left America as the only feasible object of corporate identification.

64. Whatever else we might say about the revivals, and there is much to say, it is undeniable that they undermined the authority and cohesion that existed in the churches. See Kidd, *Great Awakening*; on the revivals of the early nineteenth century, Nathan O. Hatch, *The Democratization of American Religion* (New Haven: Yale University Press, 1989).

65. The first is from Samuel Langdon, the second two analogies from Ezra Stiles, all in Cherry, ed., *God's New Israel*, 69, 88, 93–105.

66. Edwards, "The Latter-Day Glory Is Probably To Begin in America," in Cherry, ed., *God's New Israel*, 54.

67. Bercovitch, *Puritan Origins*, 146.

68. Quoted in Mark A. Noll, Nathan O. Hatch, and George M. Marsden, *The Search for Christian America* (Westchester, IL: Crossway, 1983) 62.

69. Quoted in Bercovitch, *Puritan Origins*, 144–45. On the development of nationalist millennialism, see Hamburger, *Separation*, 133–43.

70. Philip Freneau envisioned America as "a new Jerusalem sent down from heaven," which, like the tabernacle, would serve as a "pattern for the world beside" (quoted in Nye, *Almost Chosen*, 169).

71. Quoted in Mark A. Noll, *America's God: From Jonathan Edwards to Abraham Lincoln* (Oxford: Oxford University Press, 2002) 83–84.

72. Quoted in Nye, *Almost Chosen*, 107. Presbyterian preacher George Duffeld gave apocalyptic and cosmic status to the American experience by interpreting it in the light of Revelation 12's vision of the dragon's conflict with the woman. Like the woman in the vision, "America seems to have been prepared as the wilderness to which the woman should fly from the face of the dragon, and be nourished for a long series of time" (quoted in Thomas S. Kidd, *The Great Awakening: The Roots of Evangelical Christianity in Colonial America* [New Haven: Yale University Press, 2007] 296). Samuel Sherwood was more explicit, interpreting the French and Indian War as the beginning of the triumph of the true faith over "popish mysterious leaven of iniquity and absurdity." He too appealed to Revelation 12: "God has, in this American quarter of the globe, provided for the woman and her seed." Dragons cause no fear since "God Almighty, with all the powers of heaven, are on our side. Great numbers of angels, no doubt, are encamping round our coast, for our defense and protection. Michael stands ready; with all the artillery of heaven, to encounter the dragon, and to vanquish this black host" (quoted in Kidd, *Great Awakening*, 295).

73. Beecher, "A Plea for the West," in Cherry, ed., *God's New Israel*, 123.

74. Quoted in Bercovitch, *Puritan Origins*, 87–88.

75. Beecher, "A Plea," 123. On the development of Christian Republicanism, see Noll, *America's God*, chs. 4–5.

76. Quoted in Nye, *Almost Chosen*, 172.

77. Following Gunnar Myrdal, Samuel Huntington speaks of an "American Creed" consisting of the dignity of every man, rights to liberty, justice, and equality. Huntington is right that "The American Creed is the unique creation of a dissenting Protestant culture," but that is not to say that it is a Christian creed, even if it would be unthinkable without Christianity (*Who Are We? The Challenges to America's National Identity* [New York: Simon & Schuster, 2004] 67–68).

78. All quotations from Nye, *Almost Chosen People*, 169–70.

79. Quoted in ibid., 170.

80. Quote is from Bette Roth Young, *Emma Lazarus and her World: Life and Letters* (Philadelphia: Jewish Publication Society, 1997).

81. On the "inwardness" of Puritanism, see Alan Simpson, *Puritanism in Old and New England* (Chicago: University of Chicago Press, 1955). For the problems surrounding the Halfway Covenant, Edmund S. Morgan's *Visible Saints: The History of a Puritan Idea* (Ithaca: Cornell University Press, 1963) is still invaluable. On Puritan sacramental theology in general, E. Brooks Holifield, *The Covenant Sealed: The Development of*

Endnotes

Puritan Sacramental Typology in Old and New England, 1570–1720 (New Haven: Yale University Press, 1974), is still the standard.

82. On the privatization of sacramental piety, see Leigh Eric Schmidt, *Holy Fairs: Scottish Communions and American Revivals in the Early Modern Period* (Princeton: Princeton University Press, 1990) 192–212.

83. Among the loudest alarms came from John Williamson Nevin. On Nevin's career and thought, see D. G. Hart, *John Williamson Nevin: High Church Calvinist* (Philipsburg, NJ: P. & R., 2005).

84. Drew Gilpin Faust, *This Republic of Suffering: Death and the American Civil War* (New York: Knopf, 2008) xiii.

85. David Goldfield, *America Aflame: How the Civil War Created a Nation* (New York: Bloomsbury, 2011) 279.

86. The analogies were pressed: "As Christ entered into Jerusalem, the city that above all others hated, rejected and would soon slay him, so did this, His servant enter [Richmond], the city that above all others hated and rejected him, and would soon be the real if not intentional cause of his death." Rev. C. B. Crane put it succinctly: "Jesus Christ died for the world, Abraham Lincoln dies for his country." All quotations from Goldfield, *America Aflame*, 306–8.

87. Quoted in Harry S. Stout, *Upon the Altar of the Nation: A Moral History of the Civil War* (New York: Viking, 2006) 134.

88. Ibid., 55.

89. Goldfield says that through the Civil War, the United States was "born again" as a nation (*America Aflame*, 9); Stout agrees (*Upon the Altar*, xxi). This is not overblown rhetoric but a sober report of facts. See Carolyn Marvin and David W. Ingle, *Blood Sacrifice and the Nation: Totem Rituals and the American Flag* (Cambridge: Cambridge University Press, 1999) 5: "The triumph of nationalism achieved by the bloodletting of the Civil War helped restructure the American economy from a local to a national base. It also helped assimilate waves of immigrants in the late nineteenth century. In a reorganized continental community struggling to forge a national identity, the bloody flag emerged as a talisman with transforming properties."

90. Stout, *Upon the Altar*, xvii–xxii.

91. See Marvin and Ingle, *Blood Sacrifice and the Nation*.

92. Before 1861, flags were rarely seen, never in homes or churches. Then, "before the smells of powder disappeared from Charleston Harbor," John Hay wrote, "the flag floated from every newspaper office in the country" (quoted in Stout, *Upon the Altar*, 28). Henry Ward Beecher saw the flag as a sign over "all that our fathers meant in the Revolutionary War; it means all that the Declaration of Independence meant; it means all that the Constitution of our people, organizing for justice, for liberty, for happiness, meant. Our flag carries America ideas, American history and American feelings" (quoted in Stout, *Upon the Altar*, 29). Overnight, flags were everywhere—"churches, storefronts, homes, and government buildings all waved flags as a sign of loyalty and support" (Stout, *Upon the Altar*, 28).

93. Stout, *Upon the Altar*, xvi. National martyrdom was part of a "doctrine of loyalty" spelled out by Bushnell in an essay written after Gettysburg. "Loyal sentiment"—and he means loyalty to the Union—"yields up willing husbands, fathers, brothers, and sons, consenting to the fearful change of a home always desolate." Above all, loyalty expresses itself in self-sacrifice, and Bushnell was explicit that the sacrifice was offered to the nation: "It offers body and blood, and life, on the altar of its devotion. It is a fact, a political

worship, offering to seal itself by martyrdom in the field. Wonderful, grandly honorable fact, that human nature can be lifted by an inspiration so high, even in the fallen state of wrong and evil" (quoted in Stout, *Upon the Altar*, 249–50).

94. Quoted in Charles Adams, *Those Dirty Rotten Taxes: The Tax Revolts that Built America* (New York: Free Press, 1998) 98. The sacrifice was also on behalf of a particular form of economic system. Northern rage against secession was not whipped up until the newly created Confederacy reduced tariffs to create a free trade zone. Northern newspapers viewed this as a threat to the North, and to the entire Yankee way of life. Because of the difference in tariffs, wrote an editorialist for the *Boston Transcript* in 1861, "the entire Northwest must find it to their advantage to purchase their imported goods at New Orleans rather than New York. In addition to this, the manufacturing interests of the country will suffer from the increased importation resulting from low duties" (quoted in Adams, *Dirty Rotten Taxes*, 104). This could not be allowed to stand: "At once shut up every Southern port, destroy its commerce, and bring utter ruin on the Confederate states," declared an editorial for the *New York Times* (quoted in Adams, *Dirty Rotten Taxes*, 103).

95. Quoted in Adams, *Dirty Rotten Taxes*, 106.
96. Quoted in ibid., 110–11.
97. Ibid., 109.
98. See George McKenna, *The Puritan Origins of American Patriotism* (New Haven: Yale University Press, 2007) 162.
99. Quoted in Stout, *Upon the Altar*, 250.
100. Quoted in ibid., 373.
101. Ibid., xvii.
102. Ibid., xxi.
103. Quoted in ibid., 13.
104. Quoted in ibid., 460. The American experience of the frontier further embedded a belief in "regeneration through violence" in the American imagination, character, and politics. Violent clashes with Indians were seen as cosmic battles between light and darkness, and the entire American experience was mythologized in terms of the battle of cowboy and Indian. See Richard Slotkin, *Regeneration through Violence: The Mythology of the American Frontier, 1600–1860* (Norman: University of Oklahoma Press, 1973); and Slotkin, *The Fatal Environment: The Myth of the Frontier in the Age of Industrialization, 1800–1890* (New York: Atheneum, 1985). Slotkin notes, for example, how frontier motifs framed the experience of Americans in Vietnam and infused that war with mythical power (*Fatal Environment*, 17–18).
105. Hauerwas, *War and the American Difference*, 27.
106. "What Violence Is For," *First Things*.
107. Quoted in Winthrop S. Hudson, ed., *Nationalism and Religion in America: Concepts of American Identity and Mission* (New York: Harper & Row, 1970) 74.
108. From the record of the 56th Congress, available at http://www.mtholyoke.edu/acad/intrel/ajb72.htm, accessed January 13, 2012.

Chapter 5

1. Bush and Gingrich quoted in Richard H. Immerman, *Empire for Liberty: A History of American Imperialism from Benjamin Franklin to Paul Wolfowitz* (Princeton: Princeton University Press, 2010).

Endnotes

2. This reading of American history has had a significant impact on American foreign policy. The myth about ourselves is this: Early in our history, we kept pretty much to ourselves, and that worked. With the rise of the Soviet bloc, however, the world has become more dangerous and more complex, and we can no longer indulge the naïve moralisms of childhood or the gentleness of adolescence. Early American foreign policy has nothing to teach grown-ups. See Walter Russell Mead, *Special Providence: American Foreign Policy and How It Changed the World* (New York: Routledge, 2002).

3. Historians make such claims less often today than in the past, but there are still some American historians who continue to tell the American story in much this fashion. In a recent book, Thomas F. Madden argues that neither Rome nor the United States built an empire of conquest. Rather, both built empires of trust, empires of alliance. And both began from a foundation of isolationism. To build an empire of trust, one needs a "solid, stable, and peaceful civilization that wants the rest of the world to leave it alone" (Madden, *Empires of Trust: How Rome Built—and American Is Building—a New World* [New York: Dutton, 2008] 64). Both Rome and America started as "frontier societies" whose values were rooted in agriculture. Both "valued hard work, honest, piety, and virtue." They distrusted power, and "looked with suspicion on foreigners." All of these factors bred isolationism. By Madden's account, even the Spanish American War did not end American isolation: "it was a reaction to instability in Cuba under Spanish rule" (66). Some Americans accepted the European view that great nations must have great empires, but anti-imperialism remained strong. After World War I, the United States refused to enter the League of Nations, and "American isolationism was just as strong in the years leading up to World War II" (67).

4. All quoted in ibid., 65.

5. Quoted in ibid., 66.

6. Available at http://www.law.ou.edu/ushistory/monrodoc.shtml, accessed August 5, 2011.

7. Madden, *Empires of Trust*, 67.

8. Robert Kagan, *Dangerous Nation: America's Foreign Policy from Its Earliest Days to the Dawn of the Twentieth Century* (New York: Vintage, 2006) 5. Daniel Walker Howe (*What Hath God Wrought: The Transformation of America, 1815–1848* [Oxford: Oxford University Press, 2009] 707) agrees that the expansion of America is a result of deliberate planning carried out with remarkable consistency and foresight. Mead notes that America lacks a foreign policy tradition only if "foreign policy" is measured by narrow Europe-centric standards of what international politics involves. He also argues that the myth of an America innocent of foreign policy was created in the Cold War as an effort to liberate American policy toward the Soviets from the constraints of earlier American traditions of international conduct (Mead, *Special Providence*, ch. 3).

9. Of course, prior to the Revolutionary generation Americans were *part* of an empire.

10. Quoted in Immerman, *Empire For Liberty*. Jefferson endorsed Madison's logic: "the larger our association the less it will be shaken by local passions" (quoted in William Appleman Williams, *Empire as a Way of Life* [Oxford: Oxford University Press, 1980], 61). The quotations can be expanded at length: "Thomas Jefferson told James Madison that he was 'persuaded that no constitution was ever before as well calculated as ours for expanding extensive empire and self-government.' The initial 'confederacy' of thirteen would be 'the nest from which all America, North and South [would] be peopled.' Indeed, Jefferson used his inaugural address in 1801 to observe that the short history of the United States had already furnished 'a new proof for the falsehood of Montesquieu's

doctrine, that a republic can be preserved only in a small territory. The reverse is the truth.' Madison agreed, in the tenth of the Federalist Papers, he forcefully argued for 'extend[ing] the sphere' to create a larger republic" (Niall Ferguson, *Colossus: The Price of America's Empire* [New York: Penguin, 2004] 34).

11. Peter S. Onuf, *Jefferson's Empire: The Language of American Nationhood* (Charlottesville: University of Virginia Press, 2000) 1.

12. Richard Koebner, *Empire* (New York: Grosset & Dunlap, 1961) 4–5, 8. In the Renaissance, newly minted kings and princes claimed *imperium* in much the same sense. Instead of being subservient to a feudal suzerain, they were sovereign within their territory. Henry VIII claimed "The Imperial Crown of this Realm" not because he held territories outside England but because he was sovereign within it. Henry's claim to imperial authority was also part of a British mythology that connected him to Arthur and back to Constantine, crowned emperor at York. John Knox used the term in the same sense when he protested the abominable "Empire or Rule of a wicked woman." At the same time, the Humanists began to use the term to refer to the extension of power beyond the borders of a kingdom, and as *imperium* made its way into the vernacular languages of Europe, it came it came to refer to conquered territories. With Bacon, Shakespeare, and Grotius, empire was associated with domination of the seas. James Harrington used the term often in the sense of "far-flung dominance" rather than to the "countries and spaces controlled by it." By the end of the seventeenth century, Sir William Temple could use the word in what he recognized as a new sense to refer to "A nation extended over vast tracts of land, and numbers of people" (all quotations from Koebner, *Empire*, 50–60).

13. Immerman, *Empire for Liberty*, 8.

14. I take "imperial anticolonialism" from Jay Sexton, *Monroe Doctrine: Empire and Nation in Nineteenth-Century America* (New York: Hill & Wang, 2011) 5, though the phrase seems to originate with William Appleman Williams. Immerman (*Empire for Liberty*, 13) can sustain his claim that America is an empire "without settlers" only if he ignores the fact that frontier settlers were settling in "foreign" territory—that belonging to Native Americans. See below.

15. Madison letter to Jefferson, September 17, 1787. Quoted in Williams, *Empire as a Way of Life*, 46.

16. Quoted in ibid., 70.

17. Quoted in Immerman, *Empire for Liberty*, 28.

18. Quoted in ibid., 29–30.

19. Quoted in ibid., 58.

20. This vision of America's future was opposed by many, particularly by those anti-Federalists who opposed the expansion of federal power embodied in the Constitution. Many today look back to these figures for inspiration in opposing the continuing expansion of American interests and activity around the world, but the anti-Federalists, prescient though they were, lost. America as it actually exists is a Federalist polity, both domestically and internationally.

21. Kagan, *Dangerous Nation*, 130–33.

22. Immerman, *Empire for Liberty*, 68.

23. Ibid., 72.

24. Ibid., 79.

25. Ibid., 84.

26. Quoted in ibid., 85.

27. Daniel Walker Howe, *What Hath God Wrought*, 287.

Endnotes

28. Immerman, *Empire for Liberty*, 94.
29. Quoted in Howe, *What Hath God Wright*, 720.
30. Quoted in Williams, *Empire as a Way of Life*, 64.
31. This account of the context of Monroe's speech is drawn largely from Kagan, *Dangerous Nation*, ch. 6. See the similar account in Immerman, *Empire for Liberty*, 89–91.
32. Sexton, *Monroe Doctrine*, 61. Sexton wryly comments that "The political genius of Monroe's 1823 message was that it did not call for any action" (73).
33. Ferguson, *Colossus*, 42. Sexton (*Monroe Doctrine*, 6, 50–53) places the speech in the context of Anglo-American relations.
34. The reception history of Monroe's speech is the main theme of Sexton, *Monroe Doctrine*. On Polk's invention of "Monroe's Doctrine," see 85–111. For a different assessment of the intent and effect of Monroe's speech, see Harlow Giles Unger, *The Last Founding Father: James Monroe and a Nation's Call to Greatness* (Cambridge, MA: Da Capo, 2009) 315–18.
35. This summary of the debates of the 1790s depends on Kagan, *Dangerous Nation*, 104–12. Walter Russell Mead's superb *Special Providence* summarizes the entire history of American foreign policy as a complex argument and combat among "Hamiltonians," "Jeffersonians," "Wilsonians," and "Jacksonians."
36. Kagan, *Dangerous Nation*, 125.
37. Quoted in ibid., 128.
38. For obvious reasons, in this chapter I concentrate on the pre-Civil War era, the supposed era of "isolation."
39. Charles S. Maier, *Among Empires: American Ascendancy and Its Predecessors* (Cambridge: Harvard University Press, 2006) 32.
40. Mead, *Special Proviudence*, 17.
41. Max Boot, *The Savage Wars of Peace: Small Wars and the Rise of American Power* (New York: Basic Books, 2003), xiv. See Harry Allanson Ellsworth, *One Hundred Eighty Landings of United States Marines, 1800–1934*, available at http://www.marines.mil/news/publications/Documents/One%20Hundred%20Eighty%20Landings%20of%20United%20States%20Marines%201800-1934%2019000305500_1.pdf, accessed August 5, 2011.
42. Taken from the table of contents of Ellsworth, *One Hundred Eighty*. See the catalog sprinkled throughout Williams, *Empire as a Way of Life*. In many cases, these early encounters had to be followed up later. Americans fought with villagers in Liberia in 1843, and returned in 1860. The same pattern repeated itself in China: "In 1843 American marines landed in Guangzhou (Canton) to protect Americans from Chinese mobs. They returned thirteen years later and defeated five thousand Chinese troops in a pitched battle. A permanent marine presence would guard American traders and diplomats in China and participate—under foreign commanders—with European forces in the suppression of the Boxer Rebellion in 1900" (Mead, *Special Providence*, 25). The United States returned to Japan more than once: "Commodore Perry's orders directed him to shell Japan if the mikado refused his request for trade and diplomatic relations. In 1863, at the height of the Civil War, American forces landed in Japan and what is now Panama" (ibid.).
43. Mead, *Special Providence*, 26.
44. Quoted in Andrew Bacevich, *American Empire: The Realities and Consequences of U.S. Diplomacy* (Cambridge: Harvard University Press, 2004) 7.

45. Available online at http://www.potw.org/archive/potw340.html, last accessed December 16, 2011.

46. Oren, *Power, Faith, and Fantasy: America in the Middle East 1776 to the Present* (New York: Norton, 2007) 23.

47. Statistics found in Boot, *Savage Wars*, 9.

48. Quoted in ibid., 9. Another sailor, Thomas Nicholson, captured when serving aboard the *Sally*, added details of the impalement: "After they had stripped the sufferer naked, they inserted the iron pointed stake into the lower termination of the vertebrae, and thence forced it up near his back bone, until it appeared between the shoulders, avoiding the vital parts. The stake was then raised in the air and the poor sufferer exposed to the view of the other slaves, writhing in . . . insupportable agony" (quoted in Oren, *Power, Faith, Fantasy*, 71).

49. Boot, *Savage Wars*, 11. Oren's numbers are much lower: In 1790, "the Senate against rejected Jefferson's [then Secretary of State] call for war and instead earmarked the unprecedented sum of $140,000 for the purposes of ransom and tribute" (Oren, *Power, Faith, Fantasy*, 33).

50. Quoted in Oren, *Power, Faith, Fantasy*, 29.

51. Quoted in ibid., 24.

52. Ibid., 30. Oren continues, "The Reverence Thomas Thatcher reminder the Massachusetts convention that the enslavement of 'our sailors . . . in Algiers is enough to convince the most skeptical among us, of the want of general government.' Nathaniel Sargeant said it was 'preposterous' to think that the United States could continue under the ineffectual Articles of Confederation and still defend itself from 'piracies and felonies on ye high seas.' In North Carolina, Hugh Williamson 'a distinguished physician and astronomer, wondered 'What is there to prevent the Algerine Pirate from landing on your coast, and carrying your citizens into slavery?' The Kentucky attorney George Nicholas asked, 'May not the Algerines seize our vessels? Cannot they . . . pillage our ships and destroy our commerce, without subjecting themselves to any inconvenient'" (30).

Federalist #24 mounted a similar argument: "If we mean to be a commercial people . . . we must endeavor as soon as possible to have a navy." Other entries in the series of articles rang similar themes. Without a Navy (#11) "of respectable weight . . . the genius of American Merchants and Navigators would be stifled and lost." Only union under the Constitution (#41) can protect America's "maritime strength" against "the rapacious demands of pirates and barbarians." Peter Markoe published a satirical poem under the name Mehmet, an Algerian who planned to exploit American factionalism to seize women and maidens, along with Rhode Island. One historian, Thomas Bailey, wrote, "In an indirect sense, the brutal Dey of Algiers was a Founding Father of the Constitution" (quoted in Oren, *Power, Faith, Fantasy*, 31).

53. For Decatur, see Boot, *Savage Wars*, 3–6, 20–21; Oren, *Power, Faith, Fantasy*, 59–62.

54. Boot, *Savage Wars*, 6.

55. For Eaton, see Oren, *Power, Faith, Fantasy*, 63–70; Boot, *Savage Wars*, 22–27.

56. Quoted in Boot, *Savage Wars*, 23–24.

57. Ibid., 28.

58. On the commercial thrust of early American foreign policy, see ibid., xvii. Hamilton's commercial foreign policy focused on the freedom of the seas (Mead, *Special Providence*, 105–6), and in this he was followed by William Henry Seward, Lincoln's Secretary of State, who focused his energies on establishing America as a commercial empire

Endnotes

(Immerman, *Empire for Liberty*, 99–127). Mead argues that the centrality of economic policy is one of the key differences between American and European notions of foreign policy (*Special Providence*, 36–37 and passim). See also Ferguson, *Colossus*, 42–44.

59. Mead, *Special Providence*, shows that honor is an especially important value to "Jacksonians."

60. Boot, *Savage Wars*, 33–35.

61. Ibid., 36. 1831 saw another clash between American forces and Pacific islanders. Pirates attacked the American merchant vessel *Friendship* while it anchored near the Sumatran village of Quallah Battoo (Kuala Batu). Several members of the crew were killed, but the Captain, Charles Endicott, escaped and with the help of several nearby American ships was able to recover the *Friendship*, though its cargo, $40,000 of opium, was stolen. Endicott vowed that America would send a "big ship" to "punish the aggressors." Sure enough, in February 1832, the Potomac, a forty-four-gun frigate, slipped near the shore of Quallah Battoo disguised as a Dutch vessel. The impatient captain, Jack Downes, ignoring orders, refused to wait for negotiations for restitution, and early the next morning his marines stormed the fort of the village. The Sumatrans, armed with spears, sabers, and some muskets, were no match for the Americans. Three forts fell and the town was burned; two Americans died, and eleven were wounded. Downes later defended his insubordination with the claim that he knew already that "no such demand would be answered except by refusal." Back home, some Americans worried that President Jackson had ordered the attack without Congress, but their objections were ignored. Americans were back at Quallah Battoo in 1838. This time, Captain George Read attempted negotiations, but when they failed he warned the Sumatrans to evacuate and then destroyed their rebuilt fort. Sumatran pirates never troubled U.S. ships again (ibid., 46–49).

62. Ibid., 38.

63. Ibid., 55.

64. Quoted by Bruce Cumings, *Dominion from Sea to Sea: Pacific Ascendancy and American Power* (New Haven: Yale University Press, 2009) 63. Cumings's excellent book shows how America achieved its "exceptional" status during the 1840s by a reorientation toward the West and away from Europe and especially England. He notes, for instance, that what F. O. Mathiessen described as the "American Renaissance," the creation of a national literature no longer enthralled to European models, coincided with this shift of orientation.

65. The "settler ideology" that inspired movements into the far west was likewise indebted to Americanism's eschatology. Literature encouraging emigration and resettlement, in both England and America, betrayed a "paradise complex." Even apparently "economic" motives were overlaid with Americanist ones: Not just wealth, but *Eden* lay just over the next mountain range, with all its abundance. In the West, the hierarchies of European Christendom receive their final blow, because out there everyone is equal: "the working class call no man master—indeed, they are all working class—it is no uncommon thing to see a judge ploughing, or a general getting potatoes." Quoted in James Belich, *Replenishing the Earth: The Settler Revolution and the Rise of the Anglo-World, 1783–1939* (Oxford: Oxford University Press, 2009) 157. Belich (163–64) downplays the role of religion, distinguishing between "religious and secular Utopianism" and then suggesting that religious Utopianism was as likely to inhibit immigration as to encourage it. In nineteenth-century America, however, such a distinction has little basis in reality. As

Belich himself acknowledges, this was "a biblical age" in which even apparently secondary allusions to biblical hopes elicited passionately religious responses.

66. Cumings, *Dominion from Sea to Sea*, 10.
67. It would be naïve to say that the sales were all as entirely free of American pressure as the Louisiana Purchase, where France's offer is said to have taken the American ambassador completely by surprise.
68. These totals from the chart in Ferguson, *Colossus*, 40.
69. Kagan, *Dangerous Nation*, 137.
70. Ibid., 79.
71. Quoted in ibid., 88.
72. Quoted in ibid., 92.
73. See Cumings, *Dominion from Sea to Sea*, 29: "Most Indian wars, from Fallen Timbers in 1794 to the last battle at Wounded Knee in 1890, had their origin in white settlers seeking land: making treaties to push the Indians away or westward, breaking the same treaties to expand some more, killing them when they resisted."
74. Quoted in Kagan, *Dangerous Nation*, 82.
75. Quoted in ibid., 85.
76. For concise summaries, see Howe, *What Hath God Wrought*, 342–57; also Fred Anderson and Andrew Clayton, *The Dominion of War: Empire and Liberty in North America, 1500–2000* (New York: Viking, 2005) 207–46. A recent narrative history is found in Brian Hicks, *Toward the Setting Sun: John Ross, the Cherokees, and the Trail of Tears* (New York: Atlantic Monthly, 2011).
77. Cumings, *Dominion from Sea to Sea*, 29.
78. Quoted in Immerman, *Empire for Liberty*, 93.
79. Howe, *What Hath God Wrought*, 355.
80. Ibid., 357.
81. Sexton, *Monroe Doctrine*, 83.
82. Quoted in ibid., 57.
83. Ibid., 11.
84. Quoted in ibid., 106–7.
85. Howe, *What Hath God Wrought*, 658–62.
86. For a survey of this period, see Howe, *What Hath God Wrought*, 658–791. A recent narrative history of the Polk administration is Robert W. Merry, *A Country of Vast Designs: James K. Polk, the Mexican War, and the Conquest of the American Continent* (New York: Simon & Schuster, 2009).
87. Howe, *What Hath God Wrought*, 731–32. Quotation from Anderson and Clayton, *Dominion of War*, 279.
88. Quoted in Howe, *What Hath God Wrought*, 734.
89. Cumings, *Dominion from Sea to Sea*, 64–65. Cumings sees similar patterns in the outbreak of the Civil War, in the disputed attacks on the *Maine* prior to the Spanish-American war and of the *Lusitania* prior to World War I, and in the attack on Pearl Harbor.
90. Quoted in Williams, *Empire as a Way of Life*, 89.
91. Howe, *What Hath God Wrought*, 752.
92. Ibid., 708. Polk's incorporation of California achieved another of the goals of his Presidency. It received an unplanned boost from one of nineteenth-century America's freelance imperialists. The most famous of these "filibusters" was William Walker, who was involved not only in Mexico and California, but in Central America, where for

Endnotes

several years he ruled as President of Nicaragua. For a general history of filibustering, see Robert E. May, *Manifest Destiny's Underworld: Filibustering in Antebellum America* (Chapel Hill: University of North Carolina Press, 2002). Brady Harrison's *Agent of Empire: William Walker and the Imperial Self in American Literature* (Athens: University of Georgia Press, 2004), focuses mainly on Walker's presence in American literature, but provides a brief account of his life on pages 1–22. See also Eduardo Galeano, *Open Veins of Latin America: Five Centuries of the Pillage of a Continent* (New York: Monthly Review, 1997) 107.

While Polk was declaring war on Mexico over Texas, John Charles Frémont, the adventurous and well-connected son-in-law of Senator William Hart Benton, organized an uprising of American settlers in California, raided a hacienda, and stole over a hundred horses from Commandante Don Jose Castro. Frémont claimed to be acting on orders from Washington. He wasn't. But Polk had been plotting to find a way to wrest California from Mexico: "unbeknownst to Frémont, Polk had sent a secret message to the U.S. consul in Monterey, Thomas Larkin, urging him to trump up a 'revolution' to detach California in case of war with Mexico, and another one to Commodore John Sloat to seize San Francisco in the same event." With Robert Stockton, Frémont declared the independence of the Bear Flag Republic, and then pursued the goal of subduing the rest of California. The *Californios* were not pleased, and in September 1846 they revolted against U.S. occupation of the territory. Fighting continued into January 1847, when Frémont signed a peace treaty promising the residents American citizenship, and Frémont became the governor of the California Territory (Howe, *What Hath God Wrought*, 756–57). This, along with the purchase of the Oregon Territory to the 49th parallel from Britain, enabled Polk to achieve yet another aim of his Presidency, the extension of American power to the Pacific (ibid., 708).

93. Quoted in Williams, *Empire as a Way of Life*, 89.
94. Cumings, *Dominion from Sea to Sea*, 65.
95. The connection was suggested to me by Rev. Richard Bledsoe in conversation.

Chapter 6

1. *Expansion under New World-Conditions* (New York: Baker & Taylor, 1900) 247–64.
2. Ibid., 263.
3. Ibid., 272.
4. Ibid., 273.
5. Ibid., 275–78.
6. For a vivid and realistic summary of this grim episode, see William R. Everdell, *The First Moderns: Profiles in the Origins of Twentieth-Century Thought* (Chicago: University of Chicago Press, 1997) 116–26.
7. Strong, *Expansion*, 295–97.
8. Ibid., 301.
9. Walter Russell Mead details the role of American missionaries not only in the formation of a moral Wilsonian foreign policy, but also in the creation of "global civil society" (*Special Providence: American Foreign Policy and How It Changed the World* [London: Routledge, 2002] 139–62). He goes so far as to suggest that the "very concept of a global civil society comes to us out of the missionary movement" and adds, "Certainly before the missionaries no large group of people set out to build just such a world. The

concept that 'backward' countries could and should develop into Western-style industrial democracies grew up among missionaries, and missionary relief and development organizations like World Vision and Catholic Relief Services remain at the forefront of development efforts. The idea that the governments of the Western world had a positive duty to support the development of poor countries through financial aid and other forms of assistance similarly comes out of the missionary world. Most contemporary international organizations that provide relief from natural disasters, shelter refugees, train medical practitioners for poor countries, or perform other important services on an international basis can trace their origin either to missionary organizations or to the missionary milieu" (146). See also Richard M. Gamble, *The War for Righteousness: Progressive Christianity, the Great War, and the Rise of the Messianic Nation* (Wilmington, DE: ISI, 2003). For a discussion of "missionary imperialism" in Britain, see Hilary M. Carey, *God's Empire: Religion and Colonialism in the British World* (Cambridge: Cambridge University Press, 2011).

10. Gamble, *War for Righteousness*, 119.
11. Ibid., 126.
12. Quoted in ibid., 148.
13. Quoted in ibid., 151–53.
14. For the development of the martyr-soldier image in twentieth-century Europe, see George L. Mosse, *Fallen Soldiers: Reshaping the Memory of the World Wars* (New York: Oxford University Press, 1990).
15. Gamble, *War for Righteousness*, 116.
16. Quoted in ibid., 159.
17. Quoted in ibid., 160.
18. Quoted in ibid., 199. As big and loud as the chorus of the war's cheerleaders was, it could not completely drown out contrary opinion. J. Gresham Machen, for instance, blamed British imperialism for the war, and defended Germany's actions (ibid., 96–97).
19. See Peter Beinart, *The Icarus Syndrome: A History of American Hubris* (New York: Harper & Row, 2010) 34–37.
20. Immerman, *Empire for Liberty*, 173.
21. Ibid., 174–75.
22. Ibid., 175.
23. Ibid., 180–82. Stephen Ambrose and Douglas Brinkley give an airbrushed official account of this coup in *Rise to Globalism: American Foreign Policy since 1938*, 9th ed. (New York: Penguin, 2011) 148–49. Grimmer and more accurate accounts are found in Stephen Kinzer, *Overthrow: America's Century of Regime Change from Hawaii to Iraq* (New York: Times, 2006) ch. 5; Tim Weiner, *Legacy of Ashes: The History of the CIA* (New York: Anchor, 2008) 92–105; William Blum, *Killing Hope: U.S. Military and C.I.A. Interventions since World War II* (Monroe, ME: Common Courage, 2004). The original charter for the CIA did not permit the agency to engage in covert action, but the charter's authorization for the agency to "perform such other functions related to intelligence affecting the national security as the NSC may from time to time direct" was interpreted broadly to permit "propaganda, economic warfare, preventive direct action, including sabotage ... demolition and evacuation measures; subversion of hostile states, including assistance to underground resistance groups, and support of indigenous anti-Communist elements in threatened countries of the free world." Quoted in Edward Pressen, *Losing Our Souls: The American Experience in the Cold War* (Chicago: Ivan Dee, 1993) 166–67.
24. Immerman, *Empire for Liberty*, 182–83.

Endnotes

25. Bacevich, *American Empire*, 219–20.

26. Condoleeza Rice, "Rethinking the National Interest," *Foreign Affairs* (July-August 2008); quoted in William Pfaff, *The Irony of Manifest Destiny: The Tragedy of America's Foreign Policy* (New York: Walker, 2010) 92–93.

27. Plenty of recent examples may be found in Michael Northcott, *An Angel Directs the Storm: Apocalyptic Religion & American Empire* (London: Tauris, 2004); Robert Jewett, *Mission and Menace: Four Centuries of American Religious Zeal* (Minneapolis: Fortress, 2008).

28. See Richard Land, *The Divided States of America* (Nashville: Thomas Nelson, 2011) 189–210. Though many Christians accept some form of Americanism, few have been bold enough to give it a theological defense. The most impressive recent exception is Stephen H. Webb's *American Providence: A Nation With a Mission* (New York: Continuum, 2004). simultaneously a courageous and frustrating book and one that will help set up my own evaluation of American power. Webb consciously takes up Reinhold Niebuhr's task of trying to make theological sense of America and offers a refreshing and bold defense of things few theologians defend these days—providence and America, and the link between the two. On providence, he observes that in Scripture God chooses nations and rulers (e.g., Cyrus) to play a role in His providential direction of history toward its end. Webb knows that no modern nation is chosen in the unique sense that Israel was chosen, but he argues, rightly, that God hasn't stopped choosing and directing, hasn't stopped working through nations as well as individuals to achieve His purposes. Webb even has the chutzpah to suggest that Bush might actually be right in his belief that God chose him to lead America through the crisis of 9/11. Belief and disbelief in God's providential favor to the United States is, he argues, as handy a way of dividing the American political landscape as any today.

Webb demonstrates that consciousness of a historic mission has been virtually *definitive* of the American experiment. Early Americans understood that the blessings they enjoyed were gifts from God that demanded faithful stewardship, and knew too that God would judge them for their failures. Even when American conceptions of providence became secularized, detached from demands (as in the theory of Manifest Destiny), even when "racism and the lust for land" were more fundamental motivations than the spread of God's kingdom or of liberty, Americans could not shed the habit of thinking in providential terms.

Webb's understanding of providence is refreshingly forceful: "God is in charge of both history and nature, and God's governance is complete and final." Following Oliver O'Donovan's lead, he insists that providence has political results, finally emerging in "the ultimate political triumph of Jesus Christ." "All civilizations," he pithily summarizes, "are overtures to the eventual triumph of the church." His analysis of globalization has many strengths, emphasizing that the church is a truly global alternative to consumerist globalization, putting flesh on this fuzzy hope with the claim that Pentecostalism might "give voice to a truly global Christianity" (122).

Still, there are significant problems with Webb's analysis. He rightly emphasizes that God's orchestration of history is comprehensive and particular. We ought, as he urges, study Scripture so as to learn the skills necessary to read history providentially, to steady our gaze to see what God might be doing around us. Yet Webb offers very little assistance for knowing how exactly to do that. He notes that "anti-American" theologians after 9/11 are working with a providential theology just as much as Jerry Falwell. Granted; but then, So what? Both use theories of providence, but they cannot both be *right*. How does

Webb know which is right, or whether either one is? As best I can tell, Webb's answer is circular. American Christians "should be responsible advocates of the American project of freedom—precisely because the idea of America is so dependent on a flexible doctrine of providence" (75). On the face of it, that isn't much of an argument: A nation founded with a strong sense of providence might actually use it as a cover for terror. Nazis and Stalinists had a sense of destiny too. In practice Webb makes support of the American project of freedom the standard for judging between good guys and bad guys. The argument, put more baldly than Webb ever does, is: America has a providential sense of itself; America is chosen by God to fulfill a mission in the world; therefore, those who support America are supporting providence, those who attack America are resisting God.

Much of my frustration with the book boils down to my very different assessment of contemporary America. He acknowledges that someday the "trajectories" of Christianity and America might diverge and compete, but not today: "There is no immediate need to choose between these two globalisms" (145). This is rooted in a far too sanguine evaluation of America, 2012. Webb acknowledges America's sins and flaws, but he still finds very little that is disquieting in a nation whose aim is to "amuse and feed the rest of the world" (111), but he never asks what we are sending out for the world's amusement. Is it really the case today that "the American governance of global capitalism" is "within the sphere of Christian influence"? How? Modernity marginalizes religion, Webb knows, but America seems somehow to have escaped the corrosions of modernity. Webb thinks Hauerwas is wrong to say that America is "godless," but I think Hauerwas has grounds for his opinion: We've been killing babies for nearly forty years, with the full support of the American justice system. And how many more billions does the porn industry have to make, how much higher do the divorce rates have to go, how much further do sexual standards have to decline, how much more progress does the gay lobby have to make, how many more pastors and priests have to be caught in sexual sin before we are allowed to call America a "Sodom"? We can narrow down the question to this point: Arguably it was true in 1900 when Josiah Strong wrote, but is it still the case that America has a "dual commitment to exporting Christianity and democracy"?

Webb is in the end a sophisticated apologist for Americanism and the heretic nation. He identifies American ascendance with God's will, America's mission with God's mission, whose content is the spread of democracy as much as the expansion of God's *imperium*.

29. Kinzer, *Overthrow*, 56–70.

30. The best single source on these coups is Kinzer, *Overthrow*, 10–216. The CIA established itself in powerful positions throughout Latin America. Tim Weiner writes that during the mid 1960s, "The CIA was backing the leaders of eleven Latin American nations—Argentina, Bolivia, Brazil, the Dominican Republic, Ecuador, Guatemala, Guyana, Honduras, Nicaragua, Peru, and Venezuela. Once a friendly government was in power, a CIA station chief had five paths to maintain American influence over foreign leaders. 'You become their foreign intelligence service,' [Tom] Polgar said. 'They don't know what's going on in the world. So you give them a weekly briefing – doctored to meet their sensibilities. Money, definitely – that's always welcome. Procurement – toys, games, weapons. Training. And you can always take a group of officers to Fort Bragg or to Washington – a wonderful holiday.'" For the CIA of this period, "military juntas were good for the United States. . . . Law and order were better than the messy struggle for democracy and freedom" (*Legacy of Ashes*, 323). This also put the intelligence service in position if a regime change became necessary.

Endnotes

31. Blum, *Killing Hope*, 140–45.
32. Ibid., 153–56, 175–84.
33. Ibid., 99–103, 193–98.
34. Ibid., 370–82. Tim Weiner describes the later situation this way: In 1993, "Clinton set out to restore the power of the elected president of Haiti, the leftist priest Jean-Bertrand Aristide. He genuinely viewed Aristide as the legitimate ruler of the Haitian people and he wanted to see justice done. This required undoing the military junta that had ousted Aristide. Many of its leaders had been on the CIA's payroll for years, serving as trusted informants for the clandestine service. This fact was an unpleasant surprise for the White House. So was the revelation that the agency had created a Haitian intelligence service whose military leaders did little but distribute Colombian cocaine, destroy their political enemies, and preserve their power in the capital, Port-au-Prince. The agency was now placed in the awkward position of overthrowing its own agents" (*Legacy of Ashes*, 513–14).
35. See Michael Mandelbaum, *The Case for Goliath* (New York: Public Affairs, 2005) 94–115.
36. Deepak Lal, *In Praise of Empires: Globalization and Order* (New York: Palgrave Macmillan, 2004) 112.
37. Quoted in ibid., 112.
38. Ibid., 113.
39. Michael Mann, *Incoherent Empire* (London: Verso, 2003) 58–59.
40. Ibid., 59.
41. Ibid. Provocatively, Mann says, "This is not 'aid,' but ruthless price gouging."
42. Ibid., 59–61.
43. Ibid., 53.
44. Uzbekistan is a case in point: "President Karimov of Uzbekistan is as repressive as Saddam Hussein, and he is also smart. He delayed the U.S. war on Afghanistan a month until he got promises of substantial assistance, help with the IMF, and no human rights strings attached. Only then did he open up his air bases and his Friendship Bridge into Afghanistan. He got $160 million in aid in 2002" (ibid., 56).
45. Ha-Joon Chang, *Bad Samaritans: The Myth of Free Trade and the Secret History of Capitalism* (New York: Bloomsbury, 2008) 32.
46. Ibid., 32–34.
47. Ibid., 35–36. Chang argues that developing countries might not be ready to compete in an open global marketplace, since "they need time to improve their capabilities by mastering advance technologies and building effective organizations" (66). They are no more ready to enter the global market without help than a six-year-old is ready to enter the job market.
48. Ibid., 15.
49. And this is to say nothing of the charges of intimidation and bribery and worse that are regularly brought against international financial institutions. For the skullduggery of high finance, see John Perkins, *Confessions of an Economic Hit Man* (New York: Plume, 2006).
50. To repeat a mantra of the last two chapters: In pursuing national interest, we are no different from a hundred other polities. The difference is that we refuse to admit that this is what we do, and Americanism seduces us into believing that our pursuit of national interest is equivalent to doing the will of God.

51. See http://abcnews.go.com/Blotter/us-navy-rescues-iranian-sailors/story?id=15331425#.Tw1nOG_Ozw1, accessed January 11, 2012.

52. Jean Bethke Elshtain writes, "Those of us who have studied [American rules of engagement] in detail . . . know that a basic norm of U.S. military training is the combatant-noncombatant distinction—the principle of discrimination. We know that American soldiers are trained to refuse to obey illegal orders under the code of restraints called the 'laws of war,' derived in large measure from the historic evolution of the just war tradition and its spin-offs as encoded in international conventions and arrangements. U.S. military training films include generous helpings of 'what went wrong' in various operations. 'Wrong' refers not only to U.S. military losses but also to operations that led to the unintentional loss of civilian life" (*Just War Against Terror: The Burden of American Power in a Violent World* [New York: Basic Books, 2003] 21). No doubt the military efforts to minimize damage to noncombatants are sincere, but what Elshtain leaves out is revealing. I find no reference to Dresden or Tokyo in the index.

53. Mark Selden, "A Forgotten Holocaust: U.S. Bombing Strategy, the Destruction of Japanese Cities, and the American Way of War from the Pacific War to Iraq," in Yuki Tanaka and Marilyn B. Young, eds., *Bombing Civilians: A Twentieth-Century History* (New York: New Press, 2009) 78.

54. Hugo Grotius, *The Rights of War and Peace: Including the Law of Nature and of Nations* (New York: M. W. Dunne, 1901) 361–62.

55. Yuki Tanaka, "Introduction," in Tanaka and Young, eds., *Bombing Civilians*, p. 2.

56. Ibid., 3.

57. Selden, "Forgotten Holocaust," p. 80.

58. Quoted in ibid., 81.

59. Ibid., 83–86.

60. Quoted in ibid., 82.

61. Mead, *Special Providence*, 218.

62. Ibid.

63. Ibid., 219.

64. Ibid.

65. Ibid.

66. Quoted in Selden, "Forgotten Holocaust," 93.

67. Mead, *Special Providence*, 219.

68. Ibid.

69. Selden, "Forgotten Holocaust," 94.

70. Quoted in ibid., 95. Selden is quoting a study by Taylor Owen and Ben Kierman published in *Walrus* in 2006, available at http://www.walrusmagazine.com/articles/2006.10-history-bombing-cambodia/, accessed January 7, 2012.

71. Quoted in B. Young, "Bombing Civilians from the Twentieth to the Twenty-First Centuries," in Tanaka and Young, eds., *Bombing Civilians*, 171.

72. Quoted in ibid., 174.

73. Only America could produce a Francis Fukuyama. The outcry against his thesis of the "end of history" is, however, amusing, since he was only giving Hegelian expression to a settled American conviction. Maybe it was the Hegel that critics objected to.

Endnotes

CHAPTER 7

1. For the story behind this legislation and its implementation, see Thomas F. Farr, *World of Faith and Freedom: Why International Religious Liberty Is Vital to American National Security* (Oxford: Oxford University Press, 2008) 111–212. Farr was the first director of this office. Lee Marsden views the push to highlight religious liberty as a "hijacking" of the human rights agent (*For God's Sake: The Christian Right and US Foreign Policy* [London: Zed, 2008] 113–48), and Farr makes it clear that Marsden's views are widely shared within the State Department. Annual reports and other information about this office may be found at http://www.state.gov/g/drl/rls/irf/, accessed January 13, 2012.

2. According to Marsden (*For God's Sake*, 130), USAID gave over $300,000 to Voice of the Martyrs between 2001 and 2005.

3. I refer to Abdul Rahman, whose story is told in Farr, *World of Faith and Freedom*, 3–7.

4. Marsden, *For God's Sake*, 121–22.

5. This is one of the main themes of Farr, *World of Faith and Freedom*, especially chapter 2.

6. Farr notes that State Department officials resist emphasizing religious freedom by citing Supreme Court decisions and by trying to apply the Lemon Test to American foreign actions (*World of Faith and Freedom*, 13–14).

7. I refer to the Afghan Constitution, incisively critiqued by Farr, *World of Faith and Freedom*, 5–7.

8. http://pewforum.org/Government/Rising-Restrictions-on-Religion(2).aspx?src=prc-headline, accessed October 10, 2011.

9. http://www.census.gov/compendia/statab/cats/foreign_commerce_aid/foreign_aid.html, accessed October 10, 2011.

10. I am hardly the first Christian to criticize U.S. policy toward Egypt, Saudi Arabia, and other Middle Eastern Islamic nations. They have been regularly in the sights of Nina Shea (see Marsden, *For God's Sake*, 124). If I am piling on, it's for a good cause.

11. http://www.compassdirect.org/english/country/egypt/article_121244.html, accessed October 11, 2011.

12. http://www.guardian.co.uk/world/2011/oct/09/egypt-protests-cairo-clashes?newsfeed=true, accessed October 11, 2011.

13. http://www.boston.com/news/world/middleeast/articles/2011/10/10/more_clashes_erupt_in_egypt/, accessed October 11, 2011; http://www.stratfor.com/weekly/20111011-geopolitical-journey-riots-cairo?utm_source=freelist-f&utm_medium=email&utm_campaign=20111011&utm_term=gweekly&utm_content=readmore&elq=acb8b783ee5440258874c4a6bcbbd90e, accessed October 11, 2011.

14. http://www.state.gov/g/drl/rls/irf/2010/148817.htm, accessed October 11, 2011. The State Department briefing included details of a number of cases of discrimination, from petty harassments and non-cooperation to negligence to violence:

The Ministry of the Interior "continued to prevent renovation of St. John the Baptist Church at Awlad Elias in Sadfa, near Assiut, which began nine years ago. At the end of the reporting period, the congregation continued to meet for worship in a tent erected in the small courtyard of the church."

"Governmental authorities blocked renovation of other churches as well, including the Church of Mar Mina near Beni Suef, and the Archangel Mikhail Coptic Church in Ezbet al-Nakhl."

Endnotes

"The courts did not rule on the March 2008 appeal of legal counsel for Muhammad Ahmad Abduh Higazy against the January 2008 ruling of the Cairo Administrative Court that the administrative agency of the Civil Status Department was not bound to examine his client's request to have his new religious affiliation, Christianity, recorded on his national identity card. In its ruling the court wrote that principles of Islamic law forbid Muslims from converting from Islam and such conversion would constitute a disparagement of the official state religion and an enticement for other Muslims to convert. The court asserted its duty to 'protect public order from the crime of apostasy from Islam and to protect public morals, especially if the apostate petitions the administration to condone his misdeed and his corrupt caprice.'"

"On June 13, 2009, the Seventh Circuit Court of Administrative Justice ruled against Maher al-Gohary, a Muslim convert to Christianity who filed suit in 2008 seeking government recognition of his conversion, including by changing the required religion space on his national identity card to indicate 'Christian' . . . On September 17, 2009, al-Gohary attempted to leave the country. Government authorities at Cairo International Airport refused to permit him to board an airplane bound for a foreign destination and confiscated his passport. It was unclear if authorities had a legal basis for taking the passport or refusing to issue a replacement."

"On June 1, 2010, Luxor International Airport authorities reportedly confiscated 300 books from a Christian from Sohag Governorate. The individual was allowed to depart to Kuwait without the books."

"On May 24, 2010, Alexandria's Prosecution Office released 12 young persons associated with an evangelical church, who had been held in detention for two days after being accused of distributing evangelistic books and pamphlets."

"On February 15, 2010, a U.S. citizen accused of evangelizing in Egypt was reportedly arrested upon his arrival to Cairo International Airport and deported overnight. According to local contacts and press reports, the man had previously been accused of evangelizing in residential areas in Egypt."

"On September 23, 2009, police officers reportedly arrested Abd al-Masih Kamel Barsoum, who is associated with an evangelical church in Minya, while he was distributing Christian religious materials in downtown Cairo."

15. http://www.guardian.co.uk/global-development/poverty-matters/2011/jul/11/us-aid-to-pakistan, accessed October 11, 2011.

16. http://en.wikipedia.org/wiki/Persecution_of_Christians#Pakistan, accessed October 11, 2011.

17. http://www.asianews.it/news-en/Punjab:-Muslims-kidnap-14-year-old-Christian-to-convert-her-to-Islam-22456.html, accessed October 11, 2011.

18. http://www.digitaljournal.com/article/301145, accessed October 11, 2011; http://cnsnews.com/blog/terence-p-jeffrey/save-asia-bibi-mr-president, accessed October 11, 2011; http://www.cato.org/pub_display.php?pub_id=13269, accessed October 11, 2011.

19. http://cnsnews.com/blog/terence-p-jeffrey/save-asia-bibi-mr-president, accessed October 11, 2011; http://www.state.gov/g/drl/rls/irf/2010_5/168251.htm, accessed October 11, 2011.

20. http://www.independent.co.uk/opinion/commentators/mark-steel/mark-steel-why-does-saudi-arabia-need-military-aid-459786.html, accessed October 11, 2011.

21. See Craig Unger, *House of Bush, House of Saud*, who documents $1.4 billion in contracts and investments from the Saudi royal family to companies where the Bush family or close friends had significant investments. For a brief account, see http://

Endnotes

entertainment.salon.com/2004/03/16/unger_4/singleton/ and http://entertainment.salon.com/2004/03/12/unger_2/, accessed October 11, 2011.

22. Farr, *World of Faith and Freedom*, 237.

23. http://www.persecution.org/2011/04/10/saudi-arabia-where-the-public-display-of-bibles-can-lead-to-arrest/, accessed October 11, 2011; http://www.persecution.org/2010/10/08/saudi-arabia-conditional-release-for-12-filipinos-accused-of-proselytizing/, accessed October 11, 2011.

24. http://www.persecution.org/2010/10/08/saudi-arabia-conditional-release-for-12-filipinos-accused-of-proselytizing/, accessed October 11, 2011.

25. http://www.persecution.org/2011/03/22/christians-in-prison-beaten-in-saudi-arabia/, accessed October 11, 2011.

26. http://www.persecution.org/2011/07/28/india-releases-jailed-christians-after-six-month-imprisonment/, accessed October 11, 2011.

27. http://www.persecution.org/2011/07/20/eritrean-christian-faces-deportation-from-saudi-arabia-for-preaching-the-gospel/, accessed October 11, 2011.

28. Farr, *World of Faith and Freedom*, 237.

29. State's 2011 report on religious freedom in Saudi Arabia stated: "The laws and policies restrict religious freedom, and in practice, the government generally enforced these restrictions. Freedom of religion is neither recognized nor protected under the law and is severely restricted in practice. The country is an Islamic state governed by a monarchy; the king is head of both state and government. According to the basic law, Sunni Islam is the official religion and the country's constitution is the Qur'an and the Sunna (traditions and sayings of the Prophet Muhammad). . . . The public practice of any religion other than Islam is prohibited, and there is no separation between state and religion. The government did not respect religious freedom in law, but generally permitted Shia religious gatherings and non-Muslim private religious practices. Some Muslims who did not adhere to the government's interpretation of Islam faced significant political, economic, legal, social, and religious discrimination, including limited employment and educational opportunities, underrepresentation in official institutions, restrictions on religious practice, and restrictions on places of worship and community centers" (http://www.state.gov/g/drl/rls/irf/2010_5/168275.htm, accessed October 11, 2011).

30. Farr, *World of Faith and Freedom*, 240.

31. According to the 2011 State Department report, "The government continued to call for tolerance and acceptance of all religious minorities. For example on November 24, 2010, the Council of Representatives approved a document calling on the government to protect the country's Christians. Political leaders around the country in all levels of government strongly condemned the October 31 attack against the Sayidat al-Najat Church, as did religious leaders of all faiths and sects. The prime minister committed the government to funding the church's refurbishment and providing long-term extra security for all churches" (http://www.unhcr.org/refworld/country,,,,IRQ,,4e734c913a,0.html, accessed October 11, 2011). Still, Muslim-on-Muslim violence "resulted in approximately 275 deaths, over 750 injuries, significant internal displacement, some external displacement as refugees, and restricted religious freedom."

32. http://www.jpost.com/Opinion/Columnists/Article.aspx?id=241236, accessed October 11, 2011; http://www.unhcr.org/refworld/country,,,,IRQ,,4e734c913a,0.html, accessed October 11, 2011.

Endnotes

33. http://www.upi.com/Top_News/World-News/2010/10/31/At-least-30-die-in-Iraq-church-attack/UPI-77781288563737/, accessed October 11, 2011; http://www.nytimes.com/2010/11/02/world/middleeast/02iraq.html, accessed October 11, 2011.

34. http://www.unhcr.org/refworld/country,,,,IRQ,,4e734c913a,0.html, accessed October 11, 2011.

35. http://www.newsrealblog.com/2011/03/18/iraqi-christians-face-genocide-demand-separate-province-and-right-to-exist-2/, accessed October 11, 2011.

36. The Archbishop told two representative stories about persecuted Christians: "One is the story of the father of a teacher in our kindergarten in Ankawa. Last year Mr. Dahan was the first of at least eight Iraqi Christians killed in Mosul prior to the elections. The abduction that ended in his death was the second time he had been kidnapped. Two years before, he had been abducted, beaten and stuffed in the trunk of a car until the family could collect the $5000 ransom. The family says that after he returned the first time, they didn't leave Mosul because their father would not move. 'Our father said, 'if all of us Christians leave, who is going to stay in the land of the prophets and pray in our churches?' 'He said, 'we were all born in Mosul and we will die in Mosul.' A second story is about my friend Father Mazen from Qaraqosh. Father Mazen was kidnapped 4 days after he had been ordained a priest. He was released but a year later armed men entered his home and killed his father and two brothers in front of his mother and sister in law. Despite this tragedy, Father Mazen serves the displaced families in his congregation in Qaraqosh with unfaltering faith. . . . there are thousands of examples of such senseless injury and killing. The grief and sorrow in our congregations is palpable, where not one person has been uneffected by tragedy since 2003" (http://www.catholicbishops.ie/2011/03/16/christians-iraq-address-archbishop-bashar-warda-erbil-northern-iraq/, accessed October 11, 2011).

37. It should have been anticipated, argues Walter Russell Mead, who points out that the last decade accelerated trends that have been going on for a century and a half, since the Ottoman Empire collapsed. See http://blogs.the-american-interest.com/wrm/2011/09/11/persecution-spotlight-christians-in-iraq/, accessed October 11, 2011.

38. http://www.cbn.com/images4/cbnnews/PDFfiles/StateDeptChristiansinIraq.pdf, accessed October 11, 2011.

39. http://www.csi-int.org/pdfs/obama_eibner_iraq_01_11_10.pdf, accessed October 11, 2011.

40. http://blogs.the-american-interest.com/wrm/2011/09/11/persecution-spotlight-christians-in-iraq/, accessed October 11, 2011.

41. Marsden, *For God's Sake*, 122.

42. All quotations in this paragraph from the State Department Office of International Religious Freedom report on Israel, 2010, available at http://www.state.gov/g/drl/rls/irf/2010/148825.htm, accessed January 13, 2012.

43. Marsden, *For God's Sake*, 122–23.

44. Ibid., ch. 6.

45. For a controversial treatment of this, see John J. Mearsheimer and Stephen M. Walt, *The Israel Lobby and U.S. Foreign Policy* (New York: Farrar, Straus & Giroux, 2007). Also see the profile of Mearsheimer and his work in Robert Kaplan, "Why John J. Mearsheimer Is Right (About Some Things)," *The Atlantic* (January/February 2012) 80–89.

46. http://politics.salon.com/2011/09/19/obama_global_destablization/singleton/, accessed October 11, 2011; http://thenewamerican.com/world-mainmenu-26/

Endnotes

asia-mainmenu-33/7749-yemen-us-military-aid-cant-save-dictator-rebellion-escalates-, accessed October 11, 2011.

47. http://www.persecution.net/yemen.htm, accessed October 11, 2011.

48. http://www.thejakartaglobe.com/home/two-churches-torched-in-indonesia/456930, accessed October 11, 2011.

49. http://www.thejakartaglobe.com/home/bogor-authorities-give-yasmin-church-final-warning/470822, accessed October 11, 2011.

50. http://politics.salon.com/2011/02/02/american_allies_dictators/, accessed October 11, 2011.

51. http://www.state.gov/g/drl/rls/irf/2010_5/168254.htm, accessed October 11, 2011.

52. http://www.state.gov/g/drl/rls/irf/2010_5/168257.htm, accessed October 11, 2011.

53. http://www.jpost.com/Opinion/Columnists/Article.aspx?id=241236, accessed October 11, 2011.

54. Farr, *World of Faith and Freedom*, 241.

Conclusion

1. *The Tragedy of American Diplomacy*, rev. ed. (New York: Delta, 1962) 9.
2. Ibid., 9.
3. Earlier empires have had their relentless, high-placed denouncers—Bartholome de las Casas in the Spanish empire; Edmund Burke with his ferocious denunciation of British policy and actions in India. More positively, the Clapham Sect led by Wilberforce promoted one of the most impressive acts of imperial power in human history, the end of the slave trade and slavery. There are lesser examples in American history—the Christians who sided with Indians in struggles against the federal government, Davy Crockett opposing his ally Andrew Jackson in defense of the Indians. One hopes for an American Burke.

www.ingramcontent.com/pod-product-compliance
Lightning Source LLC
Chambersburg PA
CBHW031819220426
43662CB00007B/718